Feb. 2014

FOOD LOVERS'
GUIDE TO
WISCONSIN

FOOD LOVERS' SERIES

FOOD LOVERS'
GUIDE TO®
WISCONSIN

The Best Restaurants, Markets
& Local Culinary Offerings

1st Edition

Martin Hintz with Pam Percy

gpp

Guilford, Connecticut

Food Lovers' Guide to Wisconsin
is dedicated to food lovers everywhere.

To buy books in quantity for corporate use
or incentives, call **(800) 962-0973**
or e-mail **premiums@GlobePequot.com**.

Editor: Tracee Williams
Project Editor: Lauren Brancato
Layout Artist: Mary Ballachino
Text Design: Sheryl Kober
Illustrations: Jill Butler with additional art by Carleen Moira Powell and MaryAnn Dubé
Maps: Design Maps Inc. © Morris Book Publishing, LLC

ISBN 978-0-7627-9214-6

Printed in the United States of America
10 9 8 7 6 5 4 3 2 1

All the information in this guidebook is subject to change. We recommend that you call ahead to obtain current information before traveling.

Contents

Appendices, 315

About the Authors

Authors **Martin Hintz** and **Pam Percy** are longtime food writers, and their work has been published in numerous outlets around the country. In addition to interviewing chefs, writing about restaurants, and covering food events, they own a 5-acre farm north of Milwaukee and grow garlic and squash on about an acre near West Bend, Wisconsin. Through the growing and harvesting season, they serve some 40 clients in their community supported agriculture (CSA) program, as well as the occasional restaurant or special event. In addition to a wide range of produce, they also raise goats, pigs, and chickens—lots of chickens. Percy has written two books on chickens, and she and Hintz collaborated on *Wisconsin Cheese: A Cookbook and Guide to Wisconsin Cheese* for Globe Pequot Press (2008).

They also write the "Boris & Doris on the Town" column, a who's-doing-what in Milwaukee for the *Shepherd Express,* the city's premier weekly entertainment publication. This allows them to hit all the latest hot spots when it comes to cuisine. In addition to about 100 other books, Hintz has also written several guides for Globe Pequot, including 10 editions of *Off the Beaten Path: Wisconsin.* He has also authored *Wisconsin Farm Lore: Kicking Cows, Giant Pumpkins & Other Tales from the Back Forty,* a reflective look at Wisconsin's agriculture for The History Press. In addition, he has written for *Edible Milwaukee* and is a regular contributor to *M Magazine,* Milwaukee's high-end arts, culinary, personality, and fashion publication. Hintz is a Milwaukee County director of the Farm Bureau of Wisconsin and a member of the Food Council of Milwaukee. Percy is a dedicated cook, able to whip up a dinner for six or for 30 guests, with nary a quiver, under a backyard tent or in their century-old farmhouse. Hintz prepares the salads, sets the table, pours beverage, eats, and helps clean up.

Acknowledgments

The authors wish to acknowledge all those who helped with this guide to Wisconsin's marvelous restaurants, foodie shops, and food producers. In addition to our own exploration around Wisconsin, we gratefully tapped into their wealth of expertise regarding the Dairy State's culinary industry. Among the many friends, acquaintances, and professionals who offered tips, leads, and suggestions on what they considered noteworthy and delicious, plus where to eat and how to get there, were Rita and Kelly Renner, Dr. Bob and Jane Gleeson, and Mary Bergin and Gary Knowles of the Society of American Travel Writers. A special nod goes to mapmaker extraordinaire Ross Segel.

Thanks also goes to the Wisconsin Division of Tourism; the Wisconsin Department of Agriculture, Trade & Consumer Protection; the Wisconsin Milk Marketing Board; VISIT Milwaukee; the Madison Convention & Visitors Bureau (CVB); Meredith Jumisko of the Kenosha CVB; Martha Kipcak of the Food Council of Milwaukee; the Wisconsin Restaurant Association; members of the Farm Bureau of Wisconsin; the gang at SavorWisconsin; *Graze* magazine; the Midwest Organic and Sustainable Education Services; *Culture,* the international cheese magazine; our editor, Janet Raasch, at *M Magazine,* and publisher Jan Ede of *Edible Milwaukee;* plus numerous chefs, cheesemakers, farmers, restaurateurs, culinary writers/reviewers, and others in the food industry who graciously shared their insights on where to go, what's good to eat, and who makes what.

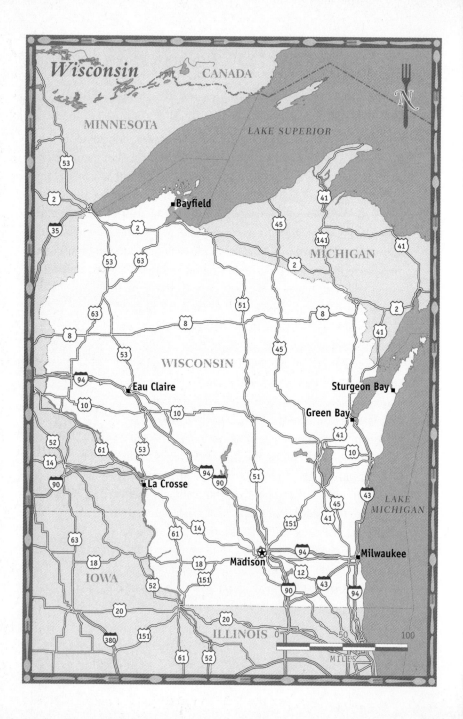

Introduction

Wisconsin's restaurant scene is concentrated in its two largest cities, Milwaukee and Madison. However, almost every town and hamlet elsewhere in the state has at least a couple of restaurants or specialty food producers of note. You can find old-fashioned supper clubs and trendy, contemporary bistros, as well as ethnic eateries and fine dining. Many hole-in-the-wall cafes and even taverns also promote delicious, nutritious fare. As such, you can munch your way from one end of Wisconsin to the other. This happy trek is fueled by steak and schnitzel; tortes, tarts, and tostadas; or fried perch and fresh baked pumpkin pie. Along the way, you can indulge in Wisconsin microbrews and distilled products, as well as milk shakes and cheese curds.

For a handy overview of the state's thousands of restaurants, utilize the handy dining guide developed by the **Wisconsin Restaurant Association** (WRA). On its website (wirestaurant.org/search/dining) you can seek out eateries by restaurant name, by type of cuisine, by metro area, by city, or even those with recreation opportunities on-site. If you have any questions about laws and regulations governing the state's restaurants, you can phone the WRA at (800) 589-3211 or (608) 270-9950, or write the organization at 2801 Fish Hatchery Rd., Madison, WI 53713.

With all this awaiting you as a culinary explorer, please take the opportunity to visit Wisconsin and experience the foodie thrill of your lifetime.

How to Use This Book

This book only ripples the surface of Wisconsin's food scene. We have concentrated on the state's major metropolitan areas but have tossed in dozens of eateries elsewhere that you will enjoy. To make it easy to find that "special place," the Milwaukee chapter is divided into neighborhoods and suburbs. The Eastern Wisconsin chapter is divided into North of Milwaukee, South of Milwaukee, and West of Milwaukee with mini sections such as Door County. We then broke the state into Central (with Madison and its surrounding communities), Northern, and Western chapters.

We conclude with easy-to-follow recipes gleaned from among the state's most skilled chefs, all of whom can flip an egg or poach a salmon with the best kitchen experts in the world.

Foodie Faves

These restaurants are either our favorites or those highly recommended by our professional foodie contacts. They attract locals as well as visitors, making for a fun time. Included are traditional locales, as well as up-and-comers.

Landmarks

These restaurants have a long history in their communities and have long been noted for excellent menus and amazing food prep. They are the legends of Wisconsin.

Specialty Stores, Markets & Producers

Wisconsin's grocers, vintners, brewers, butchers, and bakers know their stuff. A few of the many are covered here, hinting at the range of purveyors out there waiting to serve you.

Great Bars

According to historians, Milwaukee's first bar opened in 1837. By the Civil War, the number of taverns filled three pages in the city directory. These days, there are some 300 joints in which to enjoy a beverage, whether a craft cocktail or microbrew.

Recipes

Wisconsin's best chefs have contributed hearty and healthy creations that you'll enjoy making at home. It is fun trying them all.

Price Code

The price code in this guide is figured on the cost of a single entree, including tax and tip:

$	less than $10	$$$	$20–$30
$$	$10–$20	$$$$	more than $30

WISCONSIN'S AGRICULTURE SCENE

Serving the state's restaurants, Wisconsin's agriculture industry is the soul of the region's economy. It employs almost 354,000 persons, some 10 percent of the entire population. Farming makes a $59.16 billion contribution to Wisconsin's economy each year, making Wisconsin a leading state in the wide range of agricultural products. Wisconsin is home to almost 77,000 farms, encompassing 15 million acres. The average farm size in Wisconsin is 195 acres. More than 1,500 of these farms are certified organic, or at least considered "sustainable" by not using pesticides and chemical fertilizers. Some 200,000 acres are used for organic crop production, with Wisconsin having the country's largest number of organic beef and dairy farms. It also ranks first for the number of farms raising organic hogs, layer chickens, and turkeys. The state is proud that it also leads the nation in organic feed grains and forage crops. Most of the organic farms have traditionally been concentrated in Monroe, Vernon, and contiguous Western Wisconsin counties, but the number of such farms has been spreading around the state.

The Milwaukee Journal Sentinel, jsonline.com/ entertainment/dining. Award-winning food writer Carol Deptolla annually lists her top 30 Milwaukee restaurants, and also writes about food, chefs, and recipes in her weekly sections in the newspaper. Deptolla writes a regular blog on the latest food news and notes, found at jsonline.com/blogs/entertainment/mkediner.html.

The Shepherd Express, expressmilwaukee.com. Food critic Jeff Beutner and other staffers write regular dining-out columns, along with "Short Orders," which consists of a paragraph and a photo about some hot food find. *The Shepherd* is Milwaukee's major weekly entertainment, cultural, and political newspaper.

Edible Milwaukee, ediblemilwaukee.com. This free quarterly celebrates the food scene of Milwaukee and southeastern Wisconsin yet regularly branches out to capture food-related stories in other parts of the state. The magazine is part of a larger network of more than 75 Edible Communities publications in North America, each locally owned and locally oriented.

M Magazine, mmagazinemilwaukee.com. *M Magazine* is a high-gloss lifestyle publication that covers the city's personalities, culture, and, of course, food. Profiles of chefs and restaurateurs are a major component of the magazine, along with restaurant overviews and "Short Takes" on subjects ranging from where to find the best barbecue to which places have patios.

Milwaukee Magazine, milwaukeemag.com. Ann Christenson is *Milwaukee Mag's* respected food columnist, backed by other staffers and outside writers who know their food news. They cover new restaurants, review the oldies but goodies, and keep Milwaukeeans up-to-date each month on the latest trendy spot in which to dine.

Graze, **outpost.coop/connect/graze.** Distributed by the **Outpost Natural Foods** (p. 48) cooperative, *Graze* discusses food trends and issues, health, and culinary experiences. Each issue contains numerous recipes. With no advertising, each issue costs 99 cents but is free with a $20 purchase at any Outpost site around town.

Madison Capitol Times, **host.madison.com/ct.** This is the capital city's major source for news on its business scene, which often includes restaurant coverage.

The Isthmus, **isthmus.com/isthmus.** Madison's weekly alternative paper is a major source of what's happening in the city when it comes to cuisine. Its features include reviews, latest trends, and who's doing what. The newspaper's online service, *The Daily Page* (thedailypage.com), provides immediate updates on what's going on in the community, with many stories focusing on the Madison food world in its "Eats" section.

Madison Magazine, **madisonmagazine.com.** All the latest in dining, the arts, shopping, events, and business is covered by *Madison Magazine.* It offers a comprehensive dining guide, as well as stories and news about food and dining in the city.

Edible Madison, **ediblemadison.com.** This free quarterly publication is dedicated to the celebration of the food and agriculture of Southern Wisconsin. Its writers include well-known, versatile food writers such as Terese Allen, Jeanne Carpenter, Jessica Luhning, and many others.

77 Square, host.madison.com/entertainment/dining. This arts and entertainment website tells who is putting a healthy spin on popular foods, where to find fresh tacos, and how vegans and carnivores can coexist in Wisconsin's capital, plus lots more when it comes to dining out.

The Dish, union.wisc.edu/wud/publications-the-dish.htm. A project of the University of Wisconsin–Madison student programing board, The Dish provides recipes and restaurant reviews, dining guides for students with restricted diets, cooking tips and tricks, budget recipes, and monthly feature articles on the Madison food scene.

CHEESE IS GOOD!

Wisconsin is called the Cheese State for good reason. It leads the nation in the number of cheese plants, producing more than 600 varieties and turning out 2.6 billion pounds of cheese annually. Ninety percent of Wisconsin's milk goes into the production of cheese, and 90 percent of that is sold worldwide. If Wisconsin were a country, notwithstanding that Green Bay's football fans already consider themselves citizens of Packerland, it would rank fourth in total world production of cheese, just behind the total United States' output and that of Germany and France. The state makes more cheese than all of Italy! The state has also won 12 out of 16 United States Championship Cheese Contest awards since this competition began in 1981. Wisconsin is also the only state with a master cheesemaker program, a tough 3-year course that emphasizes technical skills and craftsmanship. More than 50 Wisconsin cheesemakers are considered "masters."

Madison.com, host.madison.com. This website focuses on the business, political, and culture news in Madison. To know what's opening and closing on the restaurant scene, this is the site.

Wisconsin Foodie, **wisconsinfoodie.com/about.** This weekly Emmy-nominated television program, hosted by foodie personality Kyle Cherek, is dedicated to "educating, entertaining, and connecting the community to the engaging stories and people behind their food." *Wisconsin Foodie* wraps food, cooking, and travel in an easily watchable package. Keep track of what's going on via Twitter (@WisconsinFoodie) and on Facebook (WisconsinFoodieFans).

Online Services/Blogs

Beer Barons of Milwaukee, beerbarons.org. The Beer Barons are dedicated homebrewers and all-around beer enthusiasts who love to share their knowledge of the industry.

Burp!, eatatburp.com. This food-oriented blog by Paul and Lori Fredrich features original recipes with an emphasis on local, sustainable foods. Lori is the main writer and recipe developer, while Paul is the head tester, chief marketer, party planner, and all-around foodie. As they emphasize, their core beliefs revolve around "the creation of real food that nourishes both the body and the soul."

Madison Beer Review, **madisonbeerreview.com.** This is an online niche publication that focuses on the industry and culture of craft beer. Editor in chief Jeff Glazer is a Madison attorney specializing in business law and the brewing industry.

OnMilwaukee.com, onmilwaukee.com. *OnMilwaukee* is the city's daily online magazine, with features focusing on arts and entertainment, events, and where to go and what to see. A number of knowledgeable food writers cover the restaurant scene, along with the latest on bars and clubs.

Oshkosh Beer Blog, oshkoshbeer .blogspot.com. This site is dedicated to the brewing, pouring, and history of beer in Oshkosh, Wisconsin.

SavorWisconsin.com, SavorWisconsin.com. This is an online directory and resource for consumers across the world to find food and agricultural products and services from Wisconsin.

Wisconsin Beer Geek, wisconsinbeergeek.com. In-depth interviews with brewers and others in the beer industry make up the core of this website.

Wisconsin Restaurateur **(WR)**, wirestaurant.org/ membership/wr. *WR* has an exclusive focus on Wisconsin's food service industry. All members receive a free subscription to the four-color, quarterly magazine, but you can review the archives that contain stories about carryout, safety of locally sourced food, and the farm-to-table scene.

Wisconsin Trails, wisconsintrails.com. A longtime fixture on the state's publishing and online scene, *Wisconsin Trails* consistently touches on the out-of-the-way and unusual on the culinary trail. It also covers food products and producers, in addition to restaurants and food-makers in the news.

To learn more about Wisconsin's many food and beverage events, tap into All About Wisconsin's online event website, wisconline.com. The Wisconsin Division of Tourism also has comprehensive listings of such events at its official website, travelwisconsin.com.

January

Chili Cook Off, Appleton, WI; appletondowntown.org.
Held on the last Saturday of the month, the Chili Cook-Off pits several dozen area eateries against each other. The competition is held in the downtown City Center, featuring at least one ingredient from the winter farm market. You can vote for your favorite.

February

Death by Chocolate, Appleton, WI; appletondowntown .org.
On Valentine's Day, just when you need a winter respite, munch your way along College Avenue. Sample all sorts of chocolate treats created by Appleton's premier chefs. Vote for your favorite treat and become eligible for prizes.

March

Maple Syrup Festival, Monona, WI; aldoleopoldnaturecenter .org/event/maple-syrup-fest.
Held at the Aldo Leopold Nature Center, 330 Femrite Dr., visitors can tap trees and participate in the intricate process of making maple syrup. There are cooking demos and plenty of opportunity to eat ice cream sundaes topped with maple syrup. What's most fun is hiking around the nature center and visiting

the various stations set up on the grounds that tell of the history and science of maple syruping. Proceeds benefit the Nature Center's children's programs. Advance registration is recommended, although you can still do a last-minute walk-in.

World Championship Cheese Contest, Madison, WI; worldchampioncheese.org. The biennial event, held in even-numbered years, is held at the Monona Terrace Convention Center in Madison. For more than 50 years, this competition has been the world's premier technical evaluation and contest among cheesemakers for the best of the best. Medals are awarded to the finest products in 82 classes, with up to 2,500 entries. Fame follows. An international panel of judges picks the winners. The public is invited to watch, as well as take in the final judging for the World Champion cheese. A limited number of tickets are sold to this popular event.

April

Madison Food Camp, Madison, WI; madisonfoodcamp .org. This is a daylong, hands-on event for food lovers wanting to know about beekeeping, safeguarding urban chickens, brewing beer, how to bake sourdough breads, raised-bed gardening, and how to sharpen knives, among many other topics. Try the yoga for gardeners. This is a casual, friendly day where you can talk about topics close to your culinary heart. There are no spectators here, only participants. Co-sponsored by Slow Food Madison, the event is held in the Goodman Center, 149 Waubesa St., on Madison's east side.

May

Morel Mushroom Festival, Muscoda, WI; muscoda.com. For more than three decades, Muscoda has celebrated the delicious morel each mid-May and subsequently has earned the title of the

Mushroom Capital of Wisconsin. Competitions are held for the smallest, most unusual, biggest cluster, and most pounds collected in a season. There are also chainsaw carving demonstrations, tractor pulls, basketball, softball, and horseshoe tossing tournaments. Events are held in Pickering Park, Railroad Park, the JC Ball Park, and other sites around town. Fried morels are served at Mushroom Headquarters, based on availability. On Sunday of the festival weekend, the St. John's Men's Holy Name Society hosts a pancake breakfast in St. John's Parish Hall on N. Wisconsin Avenue, adjacent to the church. The earthy, flavorful mushroom is a staple culinary delight, collected from secret places around Muscoda and elsewhere in the woods of Western Wisconsin. The morel is prized by gourmet cooks around the world.

World's Largest Brat Fest, Alliant Energy Center, Madison, WI; bratfest.com. Traditional brats are on the menu, but hot dogs and veggie brats are also available for this Memorial Day weekend eating blowout. Madison celebrities act as cashiers. Numerous bands provide the musical background. Since the fest began in 1983, more than three million brats have been sold, amounting to around 300 tons. Some 5,000 volunteers donate a combined total of more than 16,000 hours of their time. Money raised goes to local charities.

June

Brews n' Blues Festival, Oshkosh, WI; jcioshkosh.org/brews-n-blues. Held in Leach Amphitheater, the Oshkosh Jaycees throw this party each year to raise money for area charities. Among the pours presented by more than 30 of the state's top brewers, you may find Southern Tier's Plum Noir, a plum-infused porter, and New Holland's Dragon's Milk Imperial Stout.

Cheese Curd Festival, Ellsworth, WI; ellsworthchamber .com/cheese-curd-festival.html. The annual festival is hosted by the Ellsworth Cooperative Creamery, usually held in East End Park the last weekend in June. Enter Sunday's cheese-curd-eating competition, just to say you did. The squeakier the curd, the fresher and better it is. There are plenty of burger/brat stands, a parade, music, and bingo. A medallion with the respective year's logo is hidden somewhere in town, with clues provided and a $200 prize for the finder. Be sure to purchase a Cheese Curd Festival Button at one of the town's businesses so that you can claim your prize. What's not to like about this event?

July

Milwaukee Firkin Craft Beer Festival, Milwaukee, WI; milwaukeefirkin.com. More than 100 beers are available to sample, making a perfect segue for wandering through the historic Milwaukee brewing exhibits. Beer historians give talks, homebrewers show how it is done, and ArtMilwaukee showcases its members' beer-inspired art. This celebration of Milwaukee beer gets its name from the "firkin," a small cask of beer that, in medieval England, amounted to a quarter of a barrel. The event has been sponsored by Whole Foods and Hinterland Brewery. The festival packs in beer fans at Cathedral Square Park in downtown Milwaukee.

Trempealeau Lions Catfish Days, Trempealeau, WI; trempealeau.net. The Trempealeau Lions host this annual family event alongside the Mississippi River, offering dozens of food concessions plus music and a carnival. You can also take a bike or motorcycle tour (bring your own!), participate in a 5–10K walk/run, enter the bass and walleye fishing tournament, enjoy a variety show, peruse the arts and crafts, purchase something you can't live without at the flea market, take in the car show, cheer at the softball tournament, watch a parade, and settle back to enjoy the fireworks. Despite all this, don't forget to eat catfish.

August

Festival of Flavors, Eagle River, WI; eaglerivermainstreet .org. Held in Eagle River's Riverview Park on the last weekend in August, this culinary soiree features all sorts of Wisconsin foods and produce. The idea is to celebrate the foods of Wisconsin, along with bluegrass music, a Street Food Row sponsored by **Sprecher Brewery** (p. 129), a root-beer-float-drinking contest, kids' activities, a cheese carver, and chef demonstrations.

The Great Taste of the Midwest, Madison, WI; mhtg .org/great-taste-of-the-midwest. This is one of the state's most fun beer festivals. Held annually on the second Saturday in August, more than 100 brewpubs and microbreweries from the Midwest set up their stalls in Olin-Turville Park overlooking Lake Monona in Madison. Up to 6,000 beer lovers have attended in recent years, sipping, supping, and savoring ales, stouts, ambers, and all those great brews in between.

Milwaukee Irish Fest, Milwaukee, WI; irishfest.com. Milwaukee Irish Fest is the world's largest Irish cultural event of its kind, with music, theater, dance, exhibits, food, and even Irish dogs on display. Held annually on the third weekend of August, the event attracts Gaels from all over the globe. But you needn't have a whisper of Irish in you to enjoy the festivities. Major Irish politicians straight from the Auld Sod also regularly drop by to press the flesh. The festival's mission is to "Instill in Future Generations an Appreciation of Irish Heritage." To be sure, they do a grand job of it.

Seymour Burger Fest, Seymour, WI; homeofthehamburger .org. The Burger Fest honors the memory of Charles Nagreen, also known as Hamburger Charlie. Nagreen was a Seymour native who began referring to his ground beef patties served in a bun as "hamburgers." He began selling his hamburgers at age 15 at the Seymour fair in 1885 and later expanded to the Brown and Outagamie County Fairs. Since then, even the Wisconsin legislature has gotten into the act by declaring that the city is the original home of the burger, which now has a Hamburger Hall of Fame. Activities include a hot-air balloon rally, parade, car show, Bun Run, kite flying, lots of music, and loads of hamburgers, plus the hamburger-press weight-lifting competition, a thick-burger-eating competition, and a ketchup slide. Setting a record, an 8,266-pound burger was fried up August 4, 2001. Activities take place in Lake Park, usually the first week of August.

Wisconsin State Fair, 640 S. 84th St., West Allis, WI; wistatefair.com. Held in early August, the fair has been celebrating the state's agriculture heritage since the 1850s. For the best food, visit the Wisconsin Products pavilion for potatoes, bison and elk burgers, honey sticks, duck fajitas, grilled cheese sandwiches, and ice cream sundaes. Going off the deep end, try a range of deep-fried goodies such as cream puffs and deep-fried cheese curds, candy bars, and pickles. A spin on a carnival ride following this culinary excursion will certainly be an adventure.

September

Beef-A-Rama, Minocqua, WI; minocqua.com/channel/ Beef-A-Rama/2587. There is no question about "where's the beef" in Minocqua during Beef-A-Rama. A tradition for more than a half century, the fun-filled celebration is complete with the Rump Roast run, roast cook-offs, plenty of games, live music, and a craft show. Every year, at least a ton of beef is dished out to more than 12,000 people during the celebration. Participants cook their roasts in downtown, along with a beef-eating contest followed by a Parade of Roasts.

The Cumberland Rutabaga Festival, Cumberland, WI; cumberland-wisconsin.com. This fest gives a shout-out to the world's most chuckled-at vegetable on the weekend before Labor Day. Among the activities are runs/walks for charity, plus music, food vendors, and kids' programs. There might even be rutabagas on hand to sample.

Green County Cheese Day, Monroe, WI; cheesedays .com. Since 1914, Green County Cheese Days has always made for loads of family fun. The party features cheese, cheese, and more cheese, plus polka bands, cow milking competitions, and . . . did we mention cheese? The event is held on the third weekend of September in even-numbered years. In addition to eating your way along the vendors' row, you can take in the Cheesemakers' Ball and dance the night away. Be aware that throughout the evening, an occasional Swiss yodeler will step up to the microphone to showcase his or her skills. And look for the chocolate fountain.

The Warrens Cranberry Festival, Warrens, WI; cranfest .com. The cranberry is big business in the Warrens area, home of numerous berry bogs. The fest has become one of the country's largest arts and crafts fairs, as well as offering parades, bog tours, and loads of grub, much of which has a cranberry theme. The festival is held the last full weekend in September.

Watermelon Festival, Pardeeville, WI; pardeeville watermelonfestival.com. Chandler Park hosts this melon-do, with slices of cool, sweet melons offered free to guests. There are melon-carving contests, as well as seed-spitting and speed-eating competitions. In the men's category, Clark Hodgson of Pardeeville spat a seed a record 61 feet, 3 inches in 1988.

October

Bayfield Apple Festival, Bayfield, WI; bayfield.org/bayfield -activities/bayfield-apple-festival. The festival is considered one of the country's top autumn festivals, according to the Society of American Travel Writers. There are numerous booths selling cider, pies, tarts, and caramel apples. A kids' carnival with games and rides rounds out the family activity menu. Plenty of music keeps everyone up and moving.

Eagle River Cranberry Festival, Eagle River, WI; eagleriver.org/CranberryFest.asp. This cranberry fest is a family event with activities being held throughout the Northwoods community. You can try fresh, locally grown cranberries made into bratwurst and other delicacies, tour bogs, and enjoy a slice of the World's Largest Cranberry Cheesecake. The fest grounds are bounded by Division and Forest Streets and State Highway 70.

Holy Hill Art & Farm Market, 4958 Holy Hill Rd. (State Highway 167 West), Hubertus, WI; holyhillartfarm .com. The market is held on the old Loosen homestead, where barns and buildings house displays by the region's crafters and farmers. The rolling hills surrounding the market are reminiscent of Ireland, where many of the early settlers came from. The spires of the Basilica of the National Shrine of Mary, Help of Christians, are in the distance.

November

Pie Palooza, Madison, WI; reapfoodgroup.org/programs-events/pie-palooza. Pie makers all over Madison come up with sweet

 and savory pie recipes for this annual celebration held in early November. A Sunday brunch includes your choice of two slices of pie. Every selection is baked by area chefs using local products. Proceeds from Pie Palooza support REAP Food Group programs, which promote healthy foods in schools, restaurants, food stores, and home kitchens.

December

Ethnic Holiday Dinner, Old World Wisconsin, Eagle, WI; oldworldwisconsin.wisconsinhistory.org/Events/EventDetail/Event2129.aspx.

Guests love celebrating the holiday traditions of Yankee, German, Irish, and Scandinavian immigrants who came to Wisconsin in the 1800s and early 1900s. Matinee and evening seatings are available on the Sunday of the event. Old World Wisconsin, W372 S9727 State Hwy. 67, is a state historical site, comprised of an 1870s crossroads village and 10 ethnic farmsteads. The complex is located on 576 acres of wooded hills in the Southern Unit of Kettle Moraine State Forest.

ETHNIC FLAIR

Milwaukee is renowned for its range of festivals highlighting the city's many ethnic heritages, each having numerous food booths promoting the respective cultures: Polish Fest, Milwaukee Highland Games (Scottish) and Greek Fest in June; Bastille Days (French), Croatian Festival, Armenian Fest, Festa Italiana, and German Fest, July; African World Festival, Irish Fest, Mexican Fiesta, Serbian Fest, and India Fest, August; Indian Summer, September; Scandinavian, October. There is also a PrideFest in June and loads of summertime church festivals. Visit Milwaukee's website, visitmilwaukee.org, for the details.

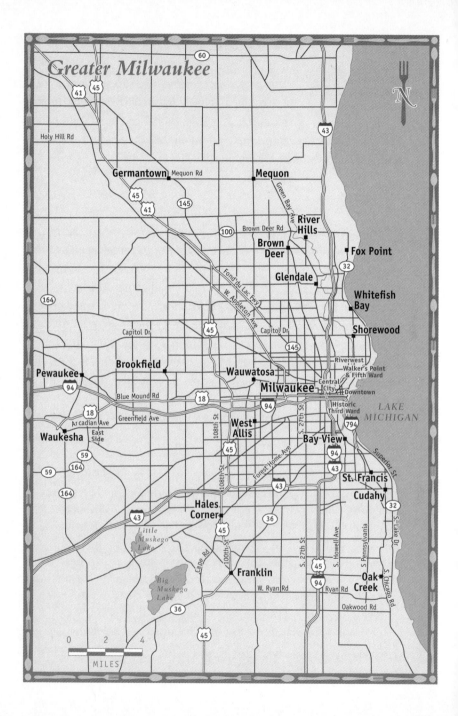

Greater Milwaukee

60

41 45

N

Holy Hill Rd

Germantown   Mequon Rd

Mequon

43

45

41   145

Green Bay Ave

100   Brown Deer Rd

River Hills

Brown Deer

Fox Point

Fond du Lac Fwy

W. Appleton Ave

Glendale

32

164

Whitefish Bay

Capitol Dr   45   Capitol Dr

Shorewood

145

Brookfield

Riverwest

Walker's Point & Fifth Ward

Pewaukee

94

Wauwatosa

Milwaukee

Central City

Downtown

Blue Mound Rd   18

Historic Third Ward

18   Greenfield Ave

Arcadian Ave

94

LAKE MICHIGAN

Waukesha

East Side

West Allis

108th St

S. 27th St

Bay View

794

45

Superior St

59

Forest Home Ave

94

164

59

43

St. Francis

164

43

Cudahy

Little Muskego Lake

Hales Corner

45

36

32

100th St

Cape Rd

S. 27th St

S. Howell Ave

S. Pennsylvania

S. Lake Dr

Big Muskego Lake

Franklin

W. Ryan Rd

45

Oak Creek

S. Chicago Rd

94

36

Ryan Rd

Oakwood Rd

45

0   2   4

MILES

Greater Milwaukee

For discussion purposes, GPS lovers, map aficionados, and out-of-towners, Milwaukee's downtown ranges along East and West Wisconsin Avenue. This main thoroughfare was called Grand Avenue in the good old 1800s. It runs directly west from Lake Michigan and a sculpture by Mark di Suvero locally called "The Sunburst," although its proper title is *The Calling.* Continue into the setting sun on to Marquette University. The north–south Milwaukee River cuts through the heart of downtown, dividing Wisconsin Avenue. The waterway is on its way to link with the west–east flowage of the Menomonee River. The downtown's northern end is Juneau Avenue, and the southern boundary is the Historic Third Ward. Within this area are the city's major office buildings, hotels, and restaurants. Among prominent civic landmarks here are City Hall, the Milwaukee County Courthouse, the main public library, the arena and auditorium, the public museum, and the Milwaukee County Historical Society.

For hundreds of years, the Menominee, Fox, Mascouten, Sauk, Potawatomi, Ojibwe (Chippewa), and Ho-Chunk (Winnebago) would gather around here, more or less in peace, to race their horses along the lake shoreline. The native nations harvested wild rice and hunted in the nearby marshes surrounding this confluence of waters. The name Milwaukee may come from the Potawatomi language *minwaking* or Ojibwe language *ominowakiing,* "Gathering Place by the Water." When settlers finally showed up in the late 17th and early 18th centuries led by the French, they used Melleorki, Milwacky, Mahn-a-waukie, Milwarck, and Milwaucki for place names. By the time the swamps were drained and filled in, many early civic records were using Milwaukie as the community's name. Finally, in the late 1800s, a newspaper utilized "Milwaukee." The term stuck and has been used ever since.

The only difference between long ago Native Americans gathering here to share stew and today's city residents dining out is that more shrimp scampi probably is eaten now than the whitetail deer of yore. Restaurants are scattered throughout this district, mostly north of Wisconsin Avenue. One of the major concentrations of eateries is along North Milwaukee Street and in the blocks surrounding Cathedral Square. For those in a walking mode, it is easy to stroll from hotel to pub to restaurant without working up a glow. To figure out where to start, check out VISIT Milwaukee's website, visitmilwaukee.org, or call (800) 554-1448 or (414) 273-3950. The convention and visitor's bureau lists numerous dining possibilities in a wide range of pricing.

Now, let's go get something to eat.

Downtown

Milwaukee's Downtown offers enough eateries to satisfy the hungriest diner, from independently owned quick-in-and-out sandwich and soup shops to high-end, linen tablecloth caravansaries. For map readers, Milwaukee's Downtown runs from Lake Michigan on the east to the Marquette University area on the west, generally along East and West Wisconsin Avenue, the city's main drag, which is divided by the Milwaukee River. To the south, the dividing line would be the elevated I-794 freeway spur, underneath which you reach the hip Third Ward. The dividing line to the north is more amorphous, so let's say the boundary would be the blocks around the Milwaukee Area Technical College.

Foodie Faves

Buckley's Restaurant and Bar, 801 N. Cass St., Milwaukee, WI 53202; (414) 277-1111; buckleysmilwaukee.com; Bistro; $$.
Emphasizing its motto of "Great Food for Great People," Buckley's is an intimate family-owned hideaway presenting a wide variety of edibles: gnocchi with short ribs; duck confit with brie, dried cherries, and ricotta; smoked beef and sun-dried tomatoes; rigatoni with pistachio pesto, paired with a dazzling serving of Graziano Sauvignon Blanc or a smooth Hitachino white ale. Grilled venison, Cornish hen, and breaded

pork loins are also on the menu. And where else can an experimenting diner get strozzapreti with wild boar, which is an artisanal, handcrafted pasta tossed with burgundy-braised boar ragù and grated Parmesan. For an extra-special night out, try out a bottle of Chateau Moncoteour Tête de Cuvée Vouvray Brut from the Loire. Buckley's also has a dynamite brunch selection that includes a mile-high quiche, Guinness-braised corned beef, and a steak and egg wrap. It also offers carryout, a popular service for surrounding apartment dwellers.

Cafe Calatrava, 700 Art Museum Dr., Milwaukee, WI 53202; (414) 224-3200; mam.org; New American; $–$$. There is hardly a better way to augment a tour of Milwaukee restaurants than to stop at the Milwaukee Art Museum for lunch in the Cafe Calatrava. The bright, cheery room honors architect Santiago Calatrava, designer of the museum's flamboyant gull-wing roof. Located in the lower level, the cafe's floor-to-ceiling windows showcase the sweeping views of Lake Michigan, with an adjoining terrace for summer dining. The menu often reflects whatever exhibits are being held in the galleries. During an Impressionist show, a simple basil gnocchi was enhanced with splashes of color by the addition of red peppers, green basil and sage, brown mushrooms, and yellow butternut squash. An art form in itself, the Sunday brunch offers a culinary palette from vegan banana pancakes to eggs Benedict. A kid-friendly menu is also available.

Carnevor Steakhouse Moderne, 724 N. Milwaukee St., Milwaukee, WI 53202; (414) 223-2200; carnevor.com; Steak House; $$$. This sleek steak house from the SURG restaurant group on Milwaukee Street's eatery row has some of the top prime steaks in the city, each offering sizzlingly exceptional flavor. Starters get modern with interesting twists, such as tuna tartare topped with

a wasabi-flavored *tobiko,* and small plates including Kobe carpaccio, thinly sliced beef with shaved Wisconsin Parmesan, local pea tendrils, smoked pine nuts, capers, truffled bread, and horseradish aioli. As far as Carnevor steaks go, the selection includes filets, New York strips, and rib eyes in varying portion sizes and cuts, plus loads of sauce selections from roasted garlic to shiitake and brandy and many in between. If you want something without red meat, there is a magnificent free-range chicken awaiting your knife and fork, or even South African lobster tail. The restaurant offers 400 varieties of wine. Desserts are supremely tempting, much to one's dismay. Among the "devil made me eat it" treats are s'mores with milk chocolate mousse, graham sponge, and marshmallow ice cream. The doughnuts made of chocolate, seasonal jam, and vanilla cream are too tempting to pass up.

City.Net Cafe, 306 E. Wisconsin Ave., Milwaukee, WI 43210; (414) 336-1723; citynetjazz.com; Casual American; $. City.Net Cafe celebrated its grand opening in February 2013, immediately garnering fans for its food and occasional live jazz in the evenings. Owned and operated by veteran restaurateur and jazz drummer Sam Belton, downtowners drop in for breakfast or lunch specials, such as Tamie's Turkey, Sam's Wrap, or a creamy broccoli soup or chili. Espresso drinks are by Abyssinia Coffee Roasters, with Belton doing his own roasting while patrons wait. He secures his coffee from Ghana, Tanzania, Indonesia, and elsewhere, favoring a powerful "red eye" espresso for himself. Honing his skills, Belton has attended roasting workshops and completed a course at the American Barista & Coffee School in Portland, Oregon. Running the kitchen, his daughter Shani acts as chef. The cafe has Wi-Fi service, with many customers sipping a latte while finishing a project on their computers. Belton always has music in the background. Performing with the likes of Milwaukee jazz greats Manty Ellis and Adekola Adedapo, he's often out on the road with the Don Lewis Quartet in Madison and elsewhere. His jazz theme extends to a gallery of musicians' photos lining the walls, with more graphics coming all the time. To find the cafe, follow the wafting aroma of fresh coffee.

Cubanitas, 728 N. Milwaukee St., Milwaukee, WI 53202; (414) 225-1760; getbianchini.com/cubanitas-restaurant.html; Cuban; $$. This is Milwaukee's only real Cuban restaurant, and it serves mojitos and piña coladas that even Hemingway would love. Generally crowded and always casual, there is street or valet parking. Among dishes we favor is the *pan con lechón,* a roasted pork and raw onion sandwich on Cuban bread with its side of mojo sauce. The *ropa vieja,* a shredded flank steak with tomato Creole sauce, onions, and peppers, also hits the spot. There are always daily specials.

Distil Milwaukee, 722 N. Milwaukee St., Milwaukee, WI 53202; (414) 220-9411; distilmilwaukee.com; Supper Club; $$. Distil's mixologists put together a rainbow of one-of-a-kind craft cocktails exclusive to the restaurant. Among the best is 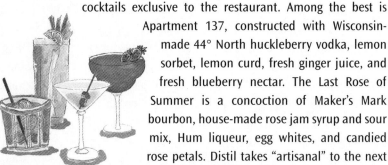 Apartment 137, constructed with Wisconsin-made 44° North huckleberry vodka, lemon sorbet, lemon curd, fresh ginger juice, and fresh blueberry nectar. The Last Rose of Summer is a concoction of Maker's Mark bourbon, house-made rose jam syrup and sour mix, Hum liqueur, egg whites, and candied rose petals. Distil takes "artisanal" to the next level with quality cheese, beer, and spirits, and products such as chorizo-stuffed dates with chèvre and a truffled chicken liver pâté. A small plate of duck *brodo* consists of butternut squash agnolotti and scallions, and the parsnip soup is worth walking on water to reach. Pastry creations here range from a sweet potato pie or a frozen yogurt with a cardamom-saffron parfait, to blackberry ganache, which is a pastry glaze. This place is trendy, overflowing with hotty models, creative arts types, trendy techies, and tall, tall pro basketball players. Scotch is often the beverage of choice, the single malts lovingly served with an eyedropper of water if an imbiber wishes.

Fajitas Grill Centro, 530 E. Mason St., Milwaukee, WI 53202; (414) 312-7799; fajitasgrillmilwaukee.com; Mexican; $–$$. Moving to this new and larger space in 2013, chef and co-owner Arturo Napoles offers several new dishes not found in his old place near Brady Street, such as appetizer scallops. Yet a true Fajitas fan will still trek the Baja for Napoles's fried plantain with tomatillo sauce. Open for a power breakfast at 7 a.m., the morning menu includes traditional huevos rancheros and delicious *chilaquiles,* handmade-from-scratch fried corn tortillas simmered in salsa and dished out with cheese, eggs, or beans. Lending an artistic touch, Hispanic-themed artwork by local painters adorns the brightly painted walls.

Harbor House, 550 N. Harbor Dr., Milwaukee, WI 53202; (414) 395-4900; harborhousemke.com; Seafood; $$–$$$. The view of Lake Michigan and the city skyline is amazing at this joint venture between the Bartolotta restaurant group and philanthropist Michael Cudahy, transporting guests to an idyllic coastal setting. Tucked between the Milwaukee Art Museum and Pier Wisconsin, diners dig into all varieties of seafood and shellfish, including oysters, clams, lump crab, soft-shell crab, mussels, and shrimp. The chefs here are also meat-friendly, presenting Strauss veal cutlets, filet mignon, and even the traditional chicken. Seasonal sitting on the verandah, gazing at stars, the harbor lights, and the illuminated downtown, makes summer all the more pleasurable when we return from a lakefront festival or are headed to the theater and are seeking a quick Champagne or martini. Scoot over here after an outdoor Fish Fry & A Flick movie night at the adjacent Discovery World museum and education center.

Mobile Food Movement

For cheap eats on the run, Milwaukeeans know to track down any one of the many meals-on-wheels wagons, trucks, and carts that roam the streets from spring to autumn. To find the most current parking sites for each traveling grill, savvy diners use Twitter and Facebook.

Pita Brothers, (262) 320-7482; pitabrothers.com. Brothers Vijay and Manoj Swearingen use Lebanese flatbread as the base for their pita wraps, assembled in a compact prep area of their battery-run vehicle. A fresh-chopped veggie pita wrap with hummus spread is $5, with a chicken-bacon-ranch delight at $6 and other menu items ranging in between. Subsequently, a diner can always be assured of an inexpensive munch, even if on the run. The vegetables can be grilled or raw. Fruit smoothies are prepared on-site, with sodas stored in a glass-front refrigerator. The Swearingens' truck is most often found at Catalano Square in the Third Ward, showing up around 11:30 a.m. weekdays or alternating to 15th and Wells near Marquette. They can be tracked on their journey via Twitter (@PitaBros) and Facebook.

Streetza Pizza, (414) 215-0021; streetza.com. Any way you slice it, Scott Baitinger and Steve Mai have an edible gold mine with their pizza-by-the-slice offering. The truck usually parks along Water Street on hot summer weekend nights for after-hours grazing, much like the famous "chippers" in Britain. The duo can also be found outside festival grounds and similar outdoor events, temptingly presenting one last snack before revelers head home. Slices are taken from a menu of daily-changing offerings, including a sausage and four cheeses to a fancier chicken Alfredo. Seek 'em out on Twitter (@streetzapizza).

Taqueria Arandas, (414) 672-3514. No one can miss the taco trucks bustling throughout the South Side. Fans of Alejandro Leon eagerly track down his fleet, coming from all over the city for their taco treat—or for a burrito, tostada, or *torta.* Leon's basic taco is merely $1.50, which means that a two-, three-, or four-taco meal isn't out of the ordinary. Fillings range from beef to chicken and beef tongue. Aficionados go for the *tripas* (chitterlings) on crisp or soft tortillas, complemented with onion and cilantro. Leon's restaurant of the same name (1531 W. Lincoln Ave.) is the "madre ship," accommodating off-season cravings.

American Euros, (414) 962-GYRO; american-euros.com. Owner Mike Miller sets up his gyro wagon at Water and Wisconsin from 10:30 a.m. to around 3 p.m., and it can be found along Water Street on Thurs and Fri from 9:30 p.m. through bar closing. Starting in 2012, business has grown enough so that Miller is even thinking of opening a storefront outlet for the winter. His basic gyro is lamb, cucumber sauce, and lettuce, topped European style with french fries. Miller also offers chicken and veggie gyros. Miller's baklava babe is his Greek mom, Alexandra Stoerri, who creates the cart's fresh pastry, a slice of the sticky, honey-sweet delicacy.

Good Food Dude, (414) 446-7372; goodfooddude.net. The Dude's large green van is seen at many East Side, Riverwest, and Downtown locales, as well as outdoor music and theater events throughout the area in the summer. Chef-Owner Bill Duvall's mission is to bring organic and locally produced goodies to the community. There is always a coffee of the month, with serving sizes ranging from the 12-ounce Normal Dude to the 16-ounce Big Dude. Espresso, cappuccino, mocha, and lattes are available as well, along with smoothies and flavored Italian soda. Experiment with the Cry Fowl hand-pattied burger, crowned with an over-easy fried egg, caramelized onions, Wisconsin cheddar cheese, and a dynamite sauce, all served on a Kaiser roll from Fred Scarina's bakery.

Hot dogs. The true harbinger of Milwaukee summer is the dog carts roaming in packs around greater Milwaukee. From May through early October, you can find wiener wagons in front of the Reuss Federal Plaza, along the River Walk, across from the Marcus Center, near City Hall, and ranging throughout the Water Street neighborhood for post-partygoers. Trimmings include sauerkraut, relish, peppers, various brown and yellow mustards, fried or raw onions, ketchup, and additional condiments. "Upscale" carts, notably **Real Dogs** at Water and Wisconsin, present even more, carrying brats, knockwurst, andouille sausage, and dynamite Hungarian sausages for the discerning diner. Chips, cookies, and related side orders are at the whim of the vendor.

Melthouse Bistro, 1857 E. Kenilworth Place, Milwaukee, WI 53202; (414) 271-6358; melthousebistro.com; Casual American; $. Gourmet grilled-cheese sandwiches, made with championship Wisconsin cheese and fresh artisan breads, are the only items on the menu, other than salads and a listing of sides that include coleslaw, soup, hash browns, waffle fries, and several other additions. All food is prepared from scratch. The comfortable little restaurant is spare, with few frills. A diner comes here for the sandwiches.

Rumpus Room, 1030 N. Water St., Milwaukee, WI 53202; (414) 292-0100; rumpusroommke.com; Bistro; $$. Situated across the street from the Marcus Center for the Performing Arts, the Rumpus Room is a wonderful spot for a laid-back dinner or a pre- or post-performance pause. The waitstaff are pros in getting guests in and out well before curtain time. Among his other culinary skills, Chef Matt Kerley is a pork expert. Everything porcine from nose to tail that comes into the Rumpus kitchen goes out on a platter in some fashion, including pigs' ears, hoisin-glazed pork belly, or footsies turned into trotter tots. Bar snacks, complementing a 30-some page booklet of drink options, range from old-school popcorn seasoned with a spice blend to rumaki, a favorite in Milwaukee of water chestnuts wrapped in bacon. For entrees, Rumpus has come up with stuffed quail, pork schnitzel, lamb Bolognese, roasted chicken, burgers, and organic salmon. Top it all off with a dessert of s'mores, a layered ice cream bar with chocolate and salted caramel gelato, fudge sauce, and graham crackers topped with marshmallow crème. Sometimes, however, a goat cheese cheesecake with a walnut crust, pickled grapes, and saba does the trick. A quick carry-out counter is just inside the front door for the rushed noontime patron.

Tutto Restaurant Bar, 1033 N. Old World 3rd St., Milwaukee, WI 53203; (414) 291-5600; tuttomilwaukee.com; Italian; $. The restaurant's name, Tutto (pronounced TOO-toe), means "everything" in Italian. Owners Sal, David, and Joe Safina have created a lively hot spot in Milwaukee's nightclub zone. They offer a menu of Italian favorites blended with American continental cuisine. Popular dishes include Dijon-crusted tilapia served with whole wheat spaghetti and a dynamite four-cheese ravioli. But the Two Buck Tuesday with $2 sliders (such as Bambino Burgers) and $2 tappers are wildly popular with the city's up-and-coming young professionals after a tough work day.

Umami Moto, 718 N. Milwaukee St., Milwaukee, WI 53202; (414) 727-9333; umamimoto.com; Asian; $$–$$$. Sashimi plates, made with salmon and roe, along with smoky bacon-dashi gelée, are grand taste treats. The classy Mr. Miyagi-tini martini is a signature Svedka vodka fusion with Kurasawa sake, muddled cucumber, simple syrup, and sour mix. The weekly fish specials are a big draw. The place was totally redone early in 2013, making it even more slick.

Ward's House of Prime, 540 E. Mason St., Milwaukee, WI 53202; (414) 223-0135; wardshouseofprime.com; Traditional American; $$$–$$$$. Neither one of us has tried the 88-ounce or the 160-ounce prime rib. If we did, and survived, we could have made it up on the restaurant's Wall of Fame along with Mike Litman, Alfred Halaka, Kurt Schmidt, and other prodigious eaters, including the demure Alyssa DiGillo, who once devoured a 72-ounce beast; Ward's even named a platter in her honor. However, go for much smaller portions or just a cup of prime rib chili. In the front is a bar with large-screen televisions for sports fans, while diners have their own quiet area in the rear. Owner Brian Ward is a scion of the famed Ward family, the multigenerational clan that helped get Milwaukee Irish Fest up and off the ground, making it the world's largest Irish cultural event. It's held each August on the lakefront festival grounds, and you bet your blarney that Ward has a major booth there. True to his heritage, he does serve a melt-in-your-mouth corned beef brisket for noon lunch.

CHECK IN & DINE WELL

Milwaukee's hotel scene features quality restaurants enjoyed not only by guests by also by locals who know good food and how to find it without having to pack a bag to get there.

Cafe at the Plaza, 1007 N. Cass St., Milwaukee, WI 53202; (414) 272-0515; cafeattheplaza.com; Traditional American; $. The cafe shares space with its mother ship, a renovated Art Deco 1920s-era Plaza Hotel. Open for breakfast and lunch, we appreciate the fresh, seasonal ingredients from local producers that go into the made in-house, from-scratch dishes. Wisconsin crafted beer, cheese, and meats are popular.

Envoy, 2308 W. Wisconsin Ave., Milwaukee, WI 53233; (414) 345-5015; envoymilwaukee.com; Supper Club; $$. The Ambassador Hotel has been a Milwaukee landmark since the 1920s, but there is nothing pretentious about the fare in Envoy. Going retro, the Great Gatsby is a four-course prix fixe. When you want to be naughty, order the caramelized Door County cherry crème brûlée with citrus zest, or a sinfully good slab of double-chocolate tres leches cake constructed with dark chocolate cake and chocolate sauce.

Hotel Metro, 411 E. Mason St., Milwaukee, WI 53202; (414) 272-1937; hotelmetro.com; Continental; $–$$$. Stop by for a drink at the award-winning Hotel Metro's beautifully redesigned bar/restaurant. Splurge on a delicious steak, cooked at 700°F in the Metro's custom-built wood-burning oven and grill, which is fired with real hardwood. Zen on Seven is the hotel's hot spot, located on the 7th floor, with an inside space for cocktail parties or dinners. The rooftop space features floor-to-ceiling windows presenting some of the best views in downtown and an exterior space that includes a waterfall, pond, and rooftop garden.

Kil@wat, 139 E. Kilbourn Ave., Milwaukee, WI 53202; (414) 291-4793; kilawatcuisine.com; Bistro; $$–$$$. Located on a flight upstairs from the lobby, the Intercontinental Hotel's main dining room presents an electrifying menu, starting with butternut squash soup and on to the mushroom pappardelle made with wild mushrooms, spinach pappardelle pasta, smoked chicken, rosemary cream, and heirloom tomatoes. Through a vaulted foyer on the first floor, the Intercontinental is linked to the Pabst Theater.

The Pfister Hotel, Mason Street Grill, 425 E. Mason St., Milwaukee, WI 53202; (414) 298-3131; masonstreetgrill.com; Traditional American; $$–$$$. This historic hotel downtown, built in 1893, is the epitome of grand elegance and truly reminiscent of an old-time transatlantic steamship. The Grill's namesake martini is The Pfister, of course. This signature drink is made with Ketel One Citroen vodka, Martini & Rossi vermouth, pomegranate juice, and sugar syrup. Adjacent to the main dining room is a special lounge and piano bar with a menu of small plates. Talented combos warm up even the coldest Wisconsin evening. Conclude an evening at the Pfister with a visit to its upper-room nightclub, Blu, for a view of the nighttime cityscape and a good pour.

Sheridan House Boutique Hotel and Cafe, 5133 S. Lake Dr., Cudahy, WI 53110; (414) 747-9800; sheridanhouseandcafe.com; New American; $–$$. Sheridan's has an illustrious history dating from 1911 as The Lakeview Inn which became The Sheridan Hotel and Palm Garden's Tavern in 1920. In 2007, it was completely renovated it to the current stylishly small hotel and bistro, returning to its former handle. Guests of a certain age go for the $5 Bistro Breakfast, geared just for seniors from 7 to 10 a.m., Tues through Fri. The meal includes two eggs done any way, a choice of sausage or bacon, one buttermilk or oatmeal pancake, and a side of fruit (no substitutions).

Smyth at the Iron Horse, 500 W. Florida St., Milwaukee, WI 53204; (414) 374-4766; theironhorsehotel.com; Bistro; $–$$. The Iron Horse Hotel is a hot spot of activity, special events, and Harley enthusiasts visiting the nearby Harley Davidson Museum. At Smyth, the small plates come in three styles: Cool, Crafted, and Classics. In the first, you can experiment with *foie gras*–crusted lamb, or chicken wings served with house-made doughnuts. For the second, the lobster deviled eggs with pickled shrimp are interestingly tasty. On the third listing are such items as tempura-battered Wisconsin cheese curds and wild Pacific salmon with shrimp and scallop hash. On the far side of the atrium is Branded, a favorite bar with grand pub grub and an outside patio for the hip and trendy in the summer. On any given day, the parking area is filled with "big iron" Harleys ridden by touring cycle fans from around the world.

Zarletti, 741 N. Milwaukee St., Milwaukee, WI 53202; (414) 225-0000; zarletti.net; Italian; $$–$$$. Chef and owner Brian C. Zarletti concentrates on regional Italian cuisine inspired by his grandmother and learned from his numerous trips to Italy. He does a marvelous job of devising intriguing meals, starting with appetizers such as whole squid stuffed with crab and bread crumbs served in a tomato sauce. For a *primi* selection, try *ravioli del giorno;* you can ask about the day's variety of stuffed, handmade pasta. The little touches count here. Who can forget the crispy breaded veal cutlets with their hint of lemon. Zarletti also has one of the city's largest Italian wine selections, featuring at least 30 varieties by the glass, mostly by small producers. The restaurant is perhaps the only place in town that serves a sinfully smooth 2004 Vietti Barolo Riserva "Villero" at $400 a bottle, but 45 bottles are under $50. Urban chic is the name of the game here. The modernist dining room has views of bustling downtown through its floor-to-ceiling windows.

Landmarks

Bacchus, 925 E. Wells St., Milwaukee, WI 53202; (414) 765-1166; bacchusmke.com; Traditional American; $$–$$$$. Located in the venerable Cudahy Tower, Bacchus is truly elegant, a perfect stage setting for romance or doing business. Small plates as well as large entrees are offered. A 900-bottle wine list is certainly cause for any celebration, but we favor perching in the bar area for burger sliders. There's no menu notice for this, so ask the bartender, and ye shall be served. For a winning foodie trifecta, complement a Bacchus burger with a four-olive Rehorst vodka martini as accompanying beverage and add a 5- or 10-cheese tasting board. Gourmands go for the Crave Brothers Les Frères, Upland Dairy's Pleasant Ridge Reserve, or any of the other Wisconsin award winners. But since Bacchus's main dining room is très chic, one must mention the lobster ravioletti and the porterhouse for two with its potato puree, sautéed mushrooms, and garlic spinach.

Butch's Old Casino Steakhouse, 555 N. James Lovell St., Milwaukee, WI 53233; (414) 271-8111; butchssteakhouse.com; Steak House; $$–$$$. For more than 30 years, Butch's has been downtown Milwaukee's premier meat lovers' getaway. Peeking into the open kitchen, guests can savor the sizzling of panfried steer tenderloin and thick-cut lamb and pork chops. Just inside the main door is a case packed with the numerous meat offerings. Select, point, and eat. Start with a dynamite martini and a platter of chicken livers, then move on to the soup or salad and a relish tray. The 20-ounce New York strip arrives with great fanfare, accompanied by baked or cottage spuds and Italian bread. Go for a muscular red wine as beverage, while admiring all the antiques, especially the vintage slots, ringing the room.

Elsa's on the Park, 833 N. Jefferson St., Milwaukee, WI 53202; (414) 765-0615; elsas.com; Bistro; $–$$. Elsa's is by far the classiest burger joint in Milwaukee, and it also serves grilled ahi tuna and smoked salmon. Overlooking Cathedral Square, the chic nightspot has flower-bedecked marble-top tables and ever-changing artwork on the walls. It is the place to see and be seen for the city's trendies of all ages, sexes, and races. Owner Karl Kopp runs a tight ship and regularly buses tables on hectic nights. Under Kopp's watchful eye, the service is always friendly and top-notch professional; many of the staff have worked alongside him for several decades. Kopp also owns Kopp's Frozen Custard outlets in Glendale, Brookfield, and several other strategic locales around Milwaukee, where hungry eaters go for towering shakes and he-man-size burgers.

Sprechen Sie Deutsch? Ja, You Bet!

Milwaukee's German heritage lives on with **Mader's** and **Karl Ratzsch's,** both serving generations of hearty eaters who love perusing a Teutonic menu. Mader's has a long and illustrious history, dating from its founding in 1902 by Charles Mader. Today, this iconic restaurant has a multimillion dollar collection of art, medieval armor, and antiques dating back to the 14th century. The Knights' Bar here is a repository of enough of this sharp-edge metalwork to outfit any castle armory. Tyler Mader, the latest in the extended family line, got his first job at the restaurant at age 6, escorting guests to their tables. Trained at the Culinary Institute of America, he's now well on his way to becoming a celebrity chef. John F. Kennedy dined at Mader's, as did Jerry Ford and Ronald Reagan. For a real German experience, the German sampler consists of wiener schnitzel, *Kasseler Rippchen,* and Rheinischer sauerbraten with potato dumplings, sauerkraut, and red cabbage. At Ratzsch's, Old World favorites include pork shank, braised beef roulade, a duck and goose combination, oodles of schnitzels, and a **Usinger Sausage** (p. 36) sampler. Valet parking is available. Ratzsch's is a 2-block walk west from the venerable **Pfister Hotel** (p. 31), another downtown landmark.

Mader's, 1041 N. Old World 3rd St., Milwaukee, WI 53203; (414) 271-3377; madersrestaurant.com; German; $$–$$$.

Karl Ratzsch's Milwaukee's Landmark German-American Restaurant, 320 E. Mason Ave., Milwaukee, WI 53202; (414) 276-2720; karlratzsch.com; German; $$–$$$.

Major Goolsbys, 340 W. Kilbourn Ave., Milwaukee, WI 53203; (414) 271-3414; Casual American; $. For more than 30 years, the Major has been the ultimate sports bar and primo gathering spot before and/or after sporting events and concerts at the nearby auditorium and arena. Hamburgers, hot dogs, brats, and sandwiches rule. The ham and cheese isn't what granny served: Six slices of ham topped with two hunks of cheese is a winner. Pregame warmups include wings, chicken tenders, sweet potato wedges, and other munchies washed down by Milwaukee-brewed beer, beer, beer. Numerous large-screen HDTVs ensure that you won't miss a pitch or a three-point shot. There is even a ticket booth inside for last-minute purchases of tickets to Milwaukee Bucks basketball games or Admirals hockey matches. Dozens of autographed photos of Milwaukee and Wisconsin athletes and loads of sports memorabilia adorn the walls.

Real Chili, 419 E. Wells St., Milwaukee, WI 53202; (414) 271-4042; realchili-milwaukee.com; Casual American; $. Founded in 1932 as a nine-stool eatery in the basement of the Jesuit residence hall at Marquette University, Real Chili has clung to tradition. You'll only get chili here, whether mild, medium, or hot-hot. Oh, sorry, there are chili dogs and chili cheese dogs, with some philistines asking for the tuna or a turkey sandwich. The downtown location is open 11 a.m. to midnight Mon to Wed, and until 3 a.m. Thurs to Sat; closed Sun. Another location is near Marquette, 1625 W. Wells St. (414-342-6955); this outlet is open until 2 a.m. Mon to Wed, 11 a.m. until 3 a.m. Thurs to Sat, and until 11 p.m. Sun. Real Chili was once featured on the Food Network's *Best Thing I Ever Ate.* In the wee hours of the morning, that's true.

The Spice House, 1031 N. Old World 3rd St., Milwaukee, WI 53203; (414) 272-0977; thespicehouse.com. In business since 1957, the Spice House is Aroma with a capital A. Spices are ground by hand in small batches to ensure freshness. For some of the spices, several selections of different origin allow guests to sample the subtleties between geographic regions. Frequent spice seminars help boost the learning curve from adobo seasoning to the versatile za'atar. Saffron, Hawaiian black lava salt, Meco brown chipotle chile peppers, Madagascar pure double-strength vanilla extract, and Chinese five-spice powder are among the store's hard-to-find-elsewhere products. Helpful staff can select a spice for whatever cuisine we are making for that night's party, whether it's Gold Classic roast lamb stock concentrate or corned beef spice that includes mustard seeds, Moroccan coriander, Jamaican allspice, Zanzibar cloves, Turkish bay leaves, Indian dill seed, China ginger, star anise, black pepper, juniper berries, mace, and cayenne red pepper.

Usinger's Sausage, 1030 N. Old World 3rd St., Milwaukee, WI 53203; (414) 276-9105; usinger.com. Ah, the perfume of blood sausage, beer brats, and braunschweiger. In the late 1870s, young German immigrant Fred Usinger showed up in Milwaukee with $400 in cash, his favorite sausage recipes, and trade tricks of the *Wurstmacher* (sausage maker) that he learned in Frankfurt. Founder Fred died in 1930, yet the fourth and fifth generations of the family are still at it, producing more than 70 varieties of links, slices, hunks, and chunks. While you can purchase Usinger's at every grocery and deli in the city, it's more fun to wander into the old-timey downtown retail showroom west of the Milwaukee River. Fanciful murals depicting happy elves making sausage rim the upper walls and gleefully grin down at patrons. Glass cases display the temptations, presided over by knowledgeable *Frauen* and *Fräulein* in white smocks, many of whom speak German.

To find great deals, seek out the seconds table. The Hessische Landleberwurst is an exquisite liver sausage, double cooked, stuffed in a natural casing, and then heavily smoked. The result is smooth as silk and tastes like heaven, especially when slabbed on a monster slice of pumpernickel black rye, with several slices of raw onion and complemented with coarse German mustard. That and a **Sprecher** (p. 129) Black Bavarian or a **Lakefront** (p. 129) India Pale Ale, both brewed in Milwaukee, make a lunch fit for the kaiser. Be sure to have a plentiful supply of gherkins or kosher dills on hand.

Wisconsin Cheese Mart, 215 W. Highland Ave., Milwaukee, WI 53203; (414) 272-3544; wisconsincheesemart.com. Playing up bragging rights since 1938, the Mart proudly presents what it calls the world's largest selection of Wisconsin cheese. Located a block north of **Usinger's Sausage** (above), the Mart is bright and cheery with lots of blond-wood finishing. Dozens of Wisconsin's most famous dairy products are showcased in the display areas. The Cheese Bar is a great locale in which to hang out on a slow Saturday (or any other afternoon if you can work it out). Try your favorite Wisconsin cheese with Wisconsin beer or wines from around the world,  or go the local route. The Mart holds regular tasting events in the Uber Tap Room where a local brewery teams up with the Cheeseheads here for a must-have experience. At the Mart, cheese comes in all configurations, sizes, and varieties, including a 2-ounce Wisconsin-shaped cheddar.

Great Bars

AJ Bombers, 1247 N. Water St., Milwaukee, WI 53202; (414) 221-9999; ajbombers.com. Kaboom! Its Milwaukee Burger was declared winner of the Travel Channel's *Food Wars*.

LONG POUR

One can't talk about Milwaukee's beer and distilling history without discussing its noteworthy bar and tavern scene, which is first noted in 1837. In that year, Louis Trayser opened his Zum Deutschen Little Tavern at State and Water Streets. At the start of the Civil War, historians estimated that there was one bar for every 98 Milwaukee residents. The list of saloons in the city covered nearly three pages of the city directory in 1873, numbering 502 establishments. In late 19th-century Milwaukee, a drinker seeking a beverage could select from at least 3,500 drinking establishments, ranging from the dilapidated rum holes to fancy bars in highbrow hotels. About 300 were owned and managed by women, most of them widows who had inherited the places from their deceased husbands.

Belmont Tavern, 784 N. Jefferson St., Milwaukee, WI 53202; (414) 988-6160; thebelmonttavern.com. Not the famous racetrack, but close enough.

Duke's on Water, 152 E. Juneau Ave., Milwaukee, WI 53202; (414) 221-0621. Can't go wrong with $1 rail cocktails and domestic beers from opening until 9 p.m.

Karma Bar and Grill, 600 E. Ogden Ave., Milwaukee, WI 53202; (414) 220-4118; karmamilwaukee.com. Good vibes, good drinks.

Mikey's, 811 N. Jefferson St., Milwaukee, WI 53202; (414) 273-5397; mikeysmilwaukee.com. Great DJs and lots of action.

My Office, 763 N. Milwaukee St., Milwaukee, WI 53202; (414) 276-9646. No lie. When your spouse calls, you are literally at "my office."

News Room Pub, 137 E. Wells St., Milwaukee, WI 53202; (414) 273-4900. Home of the oldest press club in the country, with loads of historic autographs on the walls.

Old German Beer Hall, 1009 N. Old World 3rd St., Milwaukee, WI 53203; (414) 226-2728; oldgermanbeerhall.com. *Ein Prosit, ein Prosit!*

Safe House, 779 N. Front St., Milwaukee, WI 53202; (414) 271-2007; safe-house.com. "I'm looking for a safe house" has been the password here since 1966.

HAVE A BEER WHERE
HISTORY COMES ALIVE

Best Place at the Historic Pabst Brewery, 901 W. Juneau Ave., Milwaukee, WI 53233; (414) 630-1609; bestplacemilwaukee .com. The historic Blue Ribbon Hall hosts events from union rallies to theater productions and birthday parties. A shop here features beer mugs, T-shirts, poster reproductions, and just about everything else relating to the Pabst Brewing Company. Tours of the complex are held Thurs through Sun at noon, 1, and 2 p.m. Named after Jacob Best, the Best Place Tavern is part of a redevelopment of the old brewery, with offices, a Cardinal Stritch University outreach campus, and numerous other uses. A statue of King Gambrinus, the ancient patron of breweries, is in the courtyard. Beer geeks love this place the best.

This Is It Gay Bar, 418 E. Wells St., Milwaukee, WI 53202; (414) 278-9192; thisisitbar.com. Around since 1968. What more do you need to know?

Trinity Three Irish Pubs, 125 E. Juneau Ave., Milwaukee, WI 53202; (414) 278-7033; trinitythreeirishpubs.com. What could be better than a Celtic-pub trio under one roof?

Whiskey Bar, 788 N. Jackson St., Milwaukee, WI 53202; (414) 312-8566; whiskeybarmilwaukee.com. Near Cathedral Square for a spirited experience.

Central City

Milwaukee's Central City is home to some of the oldest and best-known eateries in the community. Despite neighborhood changes, urban renewal, good economic times and bad, these landmarks remain viable.

Foodie Faves

The Five O'Clock Steakhouse, 2416 W. State St., Milwaukee, WI 53233; (414) 342-3553; fiveoclocksteakhouse.com; Steak House; $$$–$$$$. Since 1948, this steak house, formerly Coerper's Five O'Clock Club, has remained a timely Milwaukee culinary fixture, a happy caravansary where meat rules. The name came about years ago when an alarm clock behind the bar rang at 5 p.m., signaling a free round for guests. All the steaks here are served with butter-sautéed mushrooms, just as they should be. Bacon-wrapped filets, with blue cheese topping and Parmesan cream sauce, demand that you amble home, just to clear the arteries. Dinner comes with a monster tossed salad and the requisite relish tray. This is generally casual yet with a business twist because many corporate types try to show off their meat acumen to associates from out of town.

Growing Power Cafe, 2737 N. King Dr., Milwaukee, WI 53212; (414) 372-7222; growingpower.org/our_store.htm; Casual American; $. **Growing Power** (p. 47) is an urban garden center that produces veggies at 5500 W. Silver Spring Dr. in Milwaukee. In addition to its farm and operations in Chicago, it sponsors this cafe and market featuring a variety of its organic goods, plus hand-rolled butter, eggs from free-range chickens, and preservative-

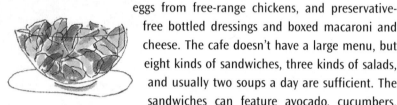

free bottled dressings and boxed macaroni and cheese. The cafe doesn't have a large menu, but eight kinds of sandwiches, three kinds of salads, and usually two soups a day are sufficient. The sandwiches can feature avocado, cucumbers, red peppers, onion, tomatoes, and Growing Power's organic mixed greens. Drink choices include **Colectivo** (see p. 69) coffee, lemonade, orange juice, bottled water, and voluptuous smoothies. For a burst of energy, try a wheatgrass shot. There are also cookies and brownies. The cafe is open every day except Sun, but only from 10 a.m. to 4 p.m.

Jake's Delicatessen, 1634 W. North Ave., Milwaukee, WI 53205; (414) 562-1272; jakes-deli.com; Jewish; $–$$. Oh, that corned beef! Ever since Jake Levin founded this deli more than 50 years ago, the message remains that "you can't fake the real thing, and we'll never try." Despite the deli's Jewish heritage, there is even a "bash o' corned beef" contest for St. Patrick's Day at the deli's Grand Avenue location (275 W. Wisconsin Ave.), when hearty eaters see how much corned beef can be downed in 10 minutes. Probably even the late Israeli prime minister Golda Meir would get a chuckle out of that feeding frenzy. As the young Golda Mabovitch, she grew up just a few blocks away from Jake's, where they still serve husky Reubens, turkey pastrami, matzo ball soup, and Philly corned beef. The basic sandwich is a mouthful, a beef brisket brined and slow-cooked, and then hand-cut fresh out of Jake's steam tables and served on fresh Miller rye. There's nothing fancy here, just battered wooden booths and a counter where those slabs of corned beef are quickly sliced and primed to go. Wash it all down with a traditional Dr. Brown's cream soda.

Landmarks

Mr. Perkins' Family Restaurant, 2001 W. Atkinson Ave., Milwaukee, WI 53209; (414) 447-6660; Casual American; $–$$. Located in the Rufus King neighborhood, Perkins' wisely takes reservations because of the crowds that pack in for pancakes and grits beginning at 6:30 a.m., as well as for lunch. Call first to determine hours. It's usually open only from Wed to Sat, but that sometimes varies. Regardless, folks here know how to dish up smothered pork chops with mac 'n' cheese and fried okra. Collards are a staple and make one of the best sides for perfectly done fried chicken. There are stories of diners who couldn't stop after only one heaping bowl of banana pudding and went on and on and on. There's no hype here, just down-home cooking, appreciated by the likes of visitors such as Danny Glover, Oprah Winfrey, Halle Berry, and Eric Benet. The late owner, Willie Perkins Jr., was an avid sports fan who could talk hours about the Green Bay Packers and Milwaukee Bucks. Unfortunately, he died of cancer in 2010. Perkins's mom, "Grandma" Hilda, and his dad, Willie Sr., started the restaurant in 1969. Young Willie started working there in high school and took over in 1999. Their tradition of serving great grub remains so strong, strong, strong that a nearby fast-food drive-through named after a certain Southern colonel shuttered after only a few years.

Riverwest

The Riverwest area on the north side of the Milwaukee River demonstrates the vitality of the community, with its explosion in small eateries, shops, galleries, and studios. There's a whole lot o' happenin' going on here—and some of the best food discoveries around.

Foodie Faves

Cafe Corazón, 3129 N. Bremen St., Milwaukee, WI 53212; (414) 810-3941; corazonmilwaukee.com; Mexican; $$. From the heart of Riverwest, the Corazón serves lunch and dinner daily except Mon. It also has a dynamite brunch pleaser on Saturday and Sunday that includes chorizo and eggs and *migas,* scrambled eggs with strips of corn tortillas and melted cheese, along with rice, beans, salsa, and bacon or sausage. There are lots of other goodies to choose from, helping "morning" become Electra, as Eugene O'Neill's play suggests. Included in breakfast tacos are hearty doses of jalapeño, a great way to jump-start any day, especially after a rollicking eve on the town. Niños dig the Abuelita hot chocolate, just like grandma used to make. A covered patio makes for a special evening in the summer, with its twinkle lights and margaritas. In the winter, the area is enclosed and heated, with serapes available on the off chance a patron becomes slightly chilly.

Centro Cafe, 808 E. Center St., Milwaukee, WI 53212; (414) 455-3751; centrocaferiverwest.com; Italian; $$. Although tiny, Centro looms large in the city's Riverwest neighborhood for its expansive service and hearty portions. It presents craft cocktails concocted with Bittercube's locally made bitters. Tables line the wall, with other guests able to sit at a bar to watch the food prepping up close and personal and to savor aromas. The two window tables fronting the door to Center Street are primo locations for watching the outside passersby. Owners Pat Moore and his wife, Peg Karpfinger, gradually rehabbed their building's old bones, making magic with both the decor and the dining when it opened in 2009. Certain dishes, as marked on the menu, can be prepared vegan and/or gluten-free.  Among our recommendations is the penne Bolognese. Musician Victor DeLorenzo has high praise for the Centro: "Whenever my wife Karen and I feel the need to scratch our Italian food itch, we head over to Centro Cafe, the perfect dining experience for anyone that dreams of all things pasta. The dish that keeps me coming back is the Pasta Pollo." In the summer, iron tables outside make for leisurely dining or a sip of our favorite Pinot Grigio or Prosecco. These are prime seats for chatting with Riverwest friends.

Filling Station, 701 E. Keefe Ave., Milwaukee, WI 53212; (414) 875-7521; the-filling-station.com; Bistro; $–$$. Opening in 2013 on the site of the old, much beloved Albanese's Italian restaurant, the Filling Station is generally packed with locals and pals from all over the city. With the face-lift, gone are the red-and-white checkered tablecloths and jukebox with Sinatra tunes, replaced by a clean and trendy look. The nice renovation by Flux Design uncovered maple floors and a tin ceiling. The Filling Station sells growlers for home consumption. The reusable 64-ounce bottles filled with tap beer were previously outlawed to prevent dishonest retailers from peddling cheap stuff instead of

THE ART OF DRINKING

Art Bar, 722 E. Burleigh St., Milwaukee, WI 53212; (414) 372-7880; artbar-riverwest.com. Artists, filmmakers, photographers, sculptors, and other creatives flock to the Art Bar in Riverwest for its exhibitions, hearty beverage pours, and general conviviality. Easily readable blackboards high up on the wall announce the latest brews and vinos. *An Entire Year of Art on One Canvas, Flesh Experts: Nude Figurative Studies,* and *Attack of the Abstracts,* as well as an annual Halloween bash have been among the quirky shows. The bar doesn't serve food, but pizza is often brought in to satisfy the gallery crawlers. Thick, rich **Colectivo** (see p. 69) coffee helps control any heady buzz after too much color or cocktailing. Wi-Fi is available, along with several gaming tables.

quality beverage. Yet the pub and city alderman Nik Kovac worked to change the law. There's more to the Filling Station, of course. The full menu ranges from fried tofu with hoisin sauce and steamed broccoli to a blackened catfish sandwich. Vegetarian sloppy joes with dynamite Indonesian scallop curry and udon noodles are worth a trip across town. The Meatwad is an 8-ounce beef patty topped with shaved New York strip, plus oodles of mushrooms, along with onions, fontina, and a mind-blowing "tiger" sauce. The Filling Station has a Friday fish special and a nightly special.

Nessun Dorma, 2778 N. Weil St., Milwaukee, WI 53212; (414) 264-8466; nessundormariverwest.com; Italian; $. When it comes to bruschetta, Riverwest's low-key Nessun Dorma has few equals. For starters, the restaurant's Crostini Pizzaiola is a thick-sliced seeded deli loaf crowned with hearty Roma tomatoes, plenty of basil and garlic, and melted fresh mozzarella. Then there is a traditional grilled Tuscan bread, topped with chopped tomatoes, fresh basil, and plenty of anti-vampire garlic. The pesto is house-made, as is the kalamata and Greek green olive tapenades. Speaking of olives, diners can also get large or small portions of red and black Bella de Cerignola and green Castelvetrano olives tossed in a house vinaigrette with capers, onions, and celery. And the beer list is *magnifico!*

Specialty Stores, Markets & Producers

Bolzano Artisan Meats, 3950 N. Holton St., Milwaukee, WI 53212; (414) 426-6380; bolzanomeats.com. Scott Buer's Bolzano Artisan Meats has brought back the lost art of dry curing. Using locally raised heirloom hogs for its various types of salamis, Bolzano is based in Milwaukee's Riverwest neighborhood, in what was once a dairy and then a distillery. Try Bolzano's seasonal Figgy Puddin' salami, a sweet/savory pairing of prosciutto and melon, mixed with dried figs that play up a sweet and salty balance along with a subtle touch of cocoa. Throughout the year, Bolzano hosts hog butchering classes where students get hands-on with pork.

Growing Power, 5500 W. Silver Spring Dr., Milwaukee, WI 53218; (414) 527-1546; growingpower.org. Growing Power (GP) is a national nonprofit organization and land trust that encourages urban agriculture ventures. Since 1993, GP has built community relationships with local organizations, offered training and hands-on experiences in composting, vermiculture, and aquaponics to volunteers and visitors. Back in the day, people used to trade chickens with GP founder Will Allen. Now his mission has expanded to Arkansas, Georgia, Kentucky, Massachusetts, and Mississippi. The operation has a farm in rural Merton, a village 20 miles west of Milwaukee, and urban farms in

Milwaukee and Chicago. It also distributes produce, grass-fed meats, and related products through 300 small family farmers in the Rainbow Cooperative and sells to many restaurants and grocery stores in Chicago, Madison, and Milwaukee.

Ma Baensch, 1025 E. Locust St., Milwaukee, WI; (414) 562-4643; mabaensch.com. Although the original Ma (Lena Baensch) is long departed, her Baensch Food Products Co., a division of Wild Foods Inc., still packs premium Atlantic herring, caught in the wild waters off Nova Scotia. Founded in 1932, the company has been at its current location since 1945 and remains a staple on most Milwaukee holiday tables. Ma's was purchased by the irrepressible Kim Wall in 1999. She still uses the original family recipes for the company's herring pieces marinated in wine sauce or sour cream and chive sauce. Baensch Foods is a member of the National Fisheries Institute and is kosher certified through the Chicago Rabbinical Council. Samples are given out at the Locust Street Festival (locust-street.com/locuststreetfestival.htm) every year, making for a hearty snack; the factory front door is right where one of the event's major stages is located.

Outpost Natural Foods, 100 E. Capitol Dr., Milwaukee, WI 53212; (414) 961-2597; outpost.coop. Even the dried fruit here is certified 100 percent organic and sulfite-free. A noontime bowl of vegetarian chili and a smoothie at the Outpost's dining area is a treat. As much as possible is sourced from nearby vendors, such as garlic from the Copper Kettle Farm, a 25-mile drive from  Colgate, Wisconsin. The Sassy Cow Creamery in Columbus, Wisconsin, where the Outpost secures much of its milk, is 80 miles away. This community of members partners with many other food-related organizations, including the Walnut Way Conservation Group, Hunger Task Forces, Urban Ecology Center, Neighbor to

Neighbor, and Think Outside the Lunchbox. The Outpost also has outlets at 2826 S. Kinnickinnic Ave. (414-755-3202) and 7000 W. State St. in Wauwatosa (414-778-2012), as well as a market cafe at Aurora Sinai Hospital, 945 N. 12th St. (414-220-9166). Ground was broken in July 2013 for another site at the corner of Mequon Road (State Highway 167) and Wauwatosa Road (State Highway 181), which will become operational in the summer of 2014.

Riverwest Co-op, 733 E. Clarke St., Milwaukee, WI 53212; (414) 264-7933; riverwestcoop.org. The co-op is the consistent winner of Best Vegetarian Chili from WMSE-FM's annual Rockabilly Chili Cook-Off. The store opened in 2001 in an old Schlitz tavern; the cafe launched in 2004 and specializes in vegan and vegetarian foods. A full breakfast menu, with old-timey goodies such as biscuits and mushroom gravy, plus an extended brunch on weekends, make this a popular neighborhood hangout. A summertime patio is usually packed with folks just hangin' and chattin'. Somebody might even bring a guitar. The co-op boasts of having 3,000 members, most of whom are active in the community's many civic, charitable, and political causes. All are fueled by locally grown produce and good vibes. WMSE-FM is the broadcast voice of the Milwaukee School of Engineering.

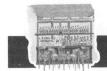

Great Bars

Club Timbuktu, 520 E. Center St., Milwaukee, WI 53212; (414) 265-7000; clubtimbuktu.us. Where else in Teutonic Milwaukee could you ever savor a *likkle ting* to good reggae and a mix of African, Afro-Caribbean, ska, and Afro-Cuban dance-hall music. This place rips on Friday and Saturday nights and hosts special events. For instance, a birthday party honoring the late Rasta star Bob Marley featured Kevin Macdonald's gritty documentary on the Jamaican music master's life and death. Beware of the head-spinning rum punch. Many of the city's African émigrés hang here for talk of home.

The Foundation, 2718 N. Bremen St., **Milwaukee, WI; (414) 374-2587; foundationbar.com.** Aloha to you at this retro tiki bar. Meanest mai tais in town.

The Mad Planet, 533 E. Center St. Milwaukee, WI 53212; (414) 263-4555; mad-planet.net. Rock 'n' roll heaven. What more needs to be said?

Polish Falcon Hall, 801 E. Clarke St., **Milwaukee, WI 53212; (414) 264-0680.** There's bowling in the basement and a kickback bar on the first floor, with a large hall for neighborhood soirees.

Savoy's Bar, 2901 N. 5th St., **Milwaukee, WI 53212; (414) 264-4202.** No cover charge here, just lots of beer and a safe, quiet place to drink. Talk about casual and laid-back, this is it. The Savoy is near Clinton Rose Park, the Martin Luther King Library, and a district police station.

Uptowner, 1032 E. Center St., **Milwaukee, WI 53212; (414) 264-3481.** Also bills itself as a tongue-in-cheek "charm school," a factor that earns points for pub crawlers. *Shepherd Express* columnist Art Kumbalek plunks down his keister here on a regular basis for wry commentary over a shot and a beer.

Historic Third Ward

South of downtown are several funky, fast-growing, restaurant-heavy neighborhoods. Where once there were mostly warehouses and factories now are condos and apartments, with plenty of eateries with chefs on the cutting edge of the city's cuisine. The Historic Third Ward, north of the Milwaukee River, was once a rice swamp during Native American days. Irish and German laborers filled in these lowlands, which quickly became the first stopover housing for newly arrived immigrants from the Auld Sod, Italy, and a host of other countries. The influx soon spilled over south of the river, where Walker's Point was a ferry crossing and then a manufacturing district.

Foodie Faves

Cafe Benelux & Market, 346 N. Broadway St., Milwaukee, WI 5320; (414) 501-2500; cafebenelux.com; Bistro; $–$$. In addition to the chicken salad and pulled pork, the Benelux has a husky Flemish beef stew with roasted fall vegetables, white cheddar pureed potatoes, pretzel bread bowl, and a bacon-wrapped meat loaf that would make grandma envious. The rooftop patio is perfect for Sunday brunching and reading the newspaper. Try the potatoes, melted cheddar, eggs, sausage, thick-cut bacon, chorizo cream gravy, and pico de gallo for a treat. Then walk 2 miles to work it all off.

Cafe La Scala, 631 E. Chicago St., Milwaukee, WI 53202; (414) 223-2185; lascalamilwaukee.com/main.html; Italian; $-$$. The Italian Conference Center (ICC) is always a hub of activity, Italian and otherwise, whether banquets, fund-raisers, weddings, or wakes. The center was founded in 1978 to celebrate the homeland's heritage and culture and has been at its current location since 1990. At its on-site Cafe La Scala, Executive Chef Jack McNeir is known for his chicken saltimbocca, a sautéed breast of chicken layered with fresh sage and prosciutto and topped with Marsala-mushroom-butter sauce served over fettuccine pasta with asparagus spears. Sam Purpero, food committee chair for Festa Italiana, favors McNeir's *braciole con uova,* which is like a thicker *spiedini,* with the meat wrapped around a hard-boiled egg and cooked in a tomato sauce. "It reminds me of what my mother made. It isn't just close, it's exactly the same," he asserts. For value-added entertainment to a meal, the center's annual Courtyard Music Series has delighted diners for 12 years from June through September.

Coquette Cafe, 316 N. Milwaukee St., Milwaukee, WI 53202; (414) 291-2655; coquettecafe.com; French; $$. Four things are de rigueur when making exceptional French onion soup, according to Chris Hatleli and Nick Burki, this cafe's chef-owners: Utilize a sharp knife, take time for proper onion caramelization, create a rich homemade chicken stock, and go naughty with Swiss-imported gruyère by adding two eighth-inch slices of the cheese per serving. Pastry Chef Hector Reyes performs double duty as head onion slicer, using an initial 300 pounds of onions in a caramelization process that extends at least 2.5

FOR A BIT OF BUBBLY

Cuvée, 177 N. Broadway St., Milwaukee, WI 53202; (414) 225-9800; cuveemke.com; $$–$$$. This cozy Champagne lounge is located on the top floor of a building that dates from 1893. Numerous restaurants are nearby, so Cuvée is great for a pre-dinner or post-dessert sip. We regularly drop in after a performance at the Skylight Music Theater across the street and aim for a window view. Cuvée (coo-VAY) is a French word for wine that means "blend." For anyone wanting bubbly in a sexy atmosphere, this is the place. Available for retail purchase are more a hundred world-renowned Champagnes, sparkling wines, reds, and whites, in addition to hearty pours at the round bar centered in the main room. The super-quick, attentive bartender—there's usually only one on duty—can whip up a delicious Belle Fleur, a purplish-pink-tinged Champagne cocktail decorated with a hibiscus flower, or an Asian Persuasion, complete with a chunk of ginger in the bottom of the glass and a yummy mix of sugar, star anise, and other spices on the rim. Comfy booths line the art-bedecked Cream City brick walls. Cuvée is one of the primary party sites in the city, with a large hall attached to the bar area. To get to the elevator, meander down a long hallway past hundreds of Buddha statues displayed in the first-floor Art Asia gallery. It is wise to call ahead, in case the place is booked for a private soiree. But once upstairs, all cares float away.

hours to get the final 50 pounds of flavorful product. Coquette's team prepares some 20 gallons of soup at a time, enough for three days' supply. A special twist is adding sherry and white wine to the soup. Croutons are made in-house from scratch. For Sunday brunch, votes go for the croque monsieur, an open-faced country ham sandwich with Dijon mustard and melted gruyère, or french toast with caramelized pears, candied pecans, maple syrup, and black-pepper bacon. Tuesday evening cooking classes cover a range of subjects.

Hinterland, 222 E. Erie St., Milwaukee, WI 53202; (414) 727-9300; hinterlandbeer.com; New American; $$–$$$. Founded in 1995 by Bill and Michelle Tressler, Hinterland also has its own award-winning beer concocted by Brewmaster Joe Karls and found  throughout Wisconsin. Hinterland does a marvelous job with fish, using such little-known varieties as arctic char. The house charcuterie is an award winner, particularly the house-made summer sausage served up on crackers complemented with 5-year-old Wisconsin cheddar. The wood-fired grill sears up everything from eggplant to duck hearts on skewers. Or try the fried veal brains and the coffee-pepper-rubbed Strauss veal chop sided by Sea Island red peas, Carolina Gold rice, grilled kale, and smoky bacon vinaigrette. Or how about the duck testicles for a real culinary experience? Reservations are helpful, though the expansive bar up front is a good place to dawdle while waiting, if necessary. Hinterland is also a great party place for after-hours social soirees, birthday parties, and job promotion celebrations.

Kanpai, 408 E. Chicago St., Milwaukee, WI 53202; (414) 220-1155; kanpaimilwaukee.com; Japanese; $$. Kanpai opened in 2012 with the idea of presenting Japanese fusion cuisine to a city eager for more Asian cuisine. Numerous foodie events are held here, where guests sample sushi, sashimi, and other Pacific Rim fare. Drink specials include 22-ounce Japanese beers or powerful saketinis—sake-infused vodka and a splash of lemon. There are two bars up front, one where patrons can watch the sushi makers at work. A number of high tops are located here, with booths facing windows that line a hallway leading to the rear dining area. In one section, you can sit Japanese style at low tables. Kanpai is about 2 blocks west of the Italian Conference Center and close to the theater district. The lakefront festival grounds are a short walk to the east.

Rustico Pizzeria, 223 N. Water St., Milwaukee, WI 53202; (414) 220-9933; rusticopizzeria.com; Italian; $. With its exposed brick walls and ceiling rafters, proximity to the River Walk, a comfortable bar near the entrance, and large TVs, Rustico emphasizes the casual. Opened by Italian restaurant maestro Brian Zarletti in 2008, Rustico is primarily a pizza place, but offers extensive salads, antipasti, and panini. Veal Bolognese is a favored dish, as is classic pasta primavera. The wine list is heavy on Italian varieties, with half prices on Tuesday's bottles. This is a handy lunch drop-in if meandering the Third Ward.

Specialty Stores, Markets & Producers

Milwaukee Public Market, 400 N. Water St., Milwaukee, WI 53202; (414) 336-1111; milwaukeepublicmarket.org. Easily visible from the I-794 freeway spur, the market offers 1 hour of free parking upon purchase of items from any of its vendors. Carry your food to the upper deck's Palm Garden if you've purchased it from the main floor. The St. Paul Fish Company has its own small table area, perfect for po' boys and lobster munching. The market also showcases cooking classes in Madame Kuony's Demonstration Kitchen on the upper level, with either local chefs or internationally known cookbook writers as instructors. The market has free Wi-Fi for ease in taking notes. With the opening of the market in 2005, the neighborhood's history of being the community's produce center has come full circle.

Murph's Original, 622 N. Water St., Milwaukee, WI 53202; (414) 270-1073; murphsoriginal.com. Kathryn (Murph) Burke launched her line of gourmet food items in 1975, just as her fifth youngster was about to be born. Her Mount Mary degrees in chemistry and home economics were pluses in initially developing a savory marinade in small batches for friends and home use, eventually evolving into a business. Next came a Bloody Mary cocktail mix, creamy garlic dressing, and shortbread cookies in chocolate chip, rosemary, and plain varieties that are bite-size perfect for even the tiniest of Santa's elves. Plus, Burke's milk or dark chocolate "Murtles" candies make for a magnificent munch of chewy caramel and pecans while wassailing. Look for her online recipes, as well.

Walker's Point & the Fifth Ward

Traveling south along 1st, 2nd, or 5th Streets through Walker's Point and into the Fifth Ward and on to Kinnickinnic Avenue, a traveler passes what was once the world largest four-sided clock, until its 40.2-foot-diameter timepiece was eclipsed by one in Saudi Arabia's Mecca at 140 feet. Yet Milwaukeeans still love their favorite civic clock high above the Allen-Bradley plant, a feature still nicknamed the "Polish Moon" in honor of all the émigré families who used to live in the district. Airplane pilots and Lake Michigan freighter captains still use the lighted clock as a nighttime beacon. The nearby Clock Tower Dairy, which makes luscious ice cream and other dairy products, takes its name from the giant A-B timepiece. The Great Lakes Water Institute, a University of Wisconsin system research facility operated by the School of Freshwater Science, is located nearby. Outside the center's front door, giant ore carriers and hustling tugboats ply the inner harbor. It's still a secret that scientists and technicians at the sprawling research complex host great chili cook-off competitions. In addition, lively perch are raised here in giant, open tanks. They are constantly being studied, from spawning until their ultimate destination via a platter at a traditional Friday fish fry.

Braise, 1101 S. 2nd St., Milwaukee, WI 53204 (414) 212-8843; braiselocalfood.com; Vegetarian/Vegetarian Friendly; $$–$$$. Chef David Swanson has long been a leader in getting restaurants to use local produce, dairy products, and other foods. Swanson has also battled for years to ensure that his farm vendors get properly compensated, founding a program called Restaurant Supported Agriculture (RSA). He remains a strong supporter of the Slow Food Wisconsin Southeast chapter and often prepares special meals for that group and others through his Braise on the Go, where owner Swanson takes his skills, fry pans, and fresh ingredients to cook off-site at a fund-raiser or for a catered dinner. Subsequently, it was great to see him opening his own new community-supported restaurant, the first in the city. He features contemporary American dishes celebrating seasonal goodies thanks to the network of area farmers he's built up over the years. Braise constantly changes its menu, depending on what items are readily available, and bakes its own bread. During the growing season, Swanson's rooftop garden ensures the freshest possible herbs and veggies. The place has an interesting history: A block or so to the north of the famed Allen-Bradley clock tower, the spacious location was once a bowling alley and then home to Jacques' French Cafe, among other residents over the years. For dessert, discerning diners dive into Swanson's lemon pudding cake with dried cherry compote. See Chef David's Swanson's recipe for **Grilled Kabocha Squash with Prosciutto & Truffle Honey** on p. 292.

c.1880, 1100 S. 1st St., Milwaukee, WI; (414) 431-9271; c1880 .com; Bistro; $$–$$$. Chef-Owner Thomas Hauck runs a tight culinary ship with a deft hand, tweaking this and that until the respective dish hits the top of his 10-point scale. His motto is "Food is the art of the earth." He earned his stripes at the Culinary Institute of America in Hyde Park, New York, and honed his skills in France and in Washington, DC, coming back to Milwaukee in 2011. Hauk emphasizes farm-fresh produce and local suppliers, going for the freshest ingredients he can find at any given time. Organic foods made from scratch, in-house cured meats, and fresh herbs and fruits are part of the experience here. Among the more interesting menu items are the veal cheeks with polenta, watercress, and cremini mushrooms. There is also rutabaga and spinach, augmented by gruyère and oyster mushrooms. Among the desserts, Hauck's olive oil cake includes blood orange, white chocolate, and almonds. The restaurant takes up the first floor of a corner building dating from the early 20th century. The dining room is open and airy with a long bar on the left as you enter.

INdustri Cafe, 524 S. 2nd St., Milwaukee, WI 53204; (414) 224-7777; industricafe.com; New American; $$. Emphasizing its motto, "Shelter from the Ordinary," the restaurant offers small plates as well as typical entree-size portions. On some nights, you can favor the traditional and go for the baked lobster mac 'n' cheese complemented with fire-roasted poblanos. Or tackle the Strauss free-raised veal meat loaf with cauliflower and mashed potatoes, wild mushroom veal demi-glace, and carrot powder. The small bar is directly underneath an upstairs lounge, with tables and chairs spread out throughout the rest of the room. Couches and chairs fill in the front bay-window platform where a musician performs on occasion. When there isn't a program, the seats there are fun for cocktail time. For an industrial-strength Bloody Mary, INdustri's comes loaded with a jumbo 7-inch grilled and skewered prawn, astride a hefty 24-ounce glass that includes roasted garlic, red onion, and poblano pepper; fresh basil; fresh horseradish;

house-infused Rehorst vodka; house-made mix; a spiced rim of mesquite chili seasoning; a beef stick; Wisconsin Gouda cheese; and oodles of pickled veggies such as asparagus, brussels sprouts, pearl mushrooms, and a pickle.

The Noble, 704 S. 2nd St., Milwaukee, WI 53205; (414) 243-4997; nobleprovisions.com; New American; $$. This quirky Walker's Point bistro brags about its "Small Space. Small Menu. Big Heart." Try to get the booth in the front window for the best view of the action throughout the place. The Noble offers three to six daily specials in meat, fish, and vegetarian. Check its Facebook page (facebook.com/TheNobleMKE) to find out what's on the griddle that night. Beer is a buck. No reservations are taken, so if the place is crowded, you can get a cocktail at the bar or even meander around the neighborhood to try another nightspot. The staff will call your cell phone when your table is ready. Don't be alarmed if someone in the place breaks out into song. It might be the owner.

The Philly Way, 405 S. 2nd St., Milwaukee, WI 53204; (414) 273-2355; thephillyway.com; Casual American; $. This hole-in-the-wall hosts cops on their break, legal beagles, artists, developers, and others from just about every walk of life. There are probably even Philadelphia ex-pats who appreciate this touch of home. The sandwiches come plain, or you can add the works, whether cheese, mushrooms, onions, sweet peppers, or loads of hot peppers.

Landmarks

Chez Jacques, 1022 S. 1st St., Milwaukee, WI 53204; (414) 672-1040; chezjacques.com; French; $$. The irrepressible Jacques Chaumet hails from Le Puy-en-Velay, a south-central French city famous for its shrines, green lentils, Verveine herbal liqueur, and lace making. Chaumet arrives early each morning, even before his staff, to quietly make his secretive soup concoction, one that brings in diners from throughout the area. Croutons are made from fresh-baked French bread drizzled with olive oil, flavored with pepper, salt, garlic, and the ever-glorious herbes de Provence, and then toasted. To locate Chez Jacques, seek out the signage with the French national symbol—the rooster—in the shadow of the Allen-Bradley clock tower. Outside, on the outer wall of the patio, is a mural painted by local artist Amanda Aquino telling the story of how Chamuet traveled from France to Milwaukee. Seeking another larger location, Chaumet saw the potential of a nearby warehouse, which he purchased and refurbished. Chaumet's Beaujolais Nouveau parties are the stuff of local legend each November.

La Merenda, 125 E. National Ave., Milwaukee, WI 53204; (414) 389-0125; lamerenda125.com; Bistro; $$. Chef-Owner Peter Sandroni's casual tapas bar has numerous tantalizing small plates that capture the marvels of local produce, meats, breads, and dairy products. For an international twist, try the *siu yuk,* a Chinese-dish made with five-spice rubbed Maple Creek Farm pork belly served over carrots, cabbage, and onions, in a kicker Chinese barbecue sauce. The *patatas bravas y chorizo* from Spain features potatoes from Igl Farms in Antigo, WI. The spuds are fried and then tossed in a spicy tomato sauce, served with garlic aioli and topped with a sautéed Tia Paquita chorizo. Sandroni loves menu items that one doesn't find elsewhere in town, making it a perfect spot for hosting visitors who might not be aware of such wonderful options in Milwaukee's foodie world.

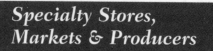

Clock Shadow Creamery, 138 W. Bruce St., Milwaukee, WI 53204; (414) 273-9711; clockshadowcreamery.com. Clock Shadow Creamery is an urban cheese factory in the Fifth Ward committed to being a model local venture. The company goal is to produce the best, freshest cheese possible from its urban setting. The site makes it convenient to dash in and pick up some Texas-style pimiento cheese or another exotic variety. The facility's Purple Door Ice Cream (purpledooricecream.com) is "locally made, naturally enjoyed." Super fine!

Great Lakes Distillery, 616 W. Virginia St., Milwaukee, WI 53204; (414) 431-8683; greatlakesdistillery.com. Located in Walker's Point, Great Lakes is the first Wisconsin distillery to open since Prohibition. Owner Guy Rehorst and his team pride themselves on their small-batch, award-winning distilled spirits. Among their products are vodkas, gins, brandies, absinthe, and Roaring Dan's Rum, named after the only man arrested (but not convicted) of piracy on the Great Lakes. A 45-minute tour of the distillery is free, though there is a slight charge for flights of five of the various beverages in the tasting room; check the website for tour times. The company belongs to the Wisconsin Artisan Food Producers, Something Special from Wisconsin, and Travel Green Wisconsin. The distillery often hosts special events for the public, including live music and book signings. Among its many awards, the distillery's Kinnickinnic Whiskey won the title of Best American Blended Whisky at the 2013 World Whisky Awards in London. Kinnickinnic is a blend of bourbon, malt, and rye whiskey by master distiller Doug MacKenzie.

Rishi Tea, 427 E. Stewart St., Milwaukee, WI 53207; (414) 747-4001; rishi-tea.com. Joshua Kaiser founded Rishi Tea in 1997 when he discovered that it was hard to find the excellent teas he had sampled on his travels in Asia. Feeling that other North American consumers felt the same way, he enlisted longtime friend Benjamin Harrison as partner. The two, along with help from friends, worked in a 400-square-foot space in Milwaukee's Historic Third Ward district, making original botanical blends by hand and individually packaging premium teas. More space was soon needed, and Rishi Tea moved into Bay View. In 2014, Rishi Tea will be again moving, this time into a larger, state-of-the-art building in the Menomonee Valley Industrial Center where they will revolutionize the procurment, processing, and packaging of the world's finest teas. The Rishi Tea Cupping Room is located at the company's headquarters, where quality-control tests are conducted on each lot of tea brought in by the company's sourcing team. The firm offers teaware and gifts in addition to its wide selections of white, green, yellow, oolong, black, and pu-erh teas, as well as masala chai, matcha tea powder, caffeine-free herbals and rooibos, and ever-changing special reserves. Included among the hard-to-get latter offerings are a rich Himalayan Royal organic black tea and a fabulous Nishi First Flush Sencha, a Japanese green tea.

Bay View

Bay View, about dozen blocks farther south down Kinnickinnic, was an independent village from 1879 to 1886. Future Milwaukee mayor Horace Chase (1862) is considered the first permanent settler, arriving around 1834. The general area is now an official historic district, roughly bounded by Lake Michigan on the east, with major streets including Superior and Lake, plus Howell and Humboldt Avenues. However, many locals toss in Morgan and Howard Avenues and a number of crisscrossing streets, making the neighborhood more of a place of mind than one of geography. In the beginning, the community was mostly a working-class neighborhood; the Milwaukee Iron Company was a major employer in the late 1800s. Currently, many artists and theater types, medical personnel, and city employees live here.

Foodie Faves

Hamburger Mary's, 2130 S. Kinnickinnic Ave., Milwaukee, WI 53207; (414) 988-9324; hamburgermarys.com/mke; Casual American; $–$$. Lolling on the lanai. Psych advice. Gluten-free bread. Half-pound Angus burgers. Definitely friendly toward the LGBT and trendy hipster communities. What more does one need dining in Bay View? Well, how about MaryOke (karaoke) sessions Friday and Saturday nights? Dining with the Divas drag revues on Saturday? Pop Quiz trivia evenings? Plus HamBINGO (this ain't yer granny's church basement game). A wildly popular Drink-'n'-Shrink on the second Tuesday of each month features clinical psychologist Dr. Julie Helmrich fielding handwritten questions from the audience. Subjects range from sex to family to omnipresent relationship issues. Hamburger Mary's has it all—a gleefully shazam joint, one where families are also welcome. Kids especially go for the Sunday brunch griddle cakes with their pecan crunchiness and sweet lather of caramel-chocolate sauce and whipped cream. Twin brothers Brandon and Ashley Wright own the Mary's franchise in Milwaukee's Bay View neighborhood. Emphasizing freshness and earning high marks from sustainable dining fans, their veggie garden out back has tomatoes and herbs galore. But bring your own boa.

Honeypie, 2643 S. Kinnickinnic Ave., Milwaukee, WI 53207; (414) 489-7437; honeypiecafe.com; Bistro; $–$$. The Pie is part of the **Braise** (p. 58) Restaurant Supported Agriculture group, a dedicated cooperative of local restaurants working together to source and purchase locally grown produce from area farms. It shows, with the fresh taste and grand presentation, making it one of our favorites in Bay View. The Lambwich is ace, with ground lamb, Creama Kasa cheese, grilled focaccia, **Growing Power** (p. 132) mixed greens, and red-pepper-flake oregano oil. Another plus is a chicken biscuit pie with fabulous chicken, potatoes, bell peppers, roasted corn, and a house-made buttermilk biscuit topping.

Odd Duck, 2352 S. Kinnickinnic Ave., Milwaukee, WI 53207; (414) 763-5881; oddduckrestaurant.com; New American; $$. Odd Duck has made a splash on the city's culinary scene ever since it opened in 2012. The Bay View restaurant is noted for an ever-changing menu that emphasizes fresh local produce, meats, and dairy products. Innovative dishes vary day to day, as in small plates or standard-size entrees. A down-home atmosphere makes patrons feel comfortable, whether they be vegan, vegetarian, or omnivore. Subsequently, a sample menu might include short rib bourguignon; a seafood curry from Goa, India; and a creative arugula salad. The Odd Duck features an open seating concept, anchored by a long curved bar to the left of the room. The bar itself is built from reclaimed wood from a family farm, and the top is made from recycled cork flooring. The tables are structured from recycled compressed sorghum straw, and the back bar evolved from bamboo shelving left behind by the building's previous owners. One blackboard indicates local producers and another relates ever-changing bar snacks.

Pastiche Bistro & Wine Bar, 3001 S. Kinnickinnic Ave., Milwaukee, WI 53207; (414) 482-1446; pastichebistro.com; French; $$. Chef Michael Engel knows his onion soup. It's one of his favorites. Engel used to add a small amount of roux to give body to his soup, but with gluten-intolerant diners these days, he now uses tomato paste that is caramelized along with the onions, adding a richness to the soup that he couldn't get with roux. He seasons the stock with all the usual suspects: thyme, bay leaf, peppercorns, a few cloves, and a pinch of marjoram. Engel also likes to combine a little caraway seed with gruyère cheese and the crouton for flavor. He puts two slices of gruyère crosswise across the top of the crock and crouton, and a small handful of shredded cheese on top. It's then browned under a high-heat broiler and sprinkled with shaved chives prior to serving. Other pluses at Pastiche include the frogs' legs, oysters on the half shell, sautéed skate, ratatouille, and undoubtedly some of the Midwest's best *ris de veau*. Sweetbreads served with a Marsala sauce were mouthwatering. Wine can be purchased on the second floor to take home.

Riviera Maya, 2258 S. Kinnickinnic Ave., Milwaukee, WI 53207; (414) 294-4848; riviera-maya-milwaukee.com; Mexican; $$. Mole sauces here rank among the city's finest, served on three styles of enchiladas. Varieties include the *encacahuatado,* peanut mole with broiled tomatoes, white onions, and chipotle peppers; the *almendrado,* a thick almond mole with broiled tomatoes, garlic, onions, and hearty morita peppers; and the *pipián verde,* a fabulous pumpkin seed mole with onion, green pepper, and cilantro. However, sometimes you may wish to go for the *pipián rojo,* a delightful sesame seed mole with broiled tomato sauce, onion, and red dried peppers, or vary the selection with mole de Oaxaca, a buttery smooth chocolate and peanut mole with blended pasilla and ancho peppers. The *vegetarianos* entree includes a cup of tortilla soup and a side of white rice with corn, which goes well with breaded plantain patties with cream cheese dished up with lettuce, avocado, and tomato. When in a rush, the *tortas,* or hot subs, are filling. The *camarones* are high on the fave list, with sautéed shrimp, Chihuahua cheese, mayo, and garlic aioli.

Landmarks

LuLu, 2261–2265 S. Howell Ave., Milwaukee, WI 53207; (414) 294-5858; lulubayview.com; New American; $–$$. LuLu is a funky bar and cafe serving burgers, pitas, and melts, along with fresh salads and a daily soup. It also has a grand list of imported and domestic beers as well as wines. Located at the intersections of Kinnickinnic, Lincoln, and Howell Avenues in Bay View makes it easy to find. LuLu fans enjoy the variety of pizzas that are unlike traditional Italian styles. Particularly tasty is the Pizza Arribiata, which utilizes capocollo ham, fontina cheese, hot pepper flakes, and a secret mix of herbs. An assortment of homemade spreads, ranging from Spanish white beans to a yummy Gorgonzola and walnut mix, can be slathered on the bread. LuLu's thick-sliced potato chips are hearty.

Palomino Bar & Restaurant, 2491 S. Superior St., Milwaukee, WI 53207; (414) 747-1007; palominobar.com; New American; $–$$. The Palomino emphasizes locally grown produce. While most of the dishes are relatively healthy, once in a while it never hurts to try goodies such as the Everest of Appetizers—a mountain of potato pieces. smothered in creamy cheese sauce and garnished with pico de gallo and shredded lettuce. Add chili for an extra few bucks. The slow-cooked beef brisket with homemade barbecue sauce, homemade baked beans, and apple slaw is a tummy filler as well. For beverages, candy's dandy as a starter, but getting down to business is the Palomino's Happy Cowgirl, with Four Roses bourbon, orange juice, sour mix, and grenadine in a pint glass. For the guys, there is the Cowboy Killer, concocted with Captain Morgan rum, Absolut vodka, and Jägermeister on the rocks. The Southern fried goodness comes out at the weekend brunches with the Misa Gringa, a vegetarian Benedict made with the vegetable of the day, two over-easy eggs topped with hollandaise, all on two potato pancakes. A heaping bowl of grits is smothered in melted cheddar cheese, bacon bits, and onions, and finished off with one fried egg.

Three Brothers, 2414 S. St. Clair St., Milwaukee, WI 53207; (414) 481-7530; Serbian; $$ For slow, relaxing dining, the Three Brothers is like a home-cooked meal, but with a Serbian feel. Located in an old Schlitz tavern, this family-operated restaurant has been a Bay View institution for decades with its high tin ceiling, old metal kitchen tables, and venerable back bar. We prefer a seating in the back of the room, quietly lit with its small table lamp, where we can snuggle in over a spinach *burek* that any Balkan grandma would prize. Dig in with an ethnic appetizer such as rolled grape leaves. Be aware that Three Brothers takes only cash or checks. A concluding glass (or two) of fiery Serbian plum brandy makes for a swell evening, ending on a high note.

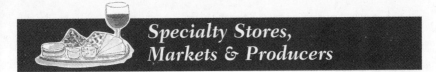

Bay View Packing Company, 1906 W. St. Paul Ave., Milwaukee, WI 53233; (414) 344-3050 or (800) 645-7976; bayviewpacking.com. As we say in Milwaukee, "Aina hey and ho, ho, ho, you betcha!" Holidays in Milwaukee mean getting pickled—with pickled Polish sausage, turkey gizzards, asparagus, garlic, and onioned eggs all laid out for Santa's midnight snacking. Let's not forget that the jolly ol' boy from the North Pole also loves his fancy boneless and bone-in pickled pork hocks and hog knuckles, as well as Nova Scotia herring in sour cream sauce. Bay View Packing was established in 1923, with five generations of Liebners in the heritage lineup, using recipes that date from the firm's beginning.

Colectivo Coffee, 2301 S. Kinnickinnic Ave., Milwaukee, WI 53207; (414) 744-6117; colectivocoffee.com. Launched in 1993 as Alterra Coffee, the firm changed its name in the summer of 2013 as part of deal made with Mars Drinks, which bought the name "Alterra" in 2010 for worldwide use. The corporate title was shared for several years when the Milwaukeeans finally decided to go their own way and subsequently needed a new handle. They were inspired by the small, brightly painted buses used throughout Latin America and thought that the concept of the little vehicles made a great branding match, especially because of the collective experience of drinking coffee with friends. The firm built a new roasting plant in 2012 at the intersection of Kinnickinnic and Lincoln in Bay View, where a full cafe menu and plenty of pastries are available. Coffee beans roasted here are served at Colectivo cafes around Greater Milwaukee and in Madison, as well as being found in many area food stores and restaurants. A favorite from this mother ship is Colectivo Lakefront (1701 N. Lincoln Memorial Dr., Milwaukee, WI 53202; 414-223-4551). This cafe is located in a former city water pumping station, whose location is perfect for business meetings. The Colectivo outlet at Mitchell International Airport is helpful for a last cuppa before heading off into the wild blue.

G. Groppi Food Market, 1441 E. Russell Ave., Milwaukee, WI 53207; (414) 747-9012; ggroppifoodmarket.com. Still bustling at a century-plus, Groppi's is one of the oldest food stores in Milwaukee. It is located in what was once a working-class neighborhood of northern Italians employed in the nearby mills and factories. Nearby is the old Club Garibaldi, scene of union rallies, political gatherings, and concerts. Forget the creaky floors, and just roam the packed aisles loaded with sausage, pasta, fresh produce, made-from-scratch pastries, and olives. Naturally, most of it is Italian themed. The Friday wine tastings and beer tastings on Saturday attract folks from around the city who know their vintages and brews. A wide range of beers, liquors, and

wines make Groppi's a one-stop shop. In addition, you'll love the to-die-for sandwich counter for midday takeout. There are some two dozen panini offerings, or you can build a personalized sandwich. In the back of the store is Louie's Pigeon Coop, a full bar named for one of the original Groppi brothers.

Klement's Sausage Co., 207 E. Lincoln Ave., Milwaukee, WI 53207; 1-800-KLEMENT; klements.com. Three brothers—John, George, and Ron Klement—purchased a small sausage company on Milwaukee's South Side in 1956 and built it into one of the largest sausage suppliers in the Midwest. It makes everything from ring bologna through a variety of summer sausages and on to breakfast

SOUTH OF THE BORDER

There are numerous Mexican restaurants scattered throughout Milwaukee's South Side, with many concentrated in the Walker's Point entertainment district. Each has its own élan, from fairly fancy to down-home comfortable. Here are several top picks:

Botanas Restaurant, 816 S. 5th St., Milwaukee WI 53204; (414) 672-3755; botanasrestaurant.com; $.

Cafe el Sol/United Community Center, 1028 S. 9th St., Milwaukee, WI 53204; (414) 384-3100; www.unitedcc.org/CafeEl Sol.htm; $.

Cielito Lindo, 739 S. 2nd St., Milwaukee 53204; (414) 649-0401; cielitolindomilwaukee.com; $.

Conejito's Place, 539 W. Virginia St., Milwaukee 53204; (414) 278-9106; conejitos-place.com; $.

El Rey Foodmart lunch counter, 1320 W. Burnham Ave., Milwaukee, WI 53204; (414) 383-7786; elreyfoods.com/locations.html; $.

Guadalajara Restaurant, 901 S. 10th St, Milwaukee, WI 53204; (414) 647-2266. $.

La Fuente, 625 S. 5th St., Milwaukee, WI 53204; (414) 271-8595; ilovelafuente.com; $–$$.

La Perla Mexican Restaurant, 734 S. 5th St., Milwaukee, WI 53204; (414) 645-9888; laperlahot.com; $–$$.

Taqueria Los Comales, 1306 S. Cesar E Chavez Dr., Milwaukee, WI 53204; (414) 384-6101; loscomales.com; $.

Terra, 600 S. 6th St., Milwaukee, WI 53204; (414) 763-7309; $.

links. When the folks here talk about sausage logs, they mean it. The factory's retail outlet stocks a goodly supply of wurst. Helping with its marketing push are the Klement's Racing Sausages, a staple at Milwaukee Brewers' baseball games. The speedy wienies include the Bratwurst (uniform #1), Polish Sausage (#2), Italian Sausage (#3), Hot Dog (#4), and the Chorizo (#5), who race around Miller Park to the cheers of baseball aficionados. They also make appearances at charity and civic events around town.

Wild Flour Bakery, 422 E. Lincoln Ave., Milwaukee, WI 53207; (414) 727-8145; wildflour.net. Breads, muffins, and bagels are baked here and then distributed to outlets throughout Milwaukee. Wild Flour is a staple at the area's seasonal farmers' markets as well. You can get breakfast sandwiches here on a variety of breads, plus lunch items that include soups and salads. For an early morning pick-me-up, a caprese focaccia includes two eggs, fried tomatoes, provolone cheese, and pesto spread on herb focaccia bread. For lunch, try the Cranberry Bog, made of roasted turkey, swiss cheese, tomato, red onions, carrots, spinach, hummus, and cranberry mustard on cranberry walnut bread.

Great Bars

At Random, 2501 S. Delaware Ave., Milwaukee, WI 53207; (414) 481-8030. Decor dating from the 1950s makes you feel like you woke up in a time warp. Blame it on the Tiki Bowl, which is served with two straws, or the ice cream drinks.

Bar LuLu, 2265 S. Howell Ave., (414) 294-5858; lulubayview.com. One of the funkiest lounges in Bay View, Bar Lulu is an expansion of LuLu (p. 67). It's big enough for live music and makes a whomping-good mojito.

Bay View Bowl, 2416 S. Kinnickinnic Ave.; (414) 483-0950. The BVB holds its own as a bar with inexpensive taps of ice-cold beer, as well as its famous Bloody Marys.

Blackbird Bar, 3007 S. Kinnickinnic Ave., Milwaukee, WI 53207; (414) 486-1344; facebook.com/blackbird.bar. Look for the avian theme, along with a photo booth and real jukebox.

Boom and the Room, 625 S. 2nd St., Milwaukee WI 53204; (414) 277-5040; boommke.com. What a blast! Music, pool, darts, and daily drink specials bring in the crowd. The place is LGBT friendly.

Boone & Crockett, 2151 S. Kinnickinnic Ave., Milwaukee, WI 53207; (414) 763-4935; booneandcrockettmke.com. If it's stuffed, you'll find it on these walls—with eyes that follow your every sip.

Burnhearts, 2599 S. Logan Ave, Milwaukee, WI 53207; (414) 294-0490. Darn good drinks are poured here.

Cactus Club, 2496 S. Wentworth Ave., Milwaukee, WI 53207; (414) 897-0663; cactusclub.dostuff.info. Fantastic live music venue for fist-pumping energy.

Cafe Centraal, 2306 S. Kinnickinnic Ave., Bay View, WI 53207; (414) 755-0378; cafecentraal.com. More than 100 tempting beers to set Bay View swinging.

Club Garibaldi, 2501 S. Superior St., Milwaukee, WI 53207; (414) 483-6335; clubgaribaldis.com. Longtime rallying place for politicos, unions, and neighborhood folks who love the back hall for speeches or music.

Historic White House Tavern, 2900 S. Kinnickinnic Ave., Milwaukee, WI 53207; (414) 483-2900; historicwhitehousetavern .com. Seems like every amateur sports team hangs out here. They've been coming here for almost a century.

La Cage, 801 S. 2nd St., Milwaukee, WI 53204; (414) 383-8330; lacagemke.com. This is the ever-fab Queen Bee of the city's gay bars.

Lucky Joe's Tiki Room, 196 S. 2nd St., Milwaukee, WI 53204; (414) 271-8454; luckyjoestiki.com. After a couple of drinks here, you'll feel lucky.

Roman's Pub, 3475 S. Kinnickinnic Ave., Milwaukee, WI 53207; (414) 481-3396; romanspub.com. Huge selection of beers from around the world.

Spin Milwaukee, 233 E. Chicago St., Milwaukee, WI 53202; (414) 831-7746; milwaukee.spingalactic.com. This ping-pong palace has a long, long bar so that you can bounce from beer to the tables.

Steny's Tavern & Grill, 800 S. 2nd St., Milwaukee, WI 53204; (414) 672-7139; stenystavern.com. Biker friendly, so bring your leathers.

Sugar Maple, 441 E. Lincoln Ave., Milwaukee, WI 53207; (414) 481-2393; mysugarmaple.com. Oh so sweet with its 60 American beers on tap and an event calendar full of live music, DJs, and comedy nights.

Tonic Tavern, 2335 S. Kinnickinnic Ave., Milwaukee, WI 53207; (414) 455-3205; tonictavern.com. Owner and guitarist Paul Jonas makes sure there is always grooving good music.

The Wicked Hop, 345 N. Broadway St., Milwaukee, WI 53202; (414) 223-0345; thewickedhop.com. Busy sports bar in the old produce warehouse district of the Historic Third Ward. Order up an award-winning Bloody Mary during Packers/Bucks/Brewers/Admirals games.

East Side

The East Side is often considered the hippest and trendiest of all the city's neighborhoods. Of course, that's usually the East Siders bragging, a situation that will get folks elsewhere ready for a heady conversation over who pours the best martini or stirs up the best soup of the day. This side of town, however, does have several pluses: Lake Michigan's beaches, Lake Drive mansions, the University of Wisconsin–Milwaukee and its Peck School for the Arts, and the iconic Downer and Oriental Theatres ensuring that creativity rules. And there are plenty of amazing bars and restaurants for anyone's beverages and food tastes.

Foodie Faves

Allium Restaurant and Bar, 2101 N. Prospect Ave., **Milwaukee, WI 53202; (414) 287-2053; alliummilwaukee.com; Bistro; $–$$.** The Allium is a cozy East Side hideaway with a small bar and about eight or nine tables. It is an intimate space with an interesting array of foods, such as a platter of Medjool dates with Clare chèvre wrapped in La Quercia prosciutto with an apple balsamic-vinegar sauce. The European-inspired restaurant is a short walk from the Oriental Theatre or the University of Wisconsin–Milwaukee's Inova, the visual arts school. It's known for its list of rotating draught beers, many from Belgium. The Allium specializes in small plates with imaginative options. We love their Duckshroom Pizza, with Nueske's smoked duck breast (p. 245), caramelized onions, and shiitake and cremini mushrooms, all perfectly paired with a glass or two of Furst Pinot Gris from the Alsace. In the summer, perch at an outdoor table to watch the passing crowd.

Brocach, 1850 N. Water St., Milwaukee, WI 53202; (414) 431-9009; brocach.com/milwaukee; Irish; $–$$. *Brocach* is Gaelic for "badger den," a perfect tie-in to Wisconsin's nickname as the Badger State. Opening in 2007, the restaurant features dinner and late-night menus, including Irish specialties. There is also a brunch on Saturday and Sunday. A ploughman's plate appetizer, with a platter of grilled sausages, Cashel blue cheese, cornichons, and pickled red onions, will take you back to the Auld Sod. The fish-and-chips would do well in Dublin, as would the Irish stout steak, a grilled New York strip with colcannon mashed potatoes, sautéed cremini mushrooms, Guinness stout sauce, and Cashel blue cheese butter; the portion size could almost feed two fiddlers and a box player. Naturally, the place is jammed with Celtic amateurs for the honored saint's March 17 High Holy Day, so we pop in regularly at other times of the year.

Cafe Hollander, 2608 N. Downer Ave., Milwaukee, WI 53211; (414) 963-6366; and 7677 W. State St., Wauwatosa, WI 53213; (414) 475-6771; cafehollander.com; New American; $–$$. Both sites serve burgers, but the menu is also overstacked with such dishes as wild-caught salmon salad, herbed chicken soup, Belgian sausages and mashed potatoes, and pork shanks. *Bier* is a serious consideration here, with dozens of varieties available. Many are privately labeled in Belgium. In both locales, the Hollander is a hub for breakfasting bicyclists and joggers who appreciate being fueled with the Green Torpedo omelet, a three-egger made with fresh spinach and basil combined with feta and goat cheeses. For everyone else, there is always cinnamon-streusel french toast, slathered in whipped cream and maple syrup.

Comet Cafe, 1947 N. Farwell Ave., Milwaukee, WI 53202; (414) 273-7677; thecometcafe.com; Casual American; $. Monday is Cheap Nite ($2 Pabst bottles). But the wow factor is a vegan house-blend Bloody Mary, made with **Furthermore** (p. 285) Knot Stock beer, with its fresh cracked black pepper and hops flavor. Comet-iers are renowned for their "hair of the dog," winning a nod as dishing up one of the area's best hangover breakfasts. So pair a Bloody Mary with a Comet breakfast burrito, devised with scrambled eggs, cheeses, and pico de gallo wrapped in a flour tortilla, lathered in ranchero sauce, and crowned with a taste-bud-exploding spicy sour cream. Mop up with hash browns—and another Bloody Mary.

Fushimi, 2116 N. Farwell Ave., Milwaukee, WI; 53202; (414) 270-1918; fushimi88.com; Japanese; $–$$. This sushi bar presents traditional rolls, sashimi, and  sushi in numerous varieties. Yet the buffet bar is the place to go, with a range of entrees, including those prepared on a hibachi. From the hot bar, try the yakitori beef or fried tofu. A hefty cold bar includes crab legs, squid and seaweed salads, and oysters, among other offerings. The prices are reasonable, so bring the family.

Harry's Bar & Grill, 3549 N. Oakland Ave., Milwaukee, WI 53211; (414) 964-6800; harrysbarandgrillmilwaukee.com; New American; $$. A Bloody Mary or a Dirty Harry—martini, that is. Sounds like date night at a bartenders' convention. Regardless, drink fans at Harry's appreciate both. This bar's traditional Bloody Mary is only $3 during Sunday brunch and is often made with Van Gogh flavored vodka,

Rehorst being another favorite base. Hearty drinkers hold out for the Queen Mary, which is served in a 22-ounce glass with a slim **Klement's** (p. 70) smoked pork sausage, a pepperoncini, celery, pickles, and cherry tomatoes. All the Bloody Marys are made with Harry's own in-house mix. Drink it down with a thin-crust breakfast pizza. The burgers are right on, as well. This place isn't large, but try to grab a table up front in the window section so that you can people gaze.

Mr. Senors, 2335 N. Murray Ave., Milwaukee, WI 53211; (414) 550-8226; mrsenors.com; Mexican; $. East Side late-night theatergoers and pub hoppers migrate to Dude Llanas's little window around bar time, seeking hearty grande burritos that cure anything that ails you. There is also a señorita burrito, billed as only "slightly" smaller than the hombre-size, as well as tacos that even Montezuma would appreciate. This is post-party fare at its finest, presented from a tiny, only-to-go, walk-up facility that opens Wed to Sat at 6 p.m. and at noon on Sun. However, there is delivery service until 9 p.m. Both the red and green sauces, plus the tortillas, are handmade. The owner is the bustling brother of noted Milwaukee vocalist Sammy Llanas of the BoDeans. Dude doesn't sing, but his late-night food sure does, as we can attest on the numerous times we've needed a quick taco fix on the way home from some late-night soiree.

North Point Custard, 2272 N. Lincoln Memorial Dr., Milwaukee, WI 53211; (414) 727-4886; northpointcustard.com; **Casual American; $.** The beach along Lake Michigan reaches almost to the front door of this frozen custard stand, so kids can race there quickly for their cones. When summer finally arrives in Milwaukee, sand volleyball players, sun worshippers, ball players, and beauteous ones on parade flock here for their simple fix, whether a hot dog or a yummy burger. Everything seems to taste better after a day of beach and water.

Oakland Gyros, 2867 N. Oakland Ave., Milwaukee, WI 53211; (414) 963-1393; **Greek; $.** To satisfy your late-night Aegean cravings, this joint is open until 3 a.m. This is where the cops, bus drivers, and students go for Greek. Copious amounts of spinach pie, dolmades, and lamb shanks are filling, not to mention Greek fries with feta cheese that are the norm. There are bus stops on each corner, making for a convenient on-off layover.

Pizza Man, 2597 N. Downer Ave., Milwaukee, WI 53211; (414) 272-1745; pizzamanmke.com; **Pizza; $$.** After a disasterous fire in 2011 that destroyed the storied original Pizza Man at the corner of  Oakland and North Avenues, owner Mike Admidzich reopened in a renovated building near the Downer Theatre in July 2013. He still produces the classic thin crust pizza in 12-, 14-, and 16-inch sizes, with Artichoke à la Mode being one of the more quirky versions. You can also get meatball sliders, grilled portobellos, and a variety of pastas. Want wine? You can get one (or more) of the 250-plus vintages by the glass here.

Simple Cafe, 2124 N. Farwell Ave., Milwaukee, WI 53202; (414) 271-2124; simplecafelakegeneva.com; **Casual American; $–$$.** An adjunct of the popular **Simple Cafe** (p. 186) in Lake Geneva, Wisconsin, the Milwaukee branch has attracted a loyal following for its breakfasts and brunches. The cafe closes at 3 p.m., but is open at 6 a.m. weekdays for the early birds on the way to the office. This is a hash-lover's mecca, but the mashed potato omelet comes in a close second if anyone is rating. Okay, okay, the chipotle beef stroganoff omelet makes for a tie. Locals have also been raving about the Korean BBQ Breakfast Bowl, tossing about words like "generous" and "amazing."

Via Downer, 2625 N. Downer Ave., Milwaukee, WI 53211; (414) 501-4510; viadowner.com; **Italian; $–$$.** This pizzeria also offers a full line of traditional Italian-Mediterranean pasta in a casual, kid- and grandkid-friendly setting. In a prime spot on the Upper East Side, the restaurant is within a block of the Downer Theatre for showings of indie and foreign films. To the south is the Boswell Book Company, with its literary food for the soul augmented by numerous author appearances. On Via Downer's appetizer list, wild rice *arancini* is a bite-size Wisconsin interpretation of the classic Italian rice ball, made with a dollop of sharp cheddar and served with marinara sauce. Then it's time to select a traditional, specialty, or garlic sauce pizza. For pasta, there's always the Bolognese, rigatoni tossed with a traditional hearty ground-beef tomato sauce with a touch of minced bacon, or a vodka salsa rosa, built high with sautéed shrimp, garlic, and oregano tossed with linguini in a vodka-tomato cream sauce. Via has an extended list of gluten-free menu items, as well, with a great deal each Tuesday and Wednesday, when you can choose any gluten-free pizza, pasta, or entree and get a gluten-free appetizer, salad, dessert, or beverage for free. New Year's Eve is fun, with all the pizza you can eat. The place hosts regular music sessions, as well, for smooth backgrounding.

Landmarks

Bartolotta's Lake Park Bistro, 3133 E. Newberry Blvd., Milwaukee, WI 53202; (414) 962-6300; lakeparkbistro.com; French; $$–$$$$. High on the bluff overlooking Lake Michigan, the Bistro is perfect for weddings, business meetings, parties, or a night out with a favorite person. The restaurant also hosts numerous tastings and dinners with notable culinary visitors. For appetizers, favorites include the *mousse de volaille,* a smoothly rich chicken liver mousse, or coquilles St.-Jacques Mornay, fresh sea scallops with mushrooms, leeks, béchamel, and gruyère cheese. Executive Chef Adam Siegel, a James Beard award winner who has worked in kitchens in France and Italy,

Enjoy a Beverage

The Hotel Foster, 2028 E. North Ave., Milwaukee, WI 53202; (414) 988-4758; thehotelfoster.com; $. No, this is not a real hotel, despite the occasional phone call asking if it has bellhop service. Located in the heart of the East Side bar district, the Parisian/American–themed bar is a popular draw whatever the time of year. We love the great discussions after the annual Milwaukee International Film Festival, which pack the house each autumn. The Foster is about a block from the grand Oriental Theatre, one of the fest's several venues. Conversation flows over the locally roasted Valentine coffees and **Rishi** (p. 62) imported teas, plus a regularly changing list of classic/craft cocktails and international beers. Wines and fine spirits round out the bill. Always questing for new twists on traditional sipping, bartenders here offer their versions of the Flying Dutchman and a delightful Gin Bramble, the alleged favorite pour of England's Queen Elizabeth. Named for the mythical ghost ship, the Dutchman is created with orange gin, orange and lemon juices, and several drops of bitters, while the Bramble is a mix of Ransom and Plymouth gin, simple syrup,

makes a marvelous rainbow trout with a warm lentil and watercress salad, plus a slow-cooked duck leg with braised French green lentils that is melt-in-your-mouth rich and luscious. Siegel is a regular at the **Fox Point Farmers' Market** (p. 133), demonstrating his skills, and he remains a great supporter of Wisconsin's sustainable agriculture scene. He has trained many of the top chefs who have spread their talents throughout Greater Milwaukee or have moved on to other high-profile restaurants around the world.

Carini's La Conca D'Oro, 3468 N. Oakland Ave., Milwaukee, WI 53211; (414) 963-9623; carinislaconcadoro.com; Italian; $$. A portrait of Guise and Francisco Carini, parents of restaurant owner Peter Carini, oversees the dining room at La Conca D'Oro, "The Shell

and Mathilde Framboise wild raspberry liqueur. There is no nonalcoholic beer here, so you may have to substitute a virgin Bloody Mary or a soft drink. **The Hamilton,** 823 E. Hamilton St., Milwaukee, WI 53202; (414) 223-1020; thehamiltonmke.com. Owner Kimberly Floyd was aided by macho drink makers Nick Kosevich and Ira Koplowitz in developing her extensive cocktail offerings, of which at least 11 are signatures, plus the traditional classics. For summer, The Hamilton's Green Ti is a daiquiri made with Admiral Nelson Rum from Martinique, pumped up with an ounce of English Harbor rum, an Antigua beauty. Then Floyd adds fresh—really fresh—lime juice and snappy green tea honey syrup, augmented by flavorful Bittercube black strong bitters. The Hamilton's back room is often used for charity events. The annual Slow Soup dinner, a fund-raiser for Slow Food Wisconsin Southeast, has been hosted here. For that, 9 or 10 local restaurants showcase delicious broths and soups ranging from West African chicken soup made by Afro Fusion Cuisine's Yollande Tchouapi to a celeriac cream soup by Andrew DNR of **c.1880** (p. 58).

of Gold." Aboard the *Anna Maria* in 1966, these elder Carinis voyaged stateside from Porticello, Sicily, with sons and daughters Peter, Rosary, Santo, Albert, Salvador, Maria, and Antonio. Peter opened his restaurant in 1996, now aided by his son Gregg as chef. Emphasizing Sicilian cooking, Carini is known for his beef, chicken, veal, swordfish, and eggplant spiedini. One of his signature dishes is La Conca D'Oro spaghetti with shrimp, scallops, mussels, clams, calamari, and crushed peppers tossed in a homemade marinara sauce or garlic wine sauce.

County Clare Irish Inn, 1234 N. Aster St., Milwaukee, WI 53202; (414) 272-5273; countyclare-inn.com; Irish; $–$$. The County Clare guesthouse is Milwaukee's premiere Irish snug, making it a home away from home for business travelers or a cozy getaway during Milwaukee Irish Fest each August. Many of the staff are from Eire, with accents as thick as the root soup served here. It's a great bar, served by staff including Barry Dodd, who makes good whiskey pour and knows what the "Guinness minute" means—for non-Gaels, that's the time it takes for the stout's rich, thick, sudsy head to sink below the glass rim prior to topping off. Often there is music, Irish and otherwise, throughout the year. As far as the menu goes, we vote for the corned beef and cabbage, shepherd's pie, and grilled salmon as favorites, regardless of the time of year. The upstairs rooms are cottagelike, albeit with Wi-Fi. For added value, each has a double whirlpool. The breakfast is complimentary.

Mimma's Cafe, 1307 E. Brady St., Milwaukee, WI 53202; (414) 271-7337; mimmas.com; Italian; $$–$$$. One never knows who might be sitting at the next table in Mimma's, a Brady Street fine-dining fixture. Owner Mimma Megna attracts major sports figures, bandleaders, and other celebrities, a clientele drawn by her hospitality and food. Megna arrived stateside in 1963 from Sicily and became a cook at the North Shore Country Club. A couple of decades later, she launched Mimma's, and this "Queen of Italian Cuisine" has not slowed down since. Megna puts a different twist on many of her pasta offerings, including vegetarian-style. Her *penne con asparagi* includes pasta with fresh asparagus and anchovies sautéed in olive oil, and her black pappardelle pasta comes with shrimp and calamari in a marinara sauce. And yes, that was ex-NYC mayor Rudy Giuliani perched over there, mopping up his sauce.

The Pasta Tree Restaurant & Wine Bar, 1503 N. Farwell Ave., Milwaukee, WI 53202; (414) 276-8867; pastatreemilwaukee .com; Italian; $$. The Pasta Tree has been one of our prime date-night choices for years, with its romantic decor emphasizing intimate dining experiences. The restaurant is about 30 years old but retains its panache and consistently earns kudos from critics and guests. It should, especially since The Pasta Tree makes its own mozzarella. One of its specialties is a sautéed chicken breast with walnuts, parsley, and garlic served over whole wheat pasta. But even we can spare time from gazing adoringly at each other to sample prosciutto-wrapped scallops or veal piccata. There are at least 20 varieties of sauces for the pasta. Among the more interesting dishes is shrimp served in an Alfredo sauce along with steamed broccoli. For vegetarians, artichoke hearts served in a traditional Alfredo sauce with garlic and herbs is always a winner. A favored specialty is the Tree's traditional Italian tomato sauce with its touch of cream, splash of vodka, and kalamata olives. To conclude a moonlight softened evening, we go for either a cup of fabled Lavazza coffee or a rich espresso.

Pitch's Lounge and Restaurant, 1801 N. Humboldt Ave., Milwaukee, WI 53202; (414) 272-9313; pitchsribs.com; Italian; $–$$. Since 1942, the Picciurro family has been serving the meanest highball on the Lower East Side, especially on Thirsty Thursday ($2 off drinks, beer, and appetizers between 4 and 7 p.m.). "Come thirsty, leave happy" is Pitch's motto. The restaurant is famous for its barbecued baby back ribs and Sicilian steak the size of that Mediterranean island. Kids love Ice Cream Social Sunday, usually going for hot fudge sundaes. Pitch's occasional cribbage tournaments are an added value. Call the bartender for winter/spring dates.

Sala da Pranzo, 2611 E. Hampshire St., Milwaukee, WI 53211; (414) 964-2611; sala-dapranzo.com; Italian; $$. While only a block east of the University of Wisconsin–Milwaukee campus, Sala da Pranzo could be in the heart of Italy. Opened in 2001 by the sibling team of Teresa and Anthony Balistreri, the two have since been joined by brother Peter. Both men perform the chef duties, making sauces by hand, using herbs from their seasonal rooftop garden, and emphasizing fresh produce. The two regularly come up with delightful new ways of

tackling weekly specials, such as their Sicilian sashimi, composed of thinly sliced raw scallops, olive oil, lemon zest, chives, capers, and pickled red onions. They readily offer many dishes prepared gluten-free, dairy-free, or vegan.

Sanford, 1547 N. Jackson St., Milwaukee, WI 53202; (414) 276-9608; sanfordrestaurant.com; New American; $$$–$$$$. After more than two decades, founders Sanford (Sandy) and Angie D'Amato sold their restaurant to Chef de Cuisine Justin Aprahamian, but the award-winning kitchen has kept that same élan and excitement as in previous years. The menu always emphasizes seasonal ingredients, but it can be lots of fun as well. For instance, try the duck corn dog with *foie gras* mustard. This is the place where business folks gather to do deals over pheasant and corn ravioli and where "special night-out" partiers go for grilled red grouper and potato-crab hash. Servers here are among the best in the city, taking their profession to the highest level and deserving a hearty tip.

Trocadero Gastrobar, 1758 N. Water St., Milwaukee, WI 53202; (414) 272-0205; trocaderogastrobar.com; Bistro; $$. The main room consists of several tables and booths and the main bar. Traffic then flows to the left, to another room, and then outside to a popular patio. Upstairs is a party room. Entrees include pork belly, truffled lobster mac 'n cheese and chicken schwarma, Dover sole, chicken coquettes, risotto, burgers, and a wide variety of sandwiches. East Siders rate the chocolate espresso mousse as one of the best desserts this side of the Mississippi.

Specialty Stores, Markets & Producers

Burke Candy, 3840 N. Fratney St., Milwaukee, WI 53212; (414) 964-7327 or (888) 287-5350; burkecandy.com. Three generations of Burkes have been making a glorious array of chocolates and confections for more than 70 years. Their goodies are particularly marvelous around the holidays; Burke's Grandmother Reilly line of toffees is perfect for holiday gifting. For the dedicated chocoholic on your gift list, how about presenting him or her with a 10-pound pail of Burke's gourmet hot fudge topping? If those lords a-leaping can't wait for the ritual unwrapping of presents, rush them to the company store, open from 10 a.m. to 5 p.m., Mon through Fri, and from 11 a.m. to 3 p.m., Sat.

Glorioso's Italian Market, 1011 E. Brady St., Milwaukee, WI 53202; (414) 272-0540; gloriosos.com. Since 1946, this well-known grocery has had one of the city's best Italian deli counters. There is enough dried pasta here to feed the ancient Roman army, whether it is calamarata, capellini spezzati, farfalline, linguine, pappardelle, and many more. Staff here can even suggest cooking times for each style, to ensure the perfect presentation. Since olive oil is the heart-healthy elixir, we appreciate the Academia Barilla's Riviera Ligure or Cori extra-virgins. For anyone who really, really loves olive oil, you can even purchase L'Olivier extra-virgin olive oil in barrels. Coming into the store is like touring Italy; the shelves overflow with goodies from the provinces as well as other European delicacies. The store hosts regular wine, oil, and vinegar tastings. For Patrice Procopio, an artist whose family came from the town of Borgia in Calabria, Glorioso's has always been a favorite because it is like eating in her grandmother's kitchen. Looking back into the city's history, Brady Street used to be one of Milwaukee's major Italian

neighborhoods. Many of its buildings were included in the 2012 filming of Terry Green's critically acclaimed *No God, No Master,* about Italian anarchists in the 1920s.

Peter Sciortino's Bakery, 1101 E. Brady St., Milwaukee, WI 53202; (414) 272-4623; petersciortinosbakery.com. Peter Sciortino's Bakery was established in 1948 by Peter C. and Grace Sciortino. In 1997, the bakery was sold to current owners and operators Giuseppe, Maria, and Luigi Vella. The new proprietors have adhered to Old World recipes for their award-winning breads, cookies, and rolls. Although we claim we count calories, the occasional trip to Sciortino's leads to a bag of macaroons, filbert kisses, or pistachio bars. On average, a pound amounts to about 20 cookies. Of course, these excursions are always for "scientific research," nothing more. Oh, don't forget the rum balls.

 *Great Bars*

Balzac, 1716 N. Arlington Place, Milwaukee, WI 53202; (414) 755-0099; balzacwinebar.com. You want wine, they have wine, which makes this a perfect place for discerning oenophiles. There is also an array of small plates, pizzas, cheese, and desserts. Check the nightly specials.

Champion's Pub, 2417 N. Bartlett Ave., Milwaukee, WI 53211; (414) 332-2440; championspub.com. Established in 1956, Champion's Pub is tucked away a block from Oakland and North Avenues.

Hi Hat Lounge, 1701 N. Arlington Place, Milwaukee, WI 53202; (414) 220-8090; hihatlounge.com. Known for its martinis; 70 beers are available in the adjoining Garage, its sister bar/cafe.

Jamo's Bar, 1800 N. Arlington Place, Milwaukee, WI 53202; (414) 276-7101. Tip a drink to the old neighborhood while admiring the kitschy, yet cool, '50s decor.

The Jazz Estate, 2423 N. Murray Ave., Milwaukee, WI 53211; (414) 964-9923; jazzestate.com. Down-home jazz chases the night tremors far, far away.

Landmark Lanes, 2220 N. Farwell Ave. Milwaukee, WI 53202; (414) 278-8770; landmarklanes.com. Funky basement bowling, with adjoining rooms for pool and pinball machines. You can always belly up to the bar here for beer, beer, beer.

Nomad World Pub, 1401 E. Brady St., Milwaukee, WI 53202; (414) 224-8111; nomadworldpub.com. In this small tavern, everyone might know your name after a second visit. This is a hub for televised soccer matches with your mates.

Paddy's Pub, 2339 N. Murray Ave., Milwaukee, WI 53211; (414) 223-3496; paddyspub.net. Sure, it's not quite the Republic of Ireland, but close enough. The pub hosts music and theatrical events in its upstairs hall, plus old-time movies are shown on a wall downstairs. An expansive patio makes for a perfect night out in good weather.

Victor's Night Club, 1230 N. Van Buren St., Milwaukee, WI 53202; (414) 272-2522; victorsnightclub.com. For nearly 50 years, Victor's has been the place to greet, grip, and grin. The dance party starts at 9 p.m. in a Las Vegas–style nightclub, one that even has a glitter ball and lighted floor for Travolta ambience. Good fish fry, as well.

Von Trier, 2235 N. Farwell Ave., Milwaukee, WI 53202; (414) 272-1775; vontriers.com. Heavily Teutonic with lovely stained-glass windows and lots of dark wood. Directly across from the Oriental Theatre.

Wolski's, 1836 N. Pulaski St., Milwaukee, WI 53202; (414) 276-8130; wolskis.com. "I Closed Wolski's" bumper stickers show up from Iraq to the Antarctic. It might be the fresh, free popcorn or the comfortable atmosphere and friendly barkeeps, but in any case, Wolski's always nabs a spot as among the top bars in the Brady Street neighborhood.

Menomonee Valley

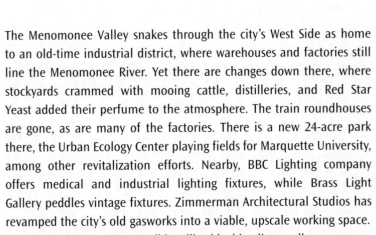

The Menomonee Valley snakes through the city's West Side as home to an old-time industrial district, where warehouses and factories still line the Menomonee River. Yet there are changes down there, where stockyards crammed with mooing cattle, distilleries, and Red Star Yeast added their perfume to the atmosphere. The train roundhouses are gone, as are many of the factories. There is a new 24-acre park there, the Urban Ecology Center playing fields for Marquette University, among other revitalization efforts. Nearby, BBC Lighting company offers medical and industrial lighting fixtures, while Brass Light Gallery peddles vintage fixtures. Zimmerman Architectural Studios has revamped the city's old gasworks into a viable, upscale working space.

The Hank Aaron State Trail is utilized by bicyclists, walkers, runners, and skaters, providing a 10-mile continuous connection via dedicated trails and marked streets between the lakefront and Milwaukee's western environs. The trail starts at Lakeshore State Park near the Henry W. Maier Festival Grounds, wends its way through the Historic Third Ward and Menomonee River Valley, past Miller Park, and links to Milwaukee County's 100-mile Oak Leaf Trail. This makes it possible to bike, or walk, from Lake Michigan to the Ice Age National Scenic Trail, Glacial Drumlin State Trail, and Military Ridge State Trail. All this certainly works up an appetite.

Dream Dance Steak, 1721 W. Canal St., Milwaukee, WI 53233; (414) 847-7883; paysbig.com/dining/dream-dance-steaks; **Steak House; $$–$$$.** Each steak is a winner here, with a side of potato, house salad, and a choice of sauce or rub. The Creekstone Farms 16-ounce rib eye is a meaty marvel. The 30-ounce porterhouse also leaves enough leftovers for more meals at home. Tables of friends can enjoy the chef's tasting menu, with five selected courses and wine pairings. Chicken breast, pork chops, venison, scallops, and lobster tail are alternatives. A separate entrance from the casino proper makes it easy for an in-and-out visit to this award-winning, top-of-the-line restaurant.

Twisted Fisherman Crab Shack, 1200 W. Canal St., Milwaukee, WI 53233 (414) 384-2722; twistedfisherman.com; **Seafood; $$.** A relative newcomer to the Valley, the Twisted Fisherman was once a boat storage structure. It now seats more than 200 patrons eager for the catch of the day served grilled, blackened, or pan-seared. A Rusty Anchor helps relieve the day's stress—that's Cruzan mango and white rum, orange and cranberry juices, and a splash of sour mix. Perching at tables on the planked patio and showing off their seasonal Wisconsin tans are popular pastimes on Friday afternoons and weekends for lithe young trendies. Owner Russ Davis also runs the Rio West Cantina, **Hubbard Park Lodge** (p. 98) restaurant, Palm Gardens inside the **Lakefront Brewery** (p. 129), and Riverwalk Boat Tours, so he knows what the restaurant business is all about. In addition to the requisite fish, he dishes up T-bones, beer sausage, salads, and even vegan and gluten-free items. If you don't have a GPS system, look for artist Mark Winter's large crab sculpture in front of the building. Scattered around are hand-painted signs by Beth Bojarski exhorting, HEY YOU, EAT SOME FISH and ALL FOR RUM AND RUM FOR ALL.

TAKING A BREAK FROM THE GAMING TABLES

At **Potawatomi Bingo Casino** (1721 W. Canal St., Milwaukee, WI 53233; 414-847-7883; paysbig.com), you won't lack for something to eat, unless your wallet or purse is cleaned out. A lot of folks like dining before or after a concert or performance at the casino's Northern Lights Theater. Many gamblers take a break from the games and off-track betting to drop in at one of the restaurants in the casino, offering choices from fine dining to casual buffets. Yet you can always bypass the slots and blackjack tables and head directly to RuYi with its Chinese, Thai, Japanese, and Korean dishes; the Fire Pit Sports Bar & Grill; the Menomonee Valley Food Court; or The Buffet. There is free parking in the structure linked to the casino. Bar 360, in the center of the action, has eight tap beers, a variety of wine, and the usual range of cocktails with appropriate names such as the Jackpot and the Valley Colada. Taking a break from the gaming tables, patrons can enjoy drink specials that pop up at times, such as domestic pints for $2.50 or the $5 margaritas.

Wild Earth Cucina, 1721 W. Canal St., Milwaukee, WI 53233; (414) 847-7626; paysbig.com/dining/wild-earth-cucina-italiana; Italian; $$. Diners win big at **Potawatomi**'s (above) Wild Earth Cucina on the upper level. The restaurant, the casino's latest eatery addition, opened in 2012 to glowing critiques. Customers enjoy the cooking area open for viewing. Chef Audrey Vandenburgh and Sous Chef Maggie Haller have come up with a compelling menu they call "a mix of contemporary and traditional interpretations with a focus on local, organic, and sustainable foods." A dish of seasonal olives as appetizers is a great way to start a dining experience that might include duck confit, porcini mushroom broth, wilted escarole, and garlic-roasted Roma tomatoes with orecchiette pasta. Conclude with *cassata,* a traditional Sicilian sweet created with ricotta and mascarpone.

Landmarks

Sobelman's Pub & Grill, 1900 W. St. Paul Ave., Milwaukee, WI 53233; (414) 931-1919; milwaukeesbestburgers.com; Casual American; $. Sobelman's is among the best joints in town for a variety of burgers, starting with the legendary Double Sobelman, hand-built with two patties and American, swiss, and cheddar cheeses, with bacon, fried onions, and diced jalapeños. The Piggyback is quirkily different, with pork belly, fried onions, and fried mushrooms coated with a bourbon sauce. The list goes on and on. Obviously, you don't come here to fast. It's no wonder that this packed place, in a building dating from the late 1800s, is consistently voted tops in town. Perhaps the rating is skewed in Dave and Melanie Sobelman's favor after judges have had several Bloody Masterpieces, featuring 13 garnishes. Sobelman's uses Jimmy Luv's Bloody Mary Mix and suggests vodka upgrades to a smooth Rehorst from **Great Lakes Distillery** (p. 62); both are locally produced. Sobelman's attracts a range of customers, which makes it a great place to mingle. Truckers, Marquette University professors, county judges, welders, baseball teams, students, lawyers, and bond traders rub elbows here.

Stone Creek Coffee Roasters, The Factory Store, 422 N. 5th St., Milwaukee, WI 53203; (414) 270-1008; stonecreekcoffee .com. Founder Eric Resch started Stone Creek Coffee in the summer of 1993 and now has eight retail stores throughout the metro area, as well as wholesale partners across the country. Look for the giant coffee cup atop the The Factory Store across from the Milwaukee Intermodal Station with its Amtrak and motorcoach connections. The station has won awards for energy efficiency, community involvement, tenant satisfaction, and curb appeal. Since it serves 1.3 million passengers a year, the Stone Creek shop is in a prime locale. The 1898 Cream City brick building was renovated in 2012, with a raw coffee prep area and a bakery. The Factory Store is on the first floor, with a kitchen and offices on the second floor. Iced Americano, cider, Cream City mint mocha, Boston latte, chai tea, and other beverages augment the extensive line of roasted coffees.

North Side

plus Brown Deer, Shorewood, Whitefish Bay, Glendale, Fox Point & Mequon

Milwaukee's North Side encapsulates the widely diversified but generally considered tonier areas of the city. There are the huge mansions along Lake Drive, duplexes near the University of Wisconsin–Milwaukee, and single-family bungalows near Alverno College and Nicolet High School. Hot spots are along East Brady Street, with a plethora of restaurants and bars lining North Oakland AVenue, particularly in suburban Shorewood. East–west streets bustling with action include Capital Drive, along with those forming the Prospect Triangle area near the Oriental Theatre. As you go farther north, you can find more fast-food and chain restaurants, particularly in Glendale and on into Mequon. But there are hidden gems, many of them family-owned hideaways, sprinkled throughout the area.

Foodie Faves

Calderone Club, 8001 N. Port Washington Rd., Fox Point, WI 53217; (414) 352-9303; calderoneclubfoxpoint.com; Italian; $–$$. For three decades, the Fazzari family has dished out oodles of noodles, platters of pizza, and gallons of sauces. The Calderone often takes first place in the Milwaukee Meatball Challenge. This comfortable, family-oriented restaurant can also turn out a champion range of Strauss veal options. Among them are Marsala, Parmigiano, scaloppine, limone, and piccata preparations. Each is served with Italian bread, mixed green salad, and rosemary-seasoned red potatoes or pasta marinara. The Calderone has expanded outside deck service during its North Shore site's summer season, with a cluster of tables in the house front and more tables plus booths ranging to the right of the entrance. The decor isn't fancy, but the place is truly foodie functional. A sister restaurant is located downtown on Old World 3rd Street, across from the Milwaukee County Historical Society (842 N. Old World 3rd St.; 414-273-3236; calderoneclub.net).

Family Table, 6598 W. Brown Deer Rd., Milwaukee, WI 53223; (414) 354-5494; familytablerestaurant.net; Casual American; $–$$. Known as the Pink Palace, this restaurant serves house-made food in a relaxed and certainly not ostentatious atmosphere. The Table has its regular diners who have made this place their own kitchen, especially for breakfast. They love the service and the pricing. There's a kids' menu and, occasionally, special prices or deals for elders. The menu items are straightforward. Don't look for flashy painting of the plates or wine pairings. You want baby beef liver with grilled onions or bacon, and that's what you get. No parsley, no chives, no nuttin'. You want thick gravy, you get it. You can cut it with a knife. Ribs are flavorful, as is the roast chicken and broiled fish of various varieties. As a test, take a first date here and check the reaction. Treat him or her with a huge slab of chocolate cake to top it all off. If all goes well without a fuss, you have a keeper.

Harvey's Central Grille, 1340 W. Towne Square Rd., Mequon, WI 53092; (262) 241-9589; harveyscentralgrille.com; Bistro; $$. This spirited bar and restaurant draws patrons from around the North Shore. We like the proximity to where we live, making it easy to meet friends and to do business. The screened-in patio is great for mosquito-buzzing summer evenings, but the outdoor patio works just as well on good nights. The MC Swingtet, chanteuse Val Barbatelli, and guitarist Eric Longreen are among the regular musicians lending extra charm to an evening out. Pistachio-crusted goat cheese and curried chicken strips are two appetizers we favor, plus the seafood stew, breaded veal, and sesame duck fettuccine for our mains.

Highland House, 12741 N. Port Washington Rd., Mequon, WI 53092; (262) 243-5844; highlandhouse.ws; Mexican; $. The original Highland House opened in 1983 for breakfast, lunch, and dinner. A margarita of the month is a popular draw. The very phrase "Turbo Tangerine" conjures up good times, especially when paired with an appetizer called a Cuban cigar roll, made of shredded pork, smoked ham, swiss cheese, and a pickle. That's all rolled in a wonton skin and quick-fried, served with honey mustard dressing. For a multiethnic twist, try the sesame ginger salmon, a Norwegian salmon fillet with an Oriental sesame sauce, served in a Mexican restaurant. This comes with garlic mashed spuds and sautéed veggies. A sister restaurant is located at 820 Indiana Ave. in Sheboygan (920-451-1500).

Hubbard Park Lodge, 3565 N. Morris Blvd., Shorewood, WI 53211; (414) 332-4207; hubbardlodge.com; Casual American; $–$$. High on a bluff overlooking the Milwaukee River, the Hubbard Park Lodge is noted for its excellent Friday fish fries and Sunday Lumberjack Brunch that includes all-you-can-eat pancakes. And don't forget the fresh doughnuts. The idyllic setting is great for weddings and other activities, from meetings of water conservationists to awards ceremonies for the Milwaukee Kickers soccer team. The wood-burning fireplace makes this rustic lodge especially cozy during the winter.

Poco Loco Cantina, 4134 W. River Ln., Brown Deer, WI 53209; (414) 355-9550; pocolococantina.com; Mexican; $–$$. This is probably the coziest of Mexican eateries, with its main dining area only a curved vintage bar where patrons perch on stools, which promotes intimacy and provides the opportunity to talk with an adjacent stoolmate if you wish. The retro look is reminiscent of the good old days when the building housed a breakfast/lunch joint. Veteran chef Dean Gardner and his crew emphasize Yucatán dishes. They do a marvelous job with their moles, seviches, and adobos; the latter are marinated dishes. For hearty eaters, the Cowboy Steak is a 16-ouncer; fish tacos are another favorite for diners who flock here, particularly in the summer when a small patio is open.

Three Lions Pub, 4515 N. Oakland Ave., Shorewood, WI 53211; (414) 763-6992; threelionspub.com; British; $. Soccer, rugby, cricket, Gaelic football, and other "overseas" sports are common on the telly here. Founded by several English "futballers" recruited to play soccer at Cardinal Stritch University, the pub has a definite Brit feel. The walls are adorned with English Premier Club memorabilia and sports photos. Inexpensive pub grub here goes beyond the typical burger. For a real international taste, try the Scotch eggs: Diners are presented with three hard-boiled eggs wrapped in house-made sausage and curry-seasoned breading, then fried and served with arugula and roasted tomato aioli. There are real bangers and mash at the Lions, with two house-made sage and onion British-style sausages, served with garlic mash and smothered in gravy. Score this one for the jolly lads!

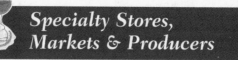

Specialty Stores, Markets & Producers

Larry's Market, 8737 N. Deerwood Dr., Milwaukee, WI 53209; (414) 355-9650; larrysmarket.com. Cheese, cheese, and more cheese. Larry's was already stocking Marieke Mature Gouda even it earned an award as 2013 US Championship Cheese. The Wisconsin cheese from **Holland's Family Cheese** (p. 242) in Thorp captured the head cheese title in a prestigious competition that has been held since 1891. That's Larry's, always on top of things. The shop is located in the old Brown Deer crossroads. Anyone on the North Shore needing catering, gift baskets, and dessert trays knows that Larry's always comes up with the biggest and the best. The deli features regular specials, such as a Friday Burger Palooza. It's clear that spring has really arrived when Larry's tent goes up on its south parking area, the grills are fired, and the sweet perfume of brats wafts throughout the neighborhood. Owner Larry Ehlers started the store in the early 1960s and still works there, spiffy in his black beret at a certain age above 80. The staff here knows all the attributes of its stock, whether the cheese is local, organic, or farmstead; how long it has been aged; and whether it is pasteurized. Tastes are encouraged, a factor we take advantage of regularly. Ehlers also hosts many food authors on tour and has a large stock of foodie books, magazines, and newspapers. There is a small eating section with tables.

Great Bars

Camp Bar, 4044 N. Oakland Ave., Shorewood, WI 53211; (414) 962-5182; campbarmke.com; $. For a faux but friendly facsimile Northwoods romp, drop into Camp Bar. This hot spot for libation is perfect for a chat with owner Paul Hackbarth, who also owns the Sound by Design disc jockey service. The cozy Rhinelander-inspired bar was designed by architect Wade Weissmann and Peabody's Interiors, complete with antler chandeliers, knotty pine, and a taxidermist's dream. Bar managers John McCarthy and Ilana Cohn-Gomez and mixologist Dan Schlax don't seem to mind  pouring under the watchful eye of Walter the Jackalope, Tucker the Growling Bear, and assorted other stuffed critters. Monday night quiz contests run from 8 to 10 p.m., with other events including Tequila Tuesday, Wine & Whiskey Wednesday, Thirsty Thursday, $5 Friday, and Funday Sunday. The Camp Van is available for birthday or work parties, or for girls' or guys' nights out. Leave the driving to them.

Thief Wine, 4512 N. Oakland Ave., Shorewood, WI 53211; (414) 906-1906; thiefwine.com. The opening of this boutique wine shop demonstrated the vitality of Oakland Avenue, where a number of new restaurants and shops have opened over the past several years. A sister shop and wine bar are situated in downtown's Public Market (400 N. Water St., Milwaukee, WI 53202; 414-336-1111). The shop hosts numerous wine tastings. Patrons perch at a long, curved bar facing shelves of wine. Guests can also sit at the tables scattered around the main room. Large windows front the street.

South Side

plus Cudahy, Oak Creek, Franklin & St. Francis

Generally considered the working-class area of greater Milwaukee, the South Side is one of the best places for finding great food and drink. Small taverns offer dozens of beers on tap, plus pub grub that consistently earn kudos for flavor, variety, and experimentation. The factories, warehouses, and freight terminals that made Milwaukee famous during its industrialization heyday are still going strong. Many small restaurants that once served blue-collar workers almost round the clock are still viable and beckoning with the perfume of almost-home-cooked meals.

Foodie Faves

Attebury's Pub and Eatery, 3807 S. Packard Ave., St. Francis, WI 53235; 414-294-3800; atteburyspub.com; Casual American; $–$$. Attebury's has become one of the most popular spots on the South Shore, especially its patio in summer. The place serves comfort food, such as cod-and-chips, mac 'n' cheese, shepherd's pie, and burgers. The Texas-style beef brisket, brined for seven days, is smoked for about 8 hours and served on a toasted baguette. That's enough to fill the hungriest cowpoke. There is a wide range of pizzas, as well.

Anyone with a powerful thirst can experiment with the 24 draft and 25 bottled options, or tackle the hearty wine list.

La Canoa, 1520 W. Lincoln Ave., Milwaukee, WI 53215; (414) 645-1140; facebook.com/pages/La-Canoa/165099926835476; Mexican; $$. *Canoa* means "canoe" in Spanish, an apt name because seafood makes up most of the extensive menu, including saltwater crayfish and red snapper not often found locally. The dishes are from various regions of Mexico, making a visit here more of an eating adventure than is generally found at the typical Tex-Mex cantina- s t y l e establishment. For the exotic, try the octopus (*pulpo*) or frogs' legs (*rana*). La Canoa's soups earn rave reviews.

Mulligans Irish Pub & Grill, 8933 S. 27th St., Franklin, WI 53132; 414-304-0300; mulliganson27th.com; Irish; $$. Reasonable prices, carefully tended food, and a happy atmosphere. What more do you need in an Irish pub? Actually, the name comes from the golfing term, rather than from some clan name. Mulligans has a full menu, including Celtic classics such as corned beef and cabbage, shepherd's pie, lamb stew, and fish-and-chips. Take up the challenge and try to down a 3-pound burger topped with a half pound of cheese, a pound of corned beef, lettuce, tomatoes, onions, pickles, and a pound of french fries in an hour to get a free meal plus a $50 gift card. There are early and late happy hours.

The National, 839 W. National Ave., Milwaukee, WI 53204; (414) 431-6551; nationaleats.com; Casual American; $. Billing itself as "Milwaukee's Neighborhood Cafe," The National opens at 7 a.m. for breakfast, serving the standards, but with a twist. The french toastwich is a fun choice, while the breakfast burrito is hearty enough for a lumberjack or two. You can even get a vegan french toast or a tofu scramble. Fresh-baked goodies direct from the kitchen are ace. Any one of these served up with a cup of Anodyne coffee or **Rishi** (p. 62) tea always gives a head start on the day. A bowl of the house-made soup of the day has always been a pleasure, especially when followed by a homemade brownie. The restaurant also sells locally made arts and crafts, ranging from clothing to botanicals. Sustainability is the key word here.

The Packing House, 900 E. Layton Ave., Milwaukee, WI 53207; 414-483-5054; packinghousemke.com; Casual American; $$. The Wiken family founded the Packing House in 1973 and still operates this longtime supper club. Grilled pork medallions, sirloin and onion shreds, and, yes, real meat loaf are staples. A barrel pickle comes with all the sandwiches, as do fries. This is a "from scratch" kitchen where dressings, sauces, soups, and stock are fresh and ever delicious. For years, Sunday brunch here after church services has been a neighborhood tradition. Folks have been known to drive for miles to secure a serving of the Wikens' famous onion shreds, which are lightly battered and fried. The late-night crowd appreciates the menu of sandwiches served only after 8 p.m.

Papa Luigi's, 3475 E. Layton Ave., Cudahy, WI 53110; (414) 483-6111; papaluigiscudahy.com; Italian; $–$$. Among its numerous authentic Italian dishes, Papa's serves broiled scampi on a skewer over a bed of vegetable rice pilaf. They know how to meld the flavors of Italian spices with a subtle hint of garlic, which makes for a lovely dish. These are positive factors for Italian food guru Betty Puccio, member of the Festa Italiana steering and food committees: "They serve this at Festa Italiana, and people love it. There is only one problem. If you don't get it early, you don't get it at all!" They run out every year." Subsequently, head down to the actual restaurant, where "plenty" is the magic word.

Tenuta's Italian Restaurant, 2995 S. Clement Ave., Milwaukee, WI 53207; (414) 431-1014; tenutasitalian.com; Italian; $–$$. Host Frank Tenuta's parents, Cesare and Antonia, came to America from southern Italy in 1961. According to family legend, they carried original family recipes gathered from throughout Italy. That attention to the old ways is still evident in the *gamberetti*, grilled shrimp with sautéed capers and baby spinach on a bed of fettuccine, drizzled with lemon garlic sauce. The original Caesar would have crossed the Rubicon twice if he had the chance to taste Tenuta's snappy *insalata di Caesar*, romaine lettuce blessed with—of course—a house dressing concocted so secretly that even Vatican archivists are envious. Jean DiMotto, Milwaukee County District Court Judge from Branch 7, can't get enough of the gnocchi with mushrooms here. The flavorful cream sauce is just the right texture. "Mmm, makes me want to stop there tonight! It is a lively place, and people come from neighborhoods near and far to enjoy it," she points out.

Thai Bar-B-Que, 3417 W. National Ave., Milwaukee, WI 53215; (414) 647-0812; thaibarbq.com; Thai; $. The first time you walk through the door, it seems like someone's home. The place is full of Thai families eating here. Kids scamper around, dads and moms talk, grandparents beam. Perfect. Pictures of each dish help negotiate the multipage menu, and there's a knowledgeable staff on hand to explain any potential puzzlements. Just about everything is made fresh. The papaya salad earns high marks, as do most of the curries, not to mention the barbecue.

Trattoria di Carlo & Pizzeria, 8469 S. Howell Ave, Oak Creek, WI 53154; (414) 768-0001; dicarlopizza.com; Italian; $. Located on South Howell Avenue just south of Drexel Avenue in Oak

Creek, this cozy, comfortable eatery with its clean, simple lines has one of the better *piatto* antipasto servings in the area. Accommodating two to four diners, the platter includes prosciutto, salami, fresh mozzarella, husky Italian olives, roasted peppers, tomatoes, and Parmesan cheese cubes, plus additional seasonal items. The trattoria's family-style option is great for any hungry group wishing to indulge in chicken Parmesan, pollo saltimbocca, filet boscaiola, or other favorites paired with pasta and choice of sauces. For high fliers, the restaurant's catering division provides in-flight meals to charter airlines and to private and corporate jets. There's nothing like a caprese salad and beef sacchettini above the clouds.

Landmarks

Caterina's Ristorante, 9104 W. Oklahoma Ave., Milwaukee, WI 543227; (414) 541-4200; caterinasristorante.com; Italian; $–$$. Antonio (Tony) Ingrilli moved to Milwaukee from Capo d'Orlando, Sicily, in 1964 and began making pizza at the tender age of 17. At 24, he opened his first restaurant and then went on to launch an Italian deli and liquor store. He and his wife, Kathy, swung open the doors at Caterina's in 1982. In 2003, their son, Tony Jr., took over the bright, cheery facility where, if anyone wants seafood, Ingrilli has it. Patrons flock here for the scampi in its numerous transformations: paired with scallops, breaded, *al française* (dipped in an egg batter and sautéed with lemon juice), and *messinese* (sautéed in tomatoes, olive oil, wine, onions, plenty of garlic, and lots of delicious fontina cheese). For meat eaters, Ingrilli's prime steer fillet is seasoned, breaded, and then sautéed with freshly sliced mushrooms, green peppers, and onions. The ristorante also has lamb, pork, and chicken. Curved as nicely as an Italian starlet, the well-stocked bar is a dining room feature.

Clifford's Supper Club, 10418 W. Forest Home Ave., Hales Corners, WI 53130; (414) 425-6226; cliffordsfinefood.com; Supper Club; $$. This Hales Corners supper club features sliced roast sirloin, ham steak (with a pineapple ring, of course), baked flounder stuffed with crabmeat, and a seafood platter hefty enough for all the hearties aboard Blackbeard's *Queen Anne's Revenge.* The jaeger schnitzel breaded veal cutlet is served with sautéed mushrooms and onions, just like Oma used to make in her kitchen. Calf's liver with onions or bacon is the perfect comfort food. Conclude with a flaming broadside of cherries jubilee, a house specialty.

Specialty Stores, Markets & Producers

Hmong Asian Food Store, 1243 S. Cesar E. Chavez Dr., Milwaukee, WI 53204; (414) 384-9990. Located in the center of Milwaukee's Hmong community, this family-owned grocery offers Asian-style produce, specialty goods, and meats.

Lovino, LLC, 2132 E. Bennett Ave., Milwaukee, WI 53207; (414) 467-6446; lovinosangria.com. Jamie and Erica Zdroik created their divine Spanish sangria after months of testing at home, sampling, and trying again. Partnering with an Algoma winery, they finally were satisfied with the concentrated blend of Cabernet Franc as a base wine, complemented with punchy citrus flavors. Think romance when dining at Di Carlo Trattoria & Pizzeria in Oak Creek or when purchasing a bottle (or two) at Ray's Wine & Spirits, **Outpost Natural Foods** (p. 48), and other outlets.

Great Bars

Bryant's Cocktail Lounge, 1579 S. 9th St., Milwaukee, WI 53204; (414) 383-2620; bryantscocktaillounge.com. Nominated for a 2013 James Beard award for Outstanding Bar Program, Bryant's boasts an impressive selection of over 400 drinks.

Club Paragon, 3578 S. 108th St., Milwaukee, WI 53228; (414) 541-9270; clubparagon.com. Described as a log cagin in the heart of the city, Club Paragon has a dart league, all-you-can-eat crab legs, and a fish fry. Promos include Ladies Night, aka "Sizzling Saturdays," from 10 p.m. to midnight.

Koz's Mini Bowl, 2078 S. 7th St., Milwaukee, WI 3204; (414) 383-0560; kozsminibowl.com. Sometimes called duckpin bowling, the pins are still set by hand on the bar's four mini-bowling lanes, with league players coming here from around the Midwest. Even the scorekeeping is manual. You can call ahead and reserve a lane, a must on weekends. There's a well-used pool table, but keep your money in your pockets. Sharks are swimming around, watching the action, so never play another man's game. The jukebox is straight out of the 1950s, and many of the crowd are reliving their glory days over a tapper. Gimme 'nother Pabst, please. Before you leave, be sure to tip the pin setters.

Redbar, 2245 E. St. Francis Ave., Milwaukee, WI 53235; (414) 212-8470; facebook.com/redbarMKE. The Redbar covers more than 3,000 square feet, with two bars on two levels. A huge game room offers shuffleboard, video machines, pool, darts, and other games. Wisconsin beers are featured here, but a determined patron can always find a frothy Guinness.

West Side

plus Wauwatosa & *West Allis*

Milwaukee's West Side has long had its traditional steak houses, where brandy manhattans and huge slabs of beef have long ruled. Lately, however, more and more slick and upscale facilities can be discovered, as well as ethnic restaurants covering a worldwide scene. Even the more staid suburb of Wauwatosa and the factory-flavored back streets of West Allis are presenting fresh opportunities for dining out. West North Avenue and West Vliet Street are great thoroughfares, taking adventurous diners to new culinary pleasures.

Foodie Faves

Antigua Latin Restaurant, 5823 W. Burnham St., West Allis, WI 53219; (414) 321-5775; antiguamilwaukee.com; Latin American; $–$$. House specials include a Spanish paella that needs about 25 to 30 minutes for cooking and prep, so you may wish to have another beer while anticipating. One popular dish is the paella Valenciana, consisting of cooked rice, with chicken breast chunks, pork, bell peppers, and onions, and then seasoned with saffron. The seafood variety, called *paella de mariscos,* is made with fish, shrimp, mussels, lobster tails, bell peppers, and onions, also seasoned with saffron.

BelAir, 6817 North Ave., Milwaukee, WI 53202; (414) 988-8533; belaircantina.com; Mexican; $–$$. The second of two BelAir restaurants, the West Side eatery opened in 2013. It features a wide patio perfect for seasonal dining and emphasizes lots of light with its almost-floor-to-ceiling windows. The old building was built in the late 1940s as an auto-repair service and car dealership. The place retains its industrial look, one with a Baja California atmosphere. The always-*bueno* original restaurant is located at 1935 N. Water St. The menus are basically the same, supervised by Jalisco-native chef Noe Zamor, who monitors both BelAir kitchens. Partners Scott Johnson, Leslie Montemurro, and Kristyn St. Denis are well known around town for their restaurant savvy. The trio also owns the **Palomino Bar** (p. 68), the Garage (9 N. Arlington Place), and the two-decades-old Fuel Cafe (818 E. Center St.). For drinks at BelAir, adding fresh-squeezed juices creates new margaritas, such as a pineapple ginger margarita, a grapefruit jalapeño margarita, and fresh-juiced strawberry margarita. Barrels of BelAir Private Label Herradura Double Reposado from Guadalajara are imported, and bottles are for sale at each location. Three pouring sizes are available for the Monte Alban and other tequilas. Both locations have more brunch items in the summer, such as huevos rancheros, chorizo and egg burritos, and *chilaquiles.* Vegan options are also available. No reservations are taken at either place.

Blue's Egg, 317 N. 76th St., Milwaukee, WI 53213; (414) 299-3180; bluesegg.com; Casual American; $$. Be aware that for Sunday breakfast, there is usually a long line, especially midmorning, but it's worth the wait. Blue's Egg is among the city's favored breakfast outlets, so try to get here before the après-church crowd arrives. Fresh products and made-from-scratch techniques support a wide variety of menu items from France, Italy, England, Germany, Belgium, Spain,

Scandinavia, North Africa, and a dash of the Far East. Omelets are ace here, especially with a side of house-made granola. The crispy blue-crab cakes are another favorite. Kids go nuts with the blueberry pancakes or french toast with almond crumble and a white chocolate sauce. The folks here serve a daily egg plate and donate $1 of every egg order to a different local charity each week. The eggs are the large brown kind from free-range birds gleaned from JRS Country Acres in Lake Mills, just to the east of Madison. Other purveyors are the Sassy Cow Creamery in Columbus, Jones Dairy Farm in Fort Atkinson, and Kinkoona Farms in Brodhead. Blue's lunch is no slouch either, especially with an avocado citrus salad with fresh avocado, orange supremes, candied almonds, feta cheese, red onion, greens, and a citrus vinaigrette. The restaurant has a long counter lined with stools, yet the two dining rooms are ample for small or large groups. Blue's Egg is open only from 7 a.m. to 2 p.m. Its sister restaurant, **Maxie's Southern Comfort** (p. 112), then takes over for the dinner crowd.

Double B's BBQ & Burgers, 7420 W. Greenfield Ave., West Allis, WI 53214; (414) 257-9150; doublebs.com; Barbecue; $. A hot-links sandwich, with slow-smoked sausages tucked into a hoagie, is a great alternative to the usual pulled pork found at all barbecue joints. The Big Texas club sandwich is Double B's signature smoked chicken served on Texas toast with smoked ham, black-pepper bacon, swiss cheese, mayo, and tomato. The ribs here are dry-rub Memphis style, coming with two sides, which could be baked beans, mac 'n' cheese, sweet potato fries, corn, or regular french fries. The house-made corn bread is a perfect addition, especially with the honey-pecan butter. There are many specials throughout the week, included no-limit Tuesday sliders. The fried catfish fillets are also pretty good.

Il Mito Trattoria e Enoteca, 6913 W. North Ave., Milwaukee, WI 53213; (414) 443-1414; ilmito.com; Italian; $$–$$$. On the city's restaurant scene since 1997, Chef Michael Feker emphasizes simple Italian cuisine, augmented by a superb wine list. Winning the chariot race for the city's best spaghetti Bolognese is Feker's tasty dance of Italian sausage, ground eye of the round, chicken sans hormones and antibiotics, plus savory herbs simmered in a red wine and tomato reduction.  Feker grows his own herbs at home in planters, which are then moved inside during the winter. Among his favorites are basil, rosemary, thyme, oregano, cilantro, and mint. Along with small plates (*piatti piccoli*), Il Mito has numerous seasonal gluten-free offerings. The restaurant is snug, with a long bar backed by tables ranging against a rustic wall. The front of the room faces Wauwatosa's bustling North Avenue, with a side area devoted to parties, tastings, and cooking demonstrations. Il Mito East opened early in 2013 at 1028 E. Juneau Ave., just off the lobby of the Knickerbocker on the Lake hotel.

Maxie's Southern Comfort, 6732 W. Fairview Ave., Milwaukee, WI 53213; (414) 292-3969; maxies.com; Casual American; $$. Owned by Dan Sidner and Chef Joe Muench, Maxie's goes for regional dishes, with taste treats including pulled pork in vinegar sauce with snappy coleslaw and hearty beans, or shrimp in tasso sauce over smooth, flavorful grits. Specials are noteworthy, such as trout *rillettes* with pickled okra and even braised bison. Fresh oysters are just as popular, whether at a table or the bar. Combine that with a shaken-not-stirred martini, and bliss awaits. Maxie's pops up all over the city, whenever and wherever there is a food fair, charity event, or another soiree featuring hearty, homespun chow.

Meritage, 5921 W. Vliet St., Milwaukee, WI 53208; (414) 479-0620; meritage.us; New American; $$–$$$. After an evening film at the Times Cinema (5906 W. Vliet St.), scamper across the street to see the latest menu offering of Chef-Owner Jan Kelly. A great starter is the ricotta and egg yolk raviolo carbonara, a house-made raviolo filled with herb ricotta cheese and a farm fresh egg yolk on wild boar bacon and brown butter. That is sometimes followed by short ribs braised with parsnips, celery root, and horseradish with carrot mashed potatoes, or a roasted poblano pepper stuffed with bison *carnitas* and Chihuahua cheese with tomatillo sauce and bison chorizo *chilaquiles,* or strips of fried corn tortillas simmered in salsa and dished up with cheese, eggs, or beans. Vegetarian and gluten-free selections are also available. The main room is comfortably soft, with a peach tone that lends itself to kicking back and getting into a Zen mode after a hectic workday or a scary monster movie at the theater. Kelly earned her culinary stripes at restaurants in Northern California before coming to Milwaukee with her husband in 1995. She worked at several high-end eateries prior to opening her own place in 2007 in the Washington Heights neighborhood. See Chef Jan Kelly's recipe for **Sauerkraut & Bacon Bread Pudding** on p. 294.

North Avenue Grill, 7225 W. North Ave., Wauwatosa, WI 53213; (414) 453-7225; www.northavenuegrill.com; Casual American; $–$$.

Billing itself as a "New American Diner," the Grill is open daily, serving breakfast from 7 a.m. all day. What could be better? This is the home for flavorful, inexpensive meals that fit any budget. Breakfast comfort food includes homemade corned beef hash and the usual omelets and egg varieties. The bacon, egg, and cheese sammie includes bacon, a fried egg, and American cheese on grilled ciabatta bread, served with American fries. Part of the fun is that every Thursday the staff picks tables at random to "throw out," after diners eat but before they pay; in other words, the meal might be on them. Neighborhood foodies often toddle in for a build-your-own-burger or a monster buffalo chicken

sandwich accompanied by a spicy sauce. Great Friday fish fry, as well, which is extended to Wednesday during Lent. Throughout it all, Chef Mike Topolovich obviously can find his way around a flattop stove.

Taqueria El Fogoncito, 10425 W. North Ave., Wauwatosa, WI 53226; (414) 331-5554; Mexican; $. Opening daily at 7 a.m., El Fogoncito is variously translated as "the little candle" or "little stove." Either way, the restaurant stands ready to scoop up at least five different huevos dishes even at that early hour. Any variety tastes best following a daybreak jog around the Mayfair Mall neighborhood. Yet night crawlers can also get a much-needed Cancún fix, with tacos as the signature dish up to 10 p.m. on weekdays and Fri and Sat until 1 a.m. There isn't any Mexican bling here. It's just basic, good grub.

Ted's Ice Cream and Restaurant, 6204 W. North Ave, Wauwatosa, WI 53213; (414) 258-5610; Casual American; $. This is the place to come on the West Side for ice cream, malts, sundaes, and bottomless cups of coffee. Simple fare and casual lunch-counter style contribute to the old-timey feel of a diner. After all, they've been on this corner for almost 70 years. The inexpensive charges make it great for hungry kids of all ages. A chalkboard special every day racks up the latest offerings for breakfast available until promptly 11:30 a.m. They mean what they say. After that hour, come the inexpensive burgers. It's a first-come, first-served sort of place, with no reservations taken.

 Landmarks

Eddie Martini's, 8612 W. Watertown Plank Rd., Wauwatosa, WI 53226; (414) 771-6680; eddiemartinis.com; Steak House; $$$$. Martinis and steak make for a powerhouse dinner, perfect for finalizing a company buyout or celebrating an anniversary of any kind. For the past several decades, Eddie's has been known for large portions, such as a hefty 24-ounce porterhouse or a bone-in rib eye. As an alternative, try broiled pheasant breast or Australian lobster tail. The bar area up front is perfect for merely sipping Champagne or a dry, dry martini. Eddie's is a short drive from Froedtert Hospital and the Medical College of Wisconsin, so a goodly supply of physicians is often here sipping their after-hours Pinots.

Le Rêve Patisserie and Cafe, 7610 Harwood Ave., Wauwatosa, WI 53213; (414) 778-3333; lerevecafe.com; French; $$.

Undergoing a renovation in 2013 that expanded an upstairs dining area, Le Rêve has perked up its charming space, still replete with Cream City brick walls and a pastry case exploding with gourmet goodies like hazelnut-chocolate cake. This bistro, consistently winning accolades as the area's best French eatery, is a great place to jump-start the day, either with a quiche or a mushroom, leek, and gruyère crepe. Croissants and muscular coffee will keep a patron going for hours. As a breakfast backup, especially on a lazy Sunday with a newspaper in hand, patrons in the know indulge in a framboise royale Champagne delight. Andrew Schneider doubles as bread baker, partner Therese Hittman handles pastry, and Chef Patrick Murphy manages the well-run kitchen. Lunch consists of French-style small plates, with late afternoon snacks of charcuterie, cheeses, *pommes frites,* and mussels as a lead-in for wine or cocktails. For dinner, we enjoy perching around one of the small forged-iron tables on the sidewalk outside for a soothing summer sip of wine while watching the passersby. It's an even better experience with braised Strauss lamb, white beans, baby root veggies, and white wine–garlic sauce. Plus, after a bowl of Schneider's bouillabaisse, anyone could easily storm and conquer the Bastille.

Ristorante Bartolotta, 7616 W. State St., Wauwatosa, WI 53213; (414) 771-7910; bartolottaristorante.com; Italian; $$–$$$. Ristorante Bartolotta serves rustic Italian dishes from central and northern Italy. Occupying a prime corner in the heart of 'Tosa Village, this Bartolotta dynasty flagship makes for a dining delight. The chefing staff can whip up a *spiedini di quaglia alla griglia,* a perfectly grilled quail breast skewered with brussels sprouts and served with baked polenta. Proud of its community links, Bartolotta is the official restaurant group for the Milwaukee Film Festival. Throughout this annual event, Bartolotta presented fun pairings between its many eateries and various movies, such as linking the Italian film *Summer Games (Giochi d'Estate)* with the restaurant's *pappardelle al ragù d'anatra,* a Tuscan dish harkening back to the movie's setting, or suggesting a particular bottle of wine for dinner prior to the showing of *Somm,* a documentary film about sommeliers. Milwaukee historian/author Bobby Tanzilo says, "As for Italian restaurants, I'm hard-pressed to think of one as good as Ristorante Bartolotta, and that most Italian expats I know won't dine out on Italian food in Milwaukee but will go there when they are entertaining for work." He praises the chef's *agnolotti al plin,* a small, traditional Piemontese ravioli.

Specialty Stores, Markets & Producers

Amaranth Bakery, 3329 W. Lisbon Ave., Milwaukee, WI 53208; (414) 934-0587. Amaranth focuses on organic ingredients, with the value-added pluses of local and fair trade. You can also order soup and sandwiches from a counter beginning at 9 a.m., then plunk down to eat at one of the small tables in the comfortable building scented with baking bread. Opening in 2006, owners Dave Boucher and Stephanie

Shipley change their dining menues daily, so you might find a black bean soup one day and something equally delicious the next. Smart shoppers load up on any one of the numerous varieties of fresh bread and take-out quarts of soup for home consumption. The motto here bears repeating: "Good bread. Good health." Amaranth always takes high kudos in any "Best Of" list for Milwaukee.

Indian Spice and Groceries, 10633 W. North Ave., Wauwatosa, WI 53226; (414) 771-3535. This cozy West Side grocery has a wide range of Asian specialties and a good selection of curries and other spices required for any Indian dishes. The place is small yet well stocked.

Treat Bake Shop, (414) 305-8937; thetreatbakeshop.com. Sarah Marx Feldner started as the early-morning baker at a co-op more than 15 years ago and was most recently the executive editor for TasteofHome.com. She secured her master's in library and information science from the University of Illinois with an emphasis on culinary collections and food research, which has helped her eat her way through 10 countries. Feldner's latest tome, *A Cook's Journey to Japan,* makes a perfect holiday companion gift for her dynamite-spiced Georgia pecans. These snazzy snacks are found at **Larry's Market** (p. 100) in Brown Deer, Grasch's in Brookfield, and other local and national outlets. To learn the spicy side of life, Feldner apprenticed with the Penzeys, Milwaukee's condiment czars. Follow her on Facebook for her next in-store promotion.

Viet HOA Supermarket, 4900 W. North Ave., Milwaukee, WI 53208; (414) 442-4016. The grocery is well stocked with items seldom heard about on the shores of Lake Michigan. But with the growing numbers of Asian families in the city, such markets stock all sorts of seemingly bizarre fish, sauces, and "things in a can." Fifty-pound bags of rice are piled in neat rows, fronting shelves of boxes, trays, and bags of tasty goodies.

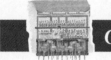

Great Bars

Colonel Hart's, 7342 W. State St., Wauwatosa, WI 53213; (414) 476-3070; colonelharts.com. Hot dogs and beer and sports. Gotta love it.

Leff's Lucky Town, 7208 W. State St., Milwaukee, WI 53213; (414) 258-9886; leffs.com. Gallons of beer, lobster roll-ups, and build your own burger on Meat Cake Monday make Leff's a standout.

Waukesha, Brookfield, Pewaukee & Germantown

Milwaukee is ringed by a cluster of suburbs, some with sidewalks and others sans. On the east is Lake Michigan, where water wings are de rigueur whether coming or going. Regardless of how one gets to these locales, each burb has eateries that have garnered accolades both from critics and from seasoned diners. Shorewood, Waukesha, Brookfield, Cudahy, St. Francis, New Berlin, and Pewaukee are only minutes from downtown Milwaukee, except during road repair season, which actually can be just about any time of the year. Don't let that be a deterrent because some of the fun is getting there, but the most enjoyable is indulging in a marvelous meal whether steak house, bistro, or pub style.

Albanese's Roadhouse & Dominic's Sports Lounge,
2301 W. Bluemound Rd., Waukesha, WI 53186; (262) 785-1930;
albanesesroadhouse.com; Italian; $. Harkening back to the days
of red-checkered tablecloths, Albanese's capitalizes on its three
generations of family owner-operators, with Joe Albanese the current
owner. House specialties include steak pizzaiola, a tenderloin sautéed
with vegetables and Marsala wine, topped with provolone cheese, and
served with a choice of spaghetti or mostacciolli, and Italian sausage
cacciatore with homemade Italian sausage and red wine married with
green peppers and oodles of mushrooms and onions. Lunch is served
Mon through Fri. A separate area has been remodeled with a lounge
and sports-bar format with pool tables, darts, pinball, and related
games. If you are into bocce ball, you can join the Roadhouse's 80-plus
member league and play on one of the six outdoor courts.

Butler Inn of Pewaukee, 742 Glacier Rd., Pewaukee, WI
53072; (262) 691-0840; butlerinnofpewaukee.com; **Supper Club;**
$$$. For a special night out, the Butler Inn offers a first-class menu with
all the trimmings. On Monday and Tuesday, surf-and-turf combinations
of charbroiled filet mignons, jumbo prawns, king crab, and Canadian
lobster tails are offered. Other specials include *saganaki,* imported
kefalograviera cheese flambéed with brandy, or a Louie's steak salad
with sliced filet mignon and blue cheese, plus bacon, tomato, cheese,
and red onions on a bed of greens. Don't miss the famous haystack
of perfectly fried onion rings. There is live entertainment on the
weekends.

Glass Nickel Pizza, 13175 W. Bluemound Rd., Brookfield, WI
53005; (262) 782-8000; glassnickelpizza.com/Locations/brookfield
.html; **Pizza; $–$$.** Madison residents Brian Glassel and Tim Nicholson

met while working in a pizza restaurant. That was a natural link since they have both worked in pizza restaurants most of their lives. The first Glass Nickel opened in 1997 in Madison, with additional outlets in Fitchburg, Sun Prairie, Oshkosh, Green Bay, Appleton, and a second Mad City eatery. The menu has an extensive array of sandwiches, subs, and appetizers. The guys emphasize green, as in environment. They use alternative fuel vehicles for deliveries, along with many in-store innovations for lighting, heating, and appliances. A pizza mail sign-up provides coupons and info on special offers.

Lagniappe Brasserie, 17001 W. Greenfield Ave., New Berlin, WI 53151; (262) 782-7530; lagniappebrasserie.com; French; $$$. The Brasserie has white tablecloths, flickering candles, and airy cathedral ceilings. The always-changing menu capitalizes on fresh herbs and vegetables, plucked from the restaurant's garden. Organic greens make up the salads, with apples from the Patterson orchard and farm market just down the road. Chef-Owner Andrew Tenaglia can do high-end entrees and also knows how to put on more comfort food, such as a one-pound Kobe beef burger.

Mr. B's, 18380 W. Capitol Dr., Brookfield, WI 53045; (262) 790-7005; mrbssteakhouse.com; Steak House; $$$–$$$$. Hey! You gotta beef? Well, plunk down at one of the tables here, dazzled up with its blue-and-white checkered tablecloth, and dig in. Steak knives the size of sabers are provided. Meat reigns at this Bartolotta steak house, with the prime bone-in rib eye an excellent dining choice. For the philistines among us who enjoy the "other white meat," however, a Berkshire pork porterhouse is a great option. For any noncarnivores going off the deep end by being in a steak house, there is a meatless rigatoni with eggplant and fresh mozzarella in a basil-tomato sauce. Chef Brent Perszyk's kitchen is classic Italian, bringing in experiences earned at the Culinary Institute of America followed by stints at top restaurants around the country before returning to hometown Milwaukee. The expansive patio out back is great for seasonal hanging out, an experience often in short supply in Wisconsin's truncated summer. Thank heavens for the outside fireplace to aid with snuggling on chilly eves. It's good to know that Mr. B's bar opens at 4:30 p.m. weekdays. Perch on a stool there and order a bottle of exceptionally tasty Pinot Noir.

Seester's Mexican Cantina, 161 W. Wisconsin Ave., Pewaukee, WI 53072; (262) 746-9400; seestersmexicancantina.com; Mexican; $. There is a five-star view of Pewaukee Lake, with a beach complete with sunbathers, swimmers, and frolicking children. So select a high-top table and flop into a colorful chair. From Memorial Day through Labor Day, Seester's is open daily, serving breakfast, lunch, and dinner (winter hours are from 4 p.m. to close on Tues through Sat). Breakfast specialties include huevos rancheros, green eggs and cactus, stuffed french toast with strawberry-jalapeño syrup, and even a banana burrito. Or try one (or two) of Seester's locally famous margaritas with fresh-squeezed lime juice. Or maybe a grapefruit margarita. Or even a grown-up Kool-Aid with adult-size portions of tequila, papaya liqueur, amaretto, margarita mix, and lemon.

Sprizzo Gallery Caffe, 363 W. Main St., Waukesha, WI 53186; (262) 513-5640; sprizzo.net; Casual American; $–$$. Sprizzo Caffe is locally owned, with a coffee shop and bar well situated in historic downtown Waukesha. Local artists display their work in an ever-changing exhibit, with area musicians lending their own charm, whether it be jazz, folk, alternative country, bluegrass, or even open mike. Lunch is especially comforting, with traditional cold or grilled sandwiches and soups on the menu. But each is always done to perfection.

Cafe Manna, 3815 N. Brookfield Rd., Brookfield, WI 53045; (262) 790-2340; cafemanna.com; Vegetarian; $$. Where's the beef? Actually, there isn't any at this 100 percent vegetarian restaurant, priding itself in using organically or sustainable farming practices, locally grown seasonal foods, and even a reverse-osmosis water purification system. The cafe is the first certified-green restaurant in Wisconsin. On the menu, you might find such delicacies as raw kale pesto pasta (raw, vegan, and gluten-free) or zucchini "noodles" tossed with shredded carrots and cherry tomatoes in a flavorful kale pesto sauce. It's all topped with sun-dried currants, pine nuts, and almond "Parmesan cheese." Or if you wish a tasty change, try the shepherd's garden pie, a hearty dish of zucchini, yellow squash, peas, and carrots in savory gravy crowned with whipped potatoes and then baked. The cafe holds cooking classes on various Sundays throughout the year, covering topics such as olive oils and vinegars, essential oils, bread baking, and gluten-free cooking. As the folks here say, "Stay healthy, love long."

Eric's Porter Haus, 229 Wisconsin Ave., Waukesha, WI 53186; (262) 542-1300; ericsporterhaus.com; Supper Club; $$. Eric's is a comfortable tuckaway in a colonnaded Greek Revival building dating from the 19th century. The façade is a page from *Gone with the Wind,* Waukesha mode. Step inside for whole roast duckling with wild rice, baby back ribs, the signature porterhouse, or enough filet mignon to pack the OK Corral. Oh, there's also beef *Rouladen* and Black Forest schnitzel. Constructed in 1844 by civic leader Isaac Lain, and then a home to banker and late Waukesha mayor Edward Estberg, the place was an American Legion post before it morphed into Eric's a generation ago.

GERMAN EATS IN LAKE COUNTRY

For decades, the Weissgerber family has had the quality restaurant business sewn up in lands far distant from downtown Milwaukee, offering a variety of German-themed and American fare lakeside properties.

Weissgerber's Gasthaus, 2720 N. Grandview Blvd., Waukesha, WI 53188; (262) 544-4460; www.weissgerbers.com/ gasthaus; $$$. The Gasthaus has all the charm of a Bavarian guesthouse. Its outdoor *Biergarten* is one of the best in the Milwaukee area, the home of real beer gardens. The Friday fish fry is renowned for its family-style presentation, so bring friends. The fried bluegill rates highly.

The Golden Mast, W349 N5293 Lacys Ln., Okauchee, WI 53069; (262) 567-7047; goldenmastinn.com; $$$. Located on Okauchee Lake, the Mast is a grand destination restaurant for dedicated diners from around the region. A veal cordon bleu sandwich, with wiener schnitzel topped with ham and melted swiss cheese, makes for a lunch on the lighter side. The German combination platter for dinner, however, provides a sampling of traditional German dishes, featuring a duck leg, beef *Rouladen,* and a schnitzel, served with the requisite spaetzle and red cabbage. There are plenty of steak and seafood options, as well.

Jake's, 21445 W. Gumina Rd., Pewaukee, WI 53072; (262) 781-7995; jakes-restaurant.com; Supper Club; $$–$$$. Although the restaurant looks like a classic supper club, the original building is a century-old barn. Jake's owners, Chef Jake and Karen Replogle, push to the cutting edge of new food. Brick-roasted chicken and a Berkshire pork chop have gained in popularity. Yet since this is Wisconsin where citizens like their meat, terrific Angus steaks remain supreme. A variety of toppings complements the taste treat, whether Cajun, blue cheese, crab and asparagus, peppercorn, truffle béarnaise, or Jake's special sauce. Trying Jake's seasonal specials is a must. Go for a fried green tomato or a beet salad with peaches and blue cheese. An adjacent lounge, Charred, is for casual pre- or post-dinner drinking, or a mere stop to say hello to friends. It has a separate pub-style menu of mostly burgers. Crispy brussels sprouts with pumpkin seeds are also on the menu.

Parkside 23, 2300 Pilgrim Place, Brookfield, WI 53005; (262) 784-7275; parkside23.com; New American; $–$$. This might be the only restaurant in Wisconsin with an on-site farm, complemented by goodies from many other local producers. No hormones and no antibiotics, and you can add additional protein to any dish (for an extra price). The place has an extensive gluten-free menu and takeout that includes braised lamb shank, broiled tenderloin, and chicken dumpling soup.

Seven Seas Seafood & Steak, 1807 Nagawicka Rd., Hartland, WI 53029; (262) 367-3903; sevenseaswi.com; Steak/Seafood $$$. Since 1981, the Seven Seas has served up excellent seafood and steaks. A Champagne Sunday brunch is always packed. *Wine Spectator* regularly passes along high honors for the wine list here.

HOP ON BOARD

Take the bus for culinary fun and leave the driving to **Milwaukee Food Tours.** Theresa Nemetz and her husband, Wade, ensure a good time, grand fun, and an exciting peek into the city's history—all rolled into one jolly excursion. The couple started their citywide ramblings as a hobby 5 years ago, combining Theresa's love of Milwaukee and Wade's love of food. Their community showcasing started as a walking food tour of the Brady Street neighborhood, but they now offer 12 different bus or walking opportunities, including those listed below. For reservations, visit online at milwaukeefoodtours.com, or call (800) 979-3370.

Milwaukee Pizza Bus: This 3-hour culinary expedition ranges from old-school joints to gourmet pizza establishments, combined with drives through historic neighborhoods, beginning in West Milwaukee at 6 p.m. Hefty slices, dessert, and transportation are included in the per-person prices. Beverages are provided at some stopovers.

Historic Third Ward Food Tour: This walking tour provides a wide variety of foods, tied together with some Wisconsin-brewed beers. Length is approximately 1 mile, with breaks and opportunities to sit down along the way. About 20 minutes is spent at each restaurant. Plan on spending about 2 to 2.5 hours, depending on whether guests are amblers or striders.

Walker's Point Dine Around: Expect to spend up to 3 hours chowing down around one of city's trendiest dining neighborhoods. Be aware that the tour is not handicap accessible because of stairs and an on-off bus route. Be sure to come hungry because of the beer/wine pairings and desserts. Included is the **Clock Shadow Creamery** (p. 62), Milwaukee's only urban cheese factory. Hit the road at 5:30 p.m.

Specialty Stores, Markets & Producers

Angelic Bakehouse, PO Box 851, Waukesha, WI 53187-0851; (262) 547-1821 or (800) 876-2253; angelicbakehouse.com. Founded as Cybros Bakery in 1969, Jenny and James Marino purchased the facility in 2009 and changed the name to Angelic Bakehouse in 2013. The firm bakes all sorts of breads and buns from sprouted grains, which are sold in numerous food stores throughout southeastern Wisconsin and can even be ordered online.

Great Bars

BuBs Irish Pub, N116 W16218 Main St., Germantown, WI 53022; (262) 255-1840; bubsirishpub.com; $-$$. In a blur of heritages, the menu's Dublin Dipper is actually a traditional french dip with the requisite roast beef, and there is a Taco Tuesday. At more than 15,000 square feet, this place says it might be "the world's largest Irish pub." But it's not so big that a thirsty drinker can't find a Guinness, or even a corned beef sandwich on the side. Bring a thousand of your closest friends.

Lucky Rabbit, 200 Madison St., Waukesha, WI 53188; (262) 542-6200; luckyrabbitwaukesha.com; $-$$. Party on down to the Rabbit for specialty pizzas and 20 craft beers, most of which are Wisconsin brewed. The bar in Waukesha's downtown is part of a push to perk up the community's central city. A DJ spins discs on Saturday night.

Slim McGinn's West, 14735 W. Lisbon Rd., Brookfield, WI 53005; (262) 373-1500; slimmcginns.com; $-$$. Look for daily specials, such as all-you-can-eat tacos on Tuesday. The gang behind the bar pours a grand pint, which brings in a crowd, particularly on weekends. It's a place where you could bring your grandma.

Milwaukee Breweries, Craft Breweries & Beer Pubs

Wisconsin ranks ninth nationally in craft breweries per capita, including large breweries that produce 6 million–plus barrels a year, regional breweries turning out 15,000 to 6 million, microbreweries brewing less than 15,000 barrels, and brewpubs. Milwaukee has a full range of brewing facilities, from small pub outlets to one of the world's largest.

Big Bay Brewing Co., 4517 N. Oakland Ave., Shorewood, WI 53211; (414) 226-6611; bigbaybrewing.com.

Horny Goat Hideaway, 2011 S. 1st St., Milwaukee, WI 53207; (414) 482-4628; hghideaway.com.

Jacob Leinenkugel Brewing Co., 1515 N. 10th St., Milwaukee, WI 53205; (414) 931-6799; leinie.com.

Lagniappe Brasserie, 17001 W. Greenfield Ave., New Berlin, WI 53151; (262) 782-7530; lagniappebrasserie.com. See full description on p. 121.

Lakefront Brewery, 1872 N. Commerce St., Milwaukee, WI 53202; (414) 372-8800; lakefrontbrewery.com.

MillerCoors LLC, 4000 W. State St., Milwaukee, WI 53208; (800) 944-5483; millercoors.com.

Milwaukee Ale House, 233 N. Water St., Milwaukee, WI 53202, (414) 276-2337; and 1208 13th Ave., Grafton, WI 53024; (262) 375-2337; ale-house.com.

Milwaukee Brewing Company, 613 S. 2nd St., Milwaukee, WI 53204; (414) 226-2337; mkebrewing.com.

Rock Bottom Restaurant & Brewery, 740 N. Plankinton Ave., Milwaukee, WI 53203; (414) 276-3030; rockbottom.com/milwaukee.

St. Francis Brewery and Restaurant, 3825 S. Kinnickinnic Ave., St. Francis, WI 53235; (414) 744-4448; stfrancisbrewery.com.

Sprecher Brewery, 701 W. Glendale Ave., Milwaukee, WI 53209; (414) 964-2739; sprecherbrewery.com.

Stonefly Brewing Company, 735 E. Center St., Milwaukee, WI 53212; (414) 212-8910; stoneflybrewery.com.

Water Street Brewery, 1101 N. Water St., Milwaukee, WI 53202, (414) 272-1195; 2615 Washington St., Grafton, WI 53024, (262) 375-2222; and 3191 Golf Rd., Delafield, WI 53018, (262) 646-7878; waterstreetbrewery.com.

Where to Get It Fresh

Brookfield Farmers' Market, 2000 N. Calhoun Rd., Brookfield, WI 53005; (262) 784-7804; brookfieldfarmersmarket .com. Sat from 7:30 a.m. to noon, end of May through end of Oct. Past vendors have been Back to Bread Bakery, Bugling Pines Elk Farm, **Schmit's Farm Produce** (p. 132), Peach Tree Gardens, Palm's Mushroom Cellar, and many more.

Brown Deer Farmers' Market, 8900 N. Deerbrook Trail, Brown Deer, WI 53233; mybrowndeernow.com. Wed from 9 a.m. to 6 p.m., late May through mid- to late October, rain or shine. Numerous Hmong families bring in fresh produce from their plots scattered around the North Shore, augmented with fruit growers, honey producers, and other purveyors.

East Side Green Market, 1901 E. North Ave., Milwaukee, WI 53202; (414) 502-9489; theeastside.org/categories/10-green-market. Sat from 10 a.m. to 2 p.m., June to Oct. Crowds of youngsters, oldsters, and in-betweens seeking locally grown goodies flock to the Beans and Barley parking lot. Take in the Tomato Romp in mid-September when hundreds of pounds of rotten tomatoes are tossed. Registration fees go to community organizations alleviating hunger.

FOOD BLOGS

Eating Milwaukee, www.eatingmilwaukee.com. This blog hits the best of Milwaukee's restaurants and talks about off-the-beaten-path eateries and traditional ethnic foods.

Burp!, eatatburp.com. In-the-know bloggers Lori and Paul Fredrich have created a foodies' delight with scrumptious recipes, nearly all of which are originals. The couple hosts food events around the community, showcasing the area's top chefs and new restaurants.

Milwaukee Brunch Reviews, milwaukeebrunchreviews.com. This site is comprehensive in its tackling of fabled Milwaukee brunch locales. The stories make for a mouthwatering read. So grab your hat and what's your hurry? Let's munch.

East Town Market, Kilbourn Avenue and Jefferson Street in Cathedral Square, Milwaukee, WI 53202; (414) 271-1416; easttown .com/events/east-town-market. Sat from 9 a.m. to 1 p.m., June to Oct. This market, hosted by the East Town Association, draws apartment and condo dwellers from downtown to mingle with suburbanites. The market is closed in mid-July for the Bastille Days street festival. Great deals can be had on spuds, flowers, and greens from the 100-plus vendors. Don't forget the yoga, live music, and Danceworks' performances.

Fondy Farmers' Market, 2200 W. Fond du Lac Ave., Milwaukee, WI 53206; (414) 933-8121; fondymarket.org/market. Sun, Tues, and Thurs from 8 a.m. to 2 p.m., and Sat from 7 a.m. to 3 p.m., early May through mid-Nov. Rain or shine, it features kids' activities and special events, such as the Saturday Taste the Season booth with cooking demos, canning classes, and tastings.

FOOD STANDS MAKE A
DELICIOUSLY FINE STOP

Dave's Fruit Stand, 3812 S. 108th St., Greenfield, WI 53228; (414) 327-0280. All the fresh vegetables and fruits you need are here.

Layton Fruit Market, 1838 E. Layton Ave., Saint Francis, WI 53235; (414) 481-3008. This locale is perfect for hungry South Siders.

Growing Power, 5500 W. Silver Spring Dr., Milwaukee, WI 53218; (414) 527-1930; growingpower.org. You'll discover fresh, seasonal produce at this urban farm located within the Milwaukee city limits. See full description on p. 42.

Pete's Fruit Market, 1400 S. Union, Milwaukee, WI 53204; (414) 383-1300. You will always find great deals on fruit and veggies.

Schmit's Farm Produce, 8013 Freistadt Rd., Mequon, WI 53097; (262) 242-3330; schmitsfarmprod@aol.com. Other sites are at 76th and Dognes Bay Road, Mequon; 93rd Street and Good Hope Road, Milwaukee; 161st Street and Capital Drive, Brookfield; 6075 N. Green Bay Rd., Glendale; W18934 County Line Rd., Germantown; and 13530 Hampton Ave., Menomonee Falls. If you like sweet corn, Schmit's offers some of the best around, plus all sorts of other Wisconsin vegetables. Vincent (Bud) Schmit also offers firewood, and he'll even plow your driveway in the winter.

Will's Roadside Farm Market, 5500 W. Silver Spring Dr., Milwaukee, WI 53218; (414) 527-1930. Green and yellow beans, onions, spuds, and other products are displayed at this market located near McGovern Park.

Fox Point Farmers' Market, 7300 N. Lombardy Rd., Fox Point, WI 53217; (414) 352-0555; localharvest.org/fox-point-farmers-market-M8259. Sat from 8 a.m. to noon, mid-June to mid-Oct. Held in the west parking lot of Stormonth School, this market features music and free chef demonstrations, as well as Greek pastry, mushrooms, free-range eggs, grass-fed beef, honey, and enough tomatoes to satisfy any ketchup lover.

West Allis Farmers Market, 6501 W. National Ave., West Allis, WI 53214; (414) 302-8600; westalliswi.gov. Established in 1919, the market is open from 1 to 6 p.m. the first Sat in May through the Sat after Thanksgiving; it is also open from noon to 6 p.m. on Tues and Thurs. The early season brings bedding plants, radishes, asparagus, and rhubarb. By June, buyers can find strawberries and raspberries, plus zucchini, peas, and snap beans. Corn arrives in July, with apples and squash later in the season.

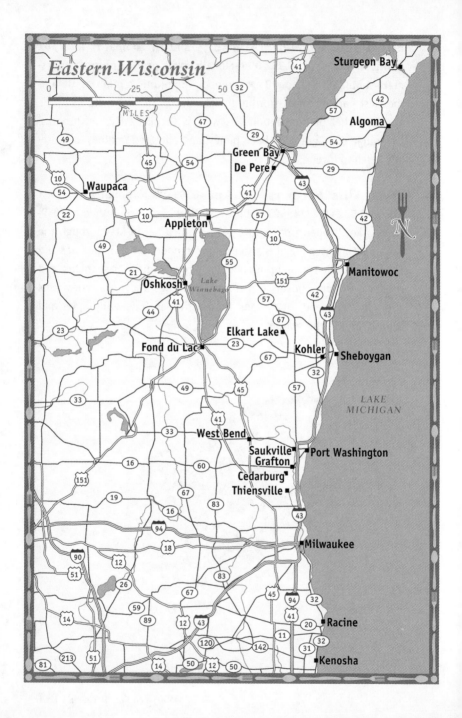

Eastern Wisconsin

Wisconsin has 1,100 miles of scenic coastline along Lake Michigan, with dozens of delightful harbor towns, bustling cities, woodsy state and county parks, and rural stretches of agricultural land. This scenic package has welcomed visitors for more than 150 years. Stretching north to south from Green Bay to the Illinois border, eastern Wisconsin is prime vacation and dining land. While eating one's way through this part of the state, visitors can also admire mammoth bones at the Kenosha Public Museum, crawl inside a World War II submarine at Manitowoc's Wisconsin Maritime Museum, and cheer competitors at the intricately winding track at Elkhart Lake's RoadAmerica. In between are breweries and wineries to salve the thirsty.

While I-94 is a quick way to roam, we often prefer the side roads, particularly State Highway 32, called the 32nd Division Memorial Highway. It honors the ferocious National Guard unit that fought its way through France in World War I. Look for the red arrows piercing a horizontal line, honoring American troops who smashed through the German divisions during that terrible conflict, helping to end the War to End All Wars. Much of Highway 32 is part of the Lake Michigan Circle Tour route marked by green signage.

The lake is the only one of the Great Lakes totally within the borders of the United States; the others are shared with Canada. Lake Michigan has a surface area of 22,400 square miles, making it the largest lake entirely within one country by surface area. Émigrés flocked here from the East Coast because of the relatively easily traversed waterway, before flooding into Wisconsin's heartland and beyond. They were drawn to the abundance of water and the fertile soil, factors still evident today with all the farms sprinkled across the landscape here. For an extensive list of farm markets and food stalls in the area, check out the website for Farm Fresh Atlas of Eastern Wisconsin (farmfresheastwi.org/about/index.htm).

Door County

Like a thumb on a mitten, Wisconsin's rocky Door County extends between Lake Michigan on the east and the choppy waters of Green Bay on the west. Several travel publications have said that "The Door" is one of the top 10 vacation destinations in North America. Others consider the 75-mile-long peninsula the "Cape Cod of the Midwest." Its 250 miles of in-and-out shoreline is a shore-hugging sailor's delight, allowing easy access to the peninsula's many eateries and specialty food shops. Think fudge, cherries, and wine.

There are five state parks and 10 lighthouses in the county, combining scenery with outdoor recreation opportunities that range from golf to skiing, plus there are community theaters and concerts for summer enjoyment, renowned art galleries, and craft shops. Lodgings range from simple to deluxe, and there's great camping for both RV and tent fans. Deer regularly wander through woods surrounding the campsites, to the awe of city kids on holiday. Exploring Potawatomi and Peninsula State Parks, hikers carry a backpack of fruit and energy bars for sustenance until reaching the next restaurant.

The waters off Door County offer trout and salmon fishing and kayaking opportunities, with numerous marina developments accommodating muscular motorboating "stinkpots" to sleek sailboats. The area also features an extensive system of biking and hiking trails. Seeking food for the mind, art lovers can meander through more than 80 galleries and museums.

Door County vacationers line up for the fish boil, which features a roaring fire under the giant iron cauldron holding fresh whitefish, oodles of onions, and bags of red skin potatoes. Kerosene is tossed on the fire at the appropriate moment, a timing that the master fish boiler has learned by experience. Cameras are at the ready to capture the dramatic explosion of boilover as it removes the oils and cooking residue. The fish is then most often served with corn on the cob lathered in melted butter. Sides include coleslaw and Bavarian dark rye bread. The dessert finale is most often fabulous Door County cherry pie à la mode, although the occasional apple pie sneaks in. Supposedly the boil was originally an inexpensive, easy way to feed large work gangs of ravenous lumbermen and fishermen.

Foodie Faves

Alexander's, 3667 State Hwy. 42, Fish Creek, WI 54234; (920) 868-3532; alexandersofdoorcounty.com; Traditional American; $$–$$$. The rule of thumb at Alexander's is casual fine dining, which means come as you are. This makes it perfect for vacationers. Specializing in seafoods and Black Angus beef, Alexander's also has top-notch soups. Every day an in-house pastry chef creates homemade pastries and desserts. As an aside, Alexander's is the longest-running, complete service caterer in Door County, catering weddings, birthdays, and reunions.

Bluefront Cafe, 86 W. Maple St., Sturgeon Bay, WI 54235; (920) 743-9218; thebluefrontcafe.com; Bistro; $–$$. Since opening in 2002, chefs Susan Guthrie and Patrick Barbercheck have provided a delightful dining experience in their cheerful, trendy cafe. A great mix of locals and tourists appreciates the fresh produce and quality of the entrees. The walleye sandwich, smoked turkey, and fish tacos are ace.

The organic coffee is smooth and hearty, while the microbrews and wine provide a bit more punch. Oh, that pot roast! Patrons can't get enough of the Angus beef braised in red wine. The dish comes with roasted root vegetables and garlic mashed potatoes. The folks here also offer an extensive kids' menu. Keeping it simple, any munchkin crowd on holiday appreciates the grilled cheese sandwiches and fries.

The Cookery, 4135 State Hwy. 42, Fish Creek, WI 54212; (920) 868-3634; cookeryfishcreek.com; New American; $–$$. The Cookery has been a family-run restaurant since 1977, serving "fresh food, expertly prepared," said one reviewer. We agree wholeheartedly. The menu is eclectic, with all items made on-site. Breakfast, lunch, and dinner are served in a building that looks like an old home, which it was. Patrons appreciate the small plates in the wine bar. There is a goodly selection of vegetarian entrees and gluten-free items. Among the favorite dishes is whole wheat linguine with wild shrimp. The caramel apple pie earns just as many raves. Jazzing up the walls are paintings by local Door County artists such as Liz Maltman.

The Danish Mill, 1934 Lobdell Point Rd., Washington Island, WI 54246; (920) 847-2632; danishmill.com; Casual American; $–$$. Established in 2010 on scenic Washington Island, the Mill features 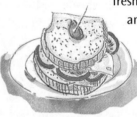 fresh-baked breads, kringle, pastries, pies, cookies, and yummy bars. Sandwiches made with Boar's Head brand deli products, homemade soups, interesting salads, and **Door County Coffee** (p. 150), tea, smoothies, and espresso drinks make a simple approach to good food. Look for the windmill.

Galileo's Italian Steakhouse & Bar, 7755 State Hwy. 42, Egg Harbor, WI 54209; (920) 868-4800; libertysquareshops.com; Italian; $$. Galileo's is located within the village's Liberty Square

Shops. Walls are colorfully adorned with panoramic murals of the Tuscan countryside. An antique mahogany bar is a featured draw for pre-meal cocktails or après-sailing. To satisfy a dinner craving after a day on the water, try the fettuccine Alfredo or the *basilico*, made with squash, mushrooms, and roasted red peppers in a basil cream sauce.

Grasse's Grill, 10663 N. Bay Shore Dr., Sister Bay, WI 54234; (920) 854-1125; grassesgrill.com; Casual American; $–$$. There are plenty of places in Door County for good music, beer, and wine. This is one of the best, especially since the folks here can provide box lunches for the beach, a concert, a boat ride, or back to work. Just call ahead to talk over options. Owners Jim and Jesse Grasse have extensive culinary experience, which is evidenced by their menu. The Beach Road brisket is slow roasted, perfect with mashed red spuds, seasonal veggies, and hearty beef gravy. For a twist on the ol' mac 'n' cheese routine, Chef Jimmy Grasse adds applewood bacon, tomatoes, and scallions.

Harbor Fish Market & Grille, 8080 State Hwy. 57, Baileys Harbor, WI 54202; (920) 839-9999; harborfishmarket-grille.com; Seafood; $$. Once you plunk down at your table draped with its crisp white tablecloth, gaze out the windows at the choppy waters of Lake Michigan. It makes for quite a view. The market is open for breakfast (try the homemade hash), lunch (ah, that lobster roll), and dinner (oysters on the half shell and snow crab). The panfried walleye, soy and honey poached salmon, and prawns always earn high marks from discerning eaters. Rib eye, prime rib, and surf and turf are faves of meat eaters, while vegetarian risotto is also available.

Joe Jo's Pizza & Gelato, 10420 State Hwy. 42, Ephraim, WI 54211; (920) 854-5455; doorcountypizza.com; Pizza; $–$$. Each thin-crusted pizza is made to order at Joe Jo's, with a dough made from scratch. Naturally, there is a seasoned sauce to go with sausage made from extra-lean ground pork. The gelato is a low-fat Italian ice cream with both fruit and cream flavors. For the diet conscious, each serving of Joe Jo's gelato has less than one gram of fat and only 120 to 160 calories. Not that we've ever counted.

KK Fiske & the Granary, 1177 Main Rd., Washington Island, WI 54246; (920) 847-2121; Seafood; $–$$. Home of the "Fish Mortician," whose daily catch includes whitefish and "lawyers," which are actually a codlike critter also called a burbot, eelpout, or mud shark. Pizzas are made to order. There are nightly specials, along with homemade bread, pies, and cookies baked fresh every day. Fish boils are held Wednesday, Friday, and Saturday. The attached Granary was once an actual grain storage facility built in the 1860s and rebuilt generations later as a pub.

Mission Grille, 10627 N. Bay Shore Dr., Sister Bay, WI 54234; (920) 854-9070; missiongrille.com; New American; $$–$$$. Many vacationers make it their mission to visit the Mission whenever passing through Sister Bay, tempted to peek at the extensive wine list, which includes interesting dessert wines. The Jackson-Triggs Vidal Icewine Proprietors' Reserve, Niagara 2004, and King Estate Vin Glacé Pinot Gris, Oregon 2006, have been hits. Try the Wisconsin artisan cheese flight, served with herb-roasted almonds, marinated olives, and a fruit compote for a starter. Tapas such as chipotle prawns or Maryland crab cakes can be found in the bar every evening. From 1911 to 1984, the Mission Grille was actually a church. St. Rosalia's was the first Catholic mission in Door County, hence the name. When a new church was built a mile south on State Highway 42, the place was transformed by Gary and Mary Ann Guterman into the restaurant. The former altar area was turned into a bar. Excuse the symbolism, but now that's the "spirits."

Mojo Rosa's Cantina and Pub, 7778 State Hwy. 42, Egg Harbor, WI 54209; (920) 868-3247; mojorosas-doorcounty.com; **Mexican; $–$$.** For casual dining fun with a sports bar atmosphere, try Mojo Rosa's. There is the standard Mexican refried beans and taco fare, but hungry vacationers can also get broasted chicken, pizza, burgers, and more! Many of the foods are based on Oaxacan recipes and are fresh daily. The bar regularly features live bands. Fund-raising parties held here have aided the Door County Humane Society, Birch Creek Music Performance Center, and other local organizations. These are usually co-hosted by such breweries as **New Glarus** (p. 243) and Tallgrass, so there's plenty o' beer. Margaritas are great here, too.

Mr. G's Logan Creek Grille, 5890 State Hwy. 57, Jacksonport, WI 54235; (920) 823-2112; mrgslogancreekgrille.com; **Supper Club; $$–$$$.** Located 2 miles south of Jacksonport, this is the quintessential Wisconsin supper club. The nightly specials run the traditional range of chicken, ribs, perch, and other supper club fare. For something new, try a tenderloin pepper steak dished out in its own brown sauce with onions and green and red peppers, all atop wild rice. For a different taste treat, try Mr. G's honey garlic pork chops. It's another great reason for staying longer on a Door vacation.

Parador, 7829 State Hwy. 42, Egg Harbor, WI 54209; (920) 868-2255; paradorwisconsin.com; **Spanish; $$.** Order one, two, or three of the small plates on Larry and Rebecca Majewski's menu. A *bomba,* a house-made pork meatball wrapped in a Yukon Gold potato puree, makes everyone dining here stand up and take notice. The pork comes from Waseda Farms in nearby Baileys Harbor. The bacon-wrapped dates are also a taste treat, but beware of the *patatas bravas,* herbed fingerling potatoes with a fiery, dynamite-good sauce. However, falling into sin here is fun with the Parador's sangria. And the Iberian touch? Larry started out as a server at the historic Hacienda del Sol in Tucson, Arizona, then worked for the Bartolotta Restaurant Group in Milwaukee and at Valentino in Las Vegas. Rebecca was born in Portugal, moving stateside as a youngster. She enjoyed a semester in Toledo, Spain, during a study-abroad program while at the University of Notre Dame. A trip back to Spain in 2010 was the primary inspiration for starting their own place.

Scaturo's Baking Company & Cafe, 19 Green Bay Rd., Sturgeon Bay, WI 54235; (920) 746-8727; scaturos.com; Casual American; $–$$. This is another Door County casual restaurant that has made its mark with fresh-from-the-oven pastries and breads. Breakfasts here could satisfy a ravenous lumberjack, with a three-egg omelet one of many early morning specials. All the soups and chilis are also made from scratch. The cafe hosts a traditional Door County fish boil, with whitefish accompanied by coleslaw, carrots, onions, potatoes, and cherry pie. The boilovers are held from mid-May through June on Friday and Saturday nights and July through mid-October on Friday, Saturday, Sunday, and Monday. The main bakery whips up loads of muffins daily, with varieties including cherry walnut, apple cinnamon pecan, blueberry, double chocolate chocolate chip, and strawberry cream cheese. The elephant ears made on-site are Dumbo size.

Shoreline Restaurant, 12747 State Hwy. 42, Gills Rock, Ellison Bay, WI 54210; (920) 854-2950; theshorelinerestaurant.com; Traditional American; $$–$$$. The Shoreline Restaurant is noted for its home-style cooking, with whitefish pesto and lightly floured, panfried perch among the most popular items. A lot of visitors also vote for the crabmeat pasta, Thai curry veggie stir-fry, or coconut shrimp tempura. Each table presents a relaxing water view for another positive touch. After getting comfortably seated, guests can watch the charter fishing boats and pleasure craft bobbing in the adjacent marina. For a twist, the restaurant offers its lighter lunch menu throughout the dinner hours. What's great are the fresh ingredients used in season. It's also worth walking on water to get to the homemade desserts, especially the Key lime pie. The Shoreline is open daily May through Oct and Fri, Sat, and Sun evenings the first 2 weeks of Nov. No reservations are taken.

White Gull Inn, 4225 Main St., Fish Creek, WI 54212; (920) 868-2018; whitegullinn.com; Traditional American; $$. For almost 50 years, the White Gull Inn has continued to earn its well-deserved reputation for being warm, friendly, and hospitable. Under their watch, innkeepers Jan and Andy Coulson have ensured that their guests would be caringly accommodated. Eggs Benedict, granola, hash browns, and stacks of pancakes are among their specialties. Traditional Door County fish boils are served Wed, Fri, and Sat evenings, a great way to wind down after a day of hiking, sailing, fishing, exploring, or loafing.

Wild Tomato Wood-Fired Pizza and Grille, 4023 State Hwy. 42, Fish Creek, WI 54212; (920) 868-3095; wildtomatopizza .com; Pizza; $–$$. This family-owned restaurant has tummy-filling wood-fired pizzas, salads, sandwiches, and burgers, all using local products. The veggie pizza scores high points with its red and green peppers, onions, mushrooms, artichoke hearts, sun-dried tomatoes, pesto, and Wisconsin goat cheese and mozzarella. For a nod to the Green Bay Packers colors, the restaurant has a Green and Gold pie, with roasted chicken, bacon, grilled broccoli, and spinach. This beauty is topped with fresh, squeaky Wisconsin cheese curds.

Al Johnson's Swedish Restaurant & Butik, 10698 N. Bay Shore Dr., Sister Bay, WI 54234; (920) 854-2626; aljohnsons.com; Swedish; $$–$$$. Goats on the roof, no kidding! It's not a baaaaad idea for an attraction. For several generations, Al Johnson's has been the premier Swedish restaurant this side of, well, Stockholm. The goats make it instantly recognizable to passing motorists, who then usually pull into the parking lot for a better look-see, followed by an appetizer of pickled herring or a platter of *pytt panna,* a dynamite roast beef hash hearty enough for any hungry Viking. Inside the carpeted dining room, servers in Scandinavian garb tempt diners with limpa bread, a rye flavored with anise seed, molasses, and a dash of orange. The menu consists of a variety of northern European fare. For breakfast, we always go for the thick pancakes slathered with lingonberries. The whitefish or meatballs, plus an extensive array of sandwiches and salads, make for memorable dining experiences. Be aware, however, of weekend crowds that flock to this popular place in the summer. The goats, which generally ignore all the photo snappers, go onto the roof at the start of each tourism season, usually in late May. They spend the winter in a barn and pasture from mid-October to the start of the next season. A "goat cam" on the roof keeps guests updated on the animals' antics. As for the menu, no, there won't be goat.

Fred & Fuzzy's Waterfront Bar and Grill, 10620 Little Sister Rd., Sister Bay, WI 54234; (920) 854-6699; fredandfuzzys.com; Casual American; $$. Fred & Fuzzy's has one of the best front-row seats in the Door for viewing the sunset. Some visitors call the place "a slice of paradise." The grill is located on the shore of Little Sister

Bay, for casual indoor or outdoor on-the-water dining. There's really nothing that can beat watching a summer storm roll up on the horizon, while snug inside sipping a Door County cherry juice margarita. *Frontier Airlines* magazine called F&F one of the best beachfront bars in the world, and we won't argue with that. F&F features quick turnarounds for food, perfect if we are heading out to see a show at the Skyway Drive-In in nearby Fish Creek or the American Folklore Theater in Ephraim. And we agree that the grilled teriyaki mahimahi and the barbecue pork sandwiches are heavenly. There's live music Tuesday nights from late June through mid-September. F&F isn't hard to find; the GPS coordinates are N 45°11.162" W 087°08.943".

Grant's Olde Stage Station Restaurant, 7778 Egg Harbor Rd. (State Highway 42), Egg Harbor, WI 54209; (920) 868-3247; Pizza; $–$$. Legend says that this was an old-time freight haulers' stop. Now, the Olde Stage is noted for its pizzas. Those long-ago teamsters probably would have loved the special blend of seven Wisconsin cheeses, baked in stone hearth ovens, that provides a base for a plethora of toppings. The restaurant also boasts having the largest selection of tap and bottled beers in Door County. Who's to argue? While we've tried more than a few, there are still dozens of labels remaining to sample. A late-night menu is offered from 10 p.m. to midnight daily. Be aware that the Olde Stage is closed Tues and Wed during the winter months.

The Hof Restaurant, 7715 Alpine Rd., Egg Harbor, WI 54209; (920) 868-3000; alpineresort.com; German; $$. *Hof* means "courtyard" or "gathering place" in German. This is a centrally located restaurant where friends can meet, even while vacationing in other nearby Door communities. There is a spectacular shoreline setting, providing a grand backdrop for dining on whitefish, prime rib and steaks, and German specialties. Breakfast is served daily, and a burger-oriented lunch on the deck is an excellent choice on a warm July noon. For dinner, do up a bratwurst, augmented with an ample addition of sauerkraut. A complement of fries rounds out a husky Teutonic lunch. An out-of-this-world schnitzel is just as good. The Hof is part of the Alpine Resort complex with its 36-hole golf course, open from late May through Oct.

Inn at Cedar Crossing, 336 Louisiana St., Sturgeon Bay, WI 54235; (920) 743-4200; innatcedarcrossing.com; Traditional American; $–$$. The Inn serves the widest variety of tastes in the area, including traditional Italian, along with American menu offerings. It's open for breakfast, Sunday brunch, lunch, and dinner. Be sure not to miss any of the scratch-made breads, pastries, and desserts. Breakfast is a treat when the homemade muffins and scones show up at the table. For dinner, the kitchen serves up scrumptious offerings of stuffed portobello mushroom caps filled with a sauté of brunoise vegetables and marinated artichoke hearts and topped with fontina cheese. Another favorite dish has been the sauteed shrimp and sea scallops over fettuccine, with sweet peas, wild mushrooms, and a smooth caper butter sauce. The guesthouse has 9 rooms, each with antiques and a different theme.

Inn at Kristofer's, 10716 N. Bay Shore Dr., Sister Bay, WI 54234; (920) 854-9419; innatkristofers.com; French; $$$. We've found the Inn at Kristofer's to be a classic waterfront restaurant at its finest, with an emphasis on French culinary experiences. On the northern outskirts of Sister Bay adjacent to the marina, the floor-to-ceiling windows allow great gazing. You can't beat a view of the sunset over the rolling waters of Green Bay and the bluffs of Sister Bay. Established in 1993, Kristofer's is known around the country, and it's has been highlighted in *Good Housekeeping, Bon Appétit, Midwest Living,* and the *Chicago Tribune.* Television's Food Network has also featured founder/owner Chef Terri Milligan, who sold her place to Mark and Catherine Antczak in late 2012. Items vary daily, depending on what's fresh and available, but you can generally find local whitefish, Alaskan halibut, and Columbia

River salmon. For meat lovers, the Wagyu flat iron steaks are melt-in-your-mouth good. The crab cakes and rack of pork are just as good. The restaurant also has an e-recipe club. Check out its website for details. Call Kristofer's for a list of its cooking classes.

The Log Den, 6626 State Hwy. 42, Egg Harbor, WI 54209; (920) 868-3888; thelogden.com; Casual American; $–$$. Just south of Egg Harbor, a rustic wooded drive leads to the The Log Den, a 10,000-square-foot restaurant and lounge designed and built by the Wayne Lautenbach family, who farmed and logged in the area for more than a century. Seventy-foot-long logs were cut on Garrett Bay Road in Ellison Bay and used in constructing the Den. The restaurant has an Abe Lincoln look about it and offers an extensive array of home-cooked goodies, ranging from patty melts to BLTs. Panfried Canadian walleye and baked Chilean sea bass lend an international feel to the menu. A traditional Wisconsin fish boil is held Wednesday nights during the summer. Be sure to get reservations.

Old Post Office Restaurant, 10040 Water St. (State Highway 42), Ephraim, WI, 54211; (920) 854-4034; oldpostoffice-doorcounty .com; Breakfast; $$. This restored building, dating from the early 1900s, once housed Ephraim's post office and a general store in an era when locals could access Ephraim only by boat. Capitalizing on its history, the Old Post Office menu offers clever titles: Letter Opener Juices, Priority Fruits, Express Mail Eggs, and Mailman Muffins. Traditional fish boils are held Monday through Saturday, as well as on holiday weekends. A cupboard in the main room is stocked with homemade  jellies, souvenir dish towels, and related gift items for sale. Be aware that the village of Ephraim is a dry community, so no alcohol is served at any restaurant here. The restaurant closes in late Oct and reopens around Mother's Day.

Pelletier's Restaurant & Fish Boil, 4199 Main St., Fish Creek, WI 54212; (920) 868-3313; doorcountyfishboil.com; Casual American; $$. This is one of our favorite fish boils, held nightly, rain or shine, starting at 4:30 p.m.; the cooking process continues every half hour until 6:30 p.m. Reservations are recommended, especially on holiday weekends. This is one of the county's longest-running fish boils, visited by generations of visitors who return year after year.

Rowleys Bay Resort, 1041 County Rd. ZZ, Ellison Bay, WI 54210; (920) 854-2385; rowleysbayresort.com; Casual American; $$–$$$. Rowleys features a traditional fish boil that also includes a buffet, as well as a full menu and bar. Breakfast, lunch, and dinner are served daily, and the restaurant's Sunday brunch includes scrumptious goodies such as pecan rolls, direct from Grandma's Swedish Bakery in Ellison Bay. There's no extra charge for the view. Rowleys says it has the only all-you-can-eat fish boil in Door County, held every Monday, Wednesday, and Saturday night. A master storyteller is usually on hand those evenings to tell of life at Rowleys Bay.

Shipwrecked Brew Pub, 7791 State Hwy. 42, Egg Harbor, WI 54209; (920) 868-2767; shipwreckedmicrobrew.com; Casual American; $–$$. Vacationers love dropping in here for casual dining in downtown Egg Harbor. Hey, this is Wisconsin, so ya gotta try the fried cheese curds. They go well with a round of the microbrewery's smooth, hearty ales. The Peninsula Porter is a special favorite, but the Bayside Blonde crisp ale also makes for a great pour. If you don't want to drive

home afterward, the Upper Deck Inn has 8 guest rooms upstairs, each with its own bathroom. Yachting fans like stopping in here because the restaurant is a short stroll to the harbor, galleries, and town shops. The original building opened in the late 1800s as a stopover for stagecoaches, and the current facility was launched in 1997. Shipwrecked brews are available in retail outlets throughout eastern Wisconsin.

Whistling Swan Inn & Restaurant, 4192 Main St., Fish Creek, WI 54212; (920) 868-3442; whistlingswan.com; New American; $$–$$$. The menu was assembled by Executive Chef Adam Schierl, who explored a wide range of contemporary American cuisine. He loves locally foraged produce, wild game, and local freshwater fish. Indulge yourself with Schierl's grilled king trumpet mushroom with beluga lentils, carrots, peas, roasted peppers, and cauliflower puree, or the seared duck breast. There is also an extensive international wine list, varieties chosen for their compatibility with menu items. Don't pass up any of the prize-winning Wisconsin cheeses such as Hook's 4-year-old cheddar, **Roth Käse** (p. 246) Buttermilk Blue, and **Carr Valley** (p. 241) Cave-Aged Marisa; the latter is served with a delicious fig preserve. A wood-burning fireplace, soft candlelight, and white linen tablecloths add to the charm.

Wilson's Restaurant and Ice Cream Parlor, 9990 Water St., Ephraim, WI 54211; (920) 854-2041; wilsonsicecream.com; Casual American; $. Wilson's Restaurant and Ice Cream Parlor has been located in the heart of Ephraim since 1906. Look for the white frame building and red-and-white-striped awnings. This Door County landmark has an old-fashioned soda fountain and numerous ice cream specialties, plus its own draft root beer to accompany broiled burgers. The juke boxes play rock 'n' roll classics. Take in the Annual Fyr Bal Firecracker Frenzy Ice Cream Eating Competition each June. There are three age groups: 10 years and younger, 11 to 17 years, and 18 years and older. Older competitors need to down a pint of firecracker ice cream, with smaller portions for the littler kids. This has long been a fun, and filling, stop on many Door County eating rounds.

Charlie's Smokehouse, 12731 State Hwy. 42, Gills Rock, WI 54210; (920) 854-2972; charliessmokehouse.com. Charlie's Smokehouse has long been known for freshly smoked fish, including delicately textured whitefish and smoked imported specialties such as Canadian lake trout, Pacific salmon, and Atlantic salmon. Charlie's overlooks Hedgehog Harbor and Garret Bay, between the rustic Door Bluff County Park and Kenosha Park on State Highway 42.

Door County Candy, 12 N. 3rd Ave., Sturgeon Bay, WI 54235; (920) 746-0924; doorcountycandy.com. This is a small shop, but the interior bursts with bags of awesome caramel corn, plus cheddar cheese corn and nutty and kettle corns. Gourmet chocolates, fresh fudge, and chocolate cherry clusters add to the calorie count. It is a challenge to pass up the Cedarcrest ice cream or roasted nuts.

Door County Coffee & Tea Company, 5773 State Hwy. 42, Carlsville, WI 54235; (920) 743-8930; doorcountycoffee.com; $–$$. Door County Coffee is a top hideaway on a warm summer morning. So indulge yourself. This is a perfectly marvelous place to grab a latte or a cup of muscular java at the espresso bar. There are dozens of available coffees, offering the chance to try a new brew every visit. A breakfast that includes a hash brown bake is on our early-morning hit list. For lunch, it's tone-down time with chicken salad or a Door County cherry salad. There is a great gift shop here as well, and guests can watch the roasting process through a window in the cafe. Orders shipped home include a complimentary package of the roastmaster's choice.

Farm Markets & Farm Stands

Baileys Harbor: Every Sun 9 a.m to noon during growing/harvest season, next to the Baileys Harbor Cornerstone Pub in the parking lot of the old Associated Bank's green space; designdoorcounty.com/baileysharbor.html.

Fish Creek: Every Wed 9:30 a.m. to 1:30 p.m. or sellout at the Settlement Shops., State Highway 42, 0.5 mile south of downtown Fish Creek. June 12 through October 16; (920) 868-3788.

Jacksonport: Every Tues morning from 9 a.m to 1 p.m., State Highway 57, Lakeside Park downtown Jacksonport. June 11 to Oct (weather dependent); (920) 823-2288; jacksonport.net.

Koepsel's Farm Market, 9669 State Hwy. 57, Baileys Harbor, WI 54202; (920) 854-2433; koepsels.com.

The Cherry Hut, 8813 State Hwy. 42, Fish Creek ,WI 54212; (920) 868-3406; doorcountycherryhut.com.

Seaquist Orchards Farm Market, 11482 State Hwy. 42, Sister Bay, WI 54234; (920) 854-4199; seaquistorchards.com.

Sister Bay: Sat, 8 a.m to noon, June 22 through Oct 12, at Corner of the Past, State Highway 57 and Fieldcrest Road. (920) 854-9242; Wed at 3:30 p.m., until produce runs out, mid-June through mid-Oct, at the Country Walk Shops, 10568 Country Walk, Sister Bay, WI 54234; (920) 358-6184.

Sturgeon Bay: Sat, 8:30 a.m to noon, June 2 through Oct 27, Market Square, corner of Michigan and 4th Avenue, (920) 746-2914; Tues, 3 to 7p.m., June 25 through Sept 24, Martin Park, 207 3rd Ave., (920) 746-2914.

Wood Orchard Market, 8112 State Hwy. 42, Egg Harbor, WI 54209; (920) 868-2334; woodorchard.com.

Open the Door to a Farm Fresh World

According to its visitor's bureau, Door County is the fourth-largest cherry producer in the United States. Depending on the weather, fragrant blossoms appear from the middle to the end of May, and the crop usually ripens in July. You can see apple blossoms soon after the cherry blossoms, with the apple crop typically ripening from mid-September to mid-October  beginning in the southern part of the county. The **Door County Visitor Bureau** can be reached at 1015 Green Bay Rd., Sturgeon Bay, WI 54235; (920) 743-4456; doorcounty.com.

Grandma Tommy's Country Store, 4020 State Hwy. 42/57, Sturgeon Bay, Wi 54235; (920) 743-2800; grandmatommys.com. Grandma Tommy's has oodles of locally made specialty foods, wines, and microbrews. Guests load up on homemade fudge, pies, cookies, hand-dipped ice cream, and cherry or root beer floats. When in season, this is a great place to get bags and boxes of Door County apples, cherries, and berries. If that's not enough, the shop also has a variety of Wisconsin cheese, along with sausage and an olive oil sampling bar. There are plenty of homemade jams, jellies, and fruit butters to choose from, some with no sugar added. Take home a jug of cherry or apple cider, bottles of maple syrup, jars of salsas, and a selection of mustards. It's all here.

Savory Spoon Cooking School, 12042 State Hwy. 42, Ellison Bay, WI 54210; (920) 854-6600; savoryspoon.com. The Savory Spoon Cooking School is a member of the International Association of Culinary Professionals. Classes are seasonal; the school is open from June through Oct each year. The hands-on sessions are led by owner Janice Thomas. The Savory Spoon was once the village schoolhouse, built in 1879 and restored in 2005 with up-to-date cooking equipment and appliances. A small store with culinary items is off the main classroom. The school also leads tours to Sicily, France, China, Mexico, and other foodie faves.

Sweetie Pies, 9106 State Hwy. 42, Fish Creek, WI 54212; (920) 868-2743; sweetiepies.us; $–$$. Sweetie Pies is among the most dangerous places we regularly visit in the Door. Oh, those handmade, old-fashioned pies. This little bakery is included in the Settlement Shops, adjacent to Settlement Courtyard Inn. Sweetie Pies started as a family business in 1995. The store features patio and indoor indulging, depending on the season. In addition to 30 flavors of pies in two sizes, there is a wide selection of cookies and handmade chocolates. Now, what did we say about danger?

Eastern Wisconsin— North of Milwaukee

How many ways can a Wisconsin visitor dine on a bratwurst, indulge in a Friday perch fry, revel in a hearty bowl of spring's nettle soup, sample an apple pie, or enjoy a connoisseur meal with vintage wine. The answer is mind-boggling, considering the vast array of food establishments up and down the Lake Michigan coastline and inland a few hops and skips. The abundance of fresh produce, well-marbled grass-fed meats, and out-of-this-world dairy products (say "champion cheese, please!") puts Wisconsin on any gourmet's culinary map. Chefs in the hinterland are known for their kitchen skills and exciting creativity, whether found in a city, town, village, or rural crossroads. There aren't any secrets to finding these places; they are everywhere. Open just about any restaurant door and step across the threshold to another culinary discovery.

A's Restaurant & Music Cafe, 112 N. Broadway, De Pere, WI 54115; (920) 336-2277; asmusiccafe.net; Traditional American; $$–$$$. A's lives up to its name, with jazz and blues to cabaret and rock on most Fridays and Saturdays. Wednesday also usually features a band or performer. The food is eclectic, with Executive Chef L. J. Weber and his team serving up hearty portions of seafood and steak. The crab and roasted red-pepper bisque has earned rave reviews from delighted patrons. The lobster ravioli is also top-notch, with a starter option of a pound of steamed blue mussels in a saffron cream sauce.

Ang and Eddie's, 7 14th St., Fond du Lac, WI 54935; (920) 933-1109; angandeddies.com; Pizza; $. Even Chicagoans on holiday stop in at Ang's for the pizza, a deep-dish, flaky-crust, Windy City–style pie slathered with tomato sauce and lots of cheese. The heartier eater can add spinach, mushrooms, and large slices of wood-fired tomatoes. You can get thin-crust pizzas, as well. The flatlanders from Illinois can also get their home-comfort-food fix with the Chicago hot dogs and Italian beef.

Anvil Pub & Grille, N70 W6340 Bridge Rd., Cedarburg, WI 53092; (262) 376-2163; anvilpubandgrille.com; Casual American; $–$$. Nestled in the Cedar Creek Settlement's restored 19th-century blacksmith's shop, the Anvil Pub & Grille is great for casual dining in a rustic atmosphere. The Anvil serves lunch and dinner daily. It specializes in what they call their own carefully baked Forge sandwiches, steak, burgers, salads, chicken, and seafood. A bar features specialty beers, wines, and mixed drinks. A dynamite Bloody Mary bar is a plus during Sunday brunch. The patio is a comfy locale for seasonal dining, with the rushing waters of Cedar Creek nearby.

GREAT FOODS AT WISCONSIN'S
TOP-RANKED RESORT

The American Club, 419 Highland Dr., Kohler, WI 53044; (800) 344-2838 or (920) 457-8000; americanclubresort.com. The American Club, a AAA Five Diamond resort, boasts several award-winning restaurants on-site or at its nearby golf courses. Each offers a different atmosphere and menu. We regularly make a run up to Kohler for a day getaway, whether for a beer or chocolate festival, a massage at the spa and an overnight, or merely a dinner. Each of the complex's restaurants is open daily, with prices ranging from moderate to expensive. The American's main building once housed Kohler Company workers laboring in its vast plumbing fixtures plant across the street.

The **Horse & Plow** restaurant and pub at the American Club was refurbished and refreshed in 2013 with a new layout, bigger bar, and a pub-fare menu created with real flair. To complement the wide range of beers, go for the tempura-fried Great Lakes smelt or pork belly wings.

Chef Anette Rose Righi has made the resort's **Craverie Chocolatier Cafe** a winner with its handmade chocolates, including seasonal chocolate Easter eggs and signature terrapins, Kohler's version of the trademarked Turtle. You can occasionally participate in beer, wine, and spirits

Black & Tan Grille, 130 E. Walnut St., Green Bay, WI 54301; (920) 430-7700; blackandtangrille.com; Irish; $$. The black and tan, a volatile mix of Guinness stout and beer, inspired the restaurant's name. Located in a renovated, tan-colored Victorian home, the Grille promotes a homey, relaxing atmosphere. Entrees include king salmon, yellowfin tuna, steak, game, and seafood dishes, plus fresh seasonal

pairings with the chocolates in tastings often hosted by the American Club's sommelier.

The Wisconsin Room at the main American Club building holds true to its heritage, located in the hotel's historic cafeteria. The kitchen incorporates locally sourced produce, meats, and cheeses into its seasonal menu. The restaurant supports small family farms with a weekly three-course farmer's tasting menu. For another taste treat, The Immigrant Restaurant is for fine-dining aficionados, with its 6 rooms tied to the region's ethnic heritages: French, Dutch, German, Norman, Danish, and English.

Other eating options at the club include The Winery Bar, an upscale, comfortable lounge adjacent to The Immigrant Restaurant. Any wine connoisseur will delight in the 500 or so label selections, along with flights of award-winning Wisconsin cheeses. For a more casual scene, zip into The Greenhouse, which was originally a solarium from Chorley, Lancashire, in England. The antique structure was dismantled and brought to Kohler, where it is now a garden cafe presenting homemade ice cream, pastries, and coffees.

Other American Club restaurants include the Italian-themed Cucina, located in the Shops of Woodlake, part of the resort complex; The Whistling Straits Restaurant, overlooking Lake Michigan at the nearby Whistling Straits golf course; and the Blackwolf Run Restaurant, with views of the Sheboygan River, located at the nationally ranked Blackwolf Run golf course.

vegetables and the always-popular Black Angus steak. Hang on to your hats here on St. Patrick's Day.

The Blind Horse Restaurant and Winery, 6018 Superior Ave., Kohler, WI 53044; (920) 467-8599; theblindhorse.com; Traditional American, $$$. The Blind Horse has merged Mediterranean cuisine into the charm of a 130-year-old brick farmhouse to create a "rustic elegance." Hidden away on 7 landscaped acres near the village of Kohler, food and wine here are eye-catching and satisfying. When in season, fresh herbs, fruits, and vegetables are from the restaurant's gardens. For appetizers, start with squash soup or seared duck breast. Then move on to spinach tagliatelle, made with seared scallops, Roma tomatoes, and roasted garlic. The walleye, chicken, and veal are exceptionally prepared.

Carmella's Italian Bistro, 716 N. Casaloma Dr., Appleton, WI 54913; (920) 882-4044; carmellasbistro.com; Italian; $$–$$$. A great first course here is the arugula salad with roasted figs, Gorgonzola, and candied walnuts with a touch of sherry vinaigrette. For the entree, you'll have a hard time deciding between the shrimp scampi and the 8-ounce filet mignon, with either the Marsala peppercorn sauce or house bacon jam and melted Gorgonzola. For a cheese round, experiment with Saxon Creamery's Evalon, Uplands' award-winning Pleasant Ridge, or **Carr Valley**'s (p. 241) Black Truffle Goat. Carmella's sells jars of its Bolognese, house marinara, and arrabbiata sauces, which can also be purchased in grocery and health food stores throughout the region.

The Cork Restaurant & Pub, 306 Ellis St., Kewaunee, WI 54216; (920) 388-2525; welcometothecork.com; Casual American; $–$$. The Cork always seems to a hopping place, with occasional live music and nightly specials, including Wednesday's 16-ounce lobster tail special. Throughout summer and early fall, the Cork is open seven nights a week. It's closed Mon from early November through mid-June. Locals flock here for the Cork's hearty portions of chicken, steak, and other seafoods. Good chef salads are also a popular item.

Where to Go for a Cuppa' Joe

Fiddleheads Espresso Bar & Cafe, W62 N605 Washington Ave., Cedarburg, WI 53012, (262) 376-1366; **Fiddleheads Coffee Roasters,** 120 N. Main St., Thiensville, WI 53092, (262) 242-1137; **Fiddlehead Espresso Bar,** 192 S. Main St., Thiensville, WI 53092, (414) 238-8737; and **Fiddlehead's Coffee Bar,** 10530 N. Port Washington Rd., Mequon, WI 53092, (262) 241-8819; fiddleheadscoffee.com. The folks at all the Fiddleheads outlets have a passion: producing great coffee from premium beans "as fresh as the day's first smile."

Java House Cafe & Micro-Roaster, W63 N653 Washington Ave., Cedarburg, WI 53012; (262) 375-8999; javahousewi.com. In the heart of historic downtown Cedarburg, the Java House has been serving java since 1992. All the beans are roasted on-site, with varieties such as Brazil yellow bourbon, espresso nuevo, Ethiopian natural sidamo, and Sumatran and Italian roast, among many others. The coffee bar boils up specialty espresso drinks and iced coffees in a number of styles.

Courthouse Pub, 1001 S. 8th St., Manitowoc, WI 54220; (920) 686-1166; courthousepub.com; Casual American; $–$$. Hear ye, hear ye! The Courthouse has captured *Wine Spectator* awards of excellence and numerous other kudos from reviewers. Capitalizing on the judicial theme, lunch entrees such as the beef tenderloin sandwiches are labeled "Burden of Proof," with "The Evidence" being the dinner selections. Our jury goes for the chicken Marsala and the cinnamon-encrusted pork. For the 12-and-under set, entrees are tagged "Juvenile Justice." It's a given that the "Closing Arguments" are desserts. The pub is close to the SS *Badger* car ferry dock and a convenient place to stop prior to boarding for a lake crossing to Michigan.

Curly's Pub, Lambeau Field, 1265 Lombardi Ave., Green Bay, WI 54304; (920) 965-6970; packers.com/lambeau-field/curlys-pub .html; Casual American; $$. This legendary eatery is infused with the spirits of several generations of Green Bay Packers. The Championship Rings, sweet colossal onions, and hand-breaded Wisconsin cheese curds are must-orders. A Door County Turkey Burger, with its layers of swiss cheese, caramelized onions, and tomatoes, is another winner. The bar and restaurant is named for the Packers' first head coach, Curly Lambeau. It's huge—nearly the length of a football field—with a sit-down dining room and fireplace as well as a sports pub.

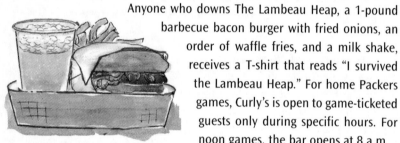

Anyone who downs The Lambeau Heap, a 1-pound barbecue bacon burger with fried onions, an order of waffle fries, and a milk shake, receives a T-shirt that reads "I survived the Lambeau Heap." For home Packers games, Curly's is open to game-ticketed guests only during specific hours. For noon games, the bar opens at 8 a.m.

Dockside Deli, 218 E. Main St., Port Washington, WI 53074; (262) 284-9440; docksidedeli.com; Sandwich Shop; $. This restaurant is mariner casual. Situated directly on the marina, you can use the free Wi-Fi, but relax; keep the computer at home and watch the comings and goings of the charter fishing boats. The menu presents vegetarian selections, sandwiches, wraps, soups, salads, smoothies, and lots of black, black coffee. Almost everything is house-made, and there are plenty of dangerous desserts, such as their cookiewich, two homemade cookies with any flavor of ice cream between them. You can also order box lunches for your day of boating.

The Firehouse Restaurant, 100 S. Main St., Saukville, WI 53080; (262) 284-8886; firehouserestaurant.webs.com; Casual American; $–$$. This comfortable eatery is located in Saukville's

FRESHNESS FIRST IN GREEN BAY

Green Bay East Side Festival Foods Farmers' Market, 3534 Steffen Ct.; (920) 434-0730. 7 a.m. to noon, Wed, mid-July through mid-Oct.

Green Bay Farmers' Market, Monroe Avenue parking lot between Cherry and Pine Streets; (920) 448-3210. 7 a.m. to noon, Sat, mid-June through end of Oct. The city has operated this farmers' market since 1917.

An extensive list of other farm market and food stands in Brown County can be found at browncountyextension.org.

former firehouse, with firefighter paraphernalia filling display cases, and art and photos adorning the walls. Some of the proceeds benefit the volunteer firefighters and other uniformed first responders in the area. The restaurant is convenient, only a few blocks from the Saukville Mill. Swing through for an early morning breakfast.

Fratellos Waterfront Restaurant, 501 W. Water St., Appleton, WI 54911; (920) 993-9087; fratelloswaterfront.com; Bistro; $$. As the Fratello's gang says, "Uncork the fun." The spacious dining room has expansive views of the Fox River to enjoy while dining on house specialties and familiar favorites. Fresh seafood, along with steaks, pastas, pizzas, and sandwiches, are simple fare and simply delicious. Handcrafted Fox River–area beers are on tap, enjoyed especially on the seasonal outdoor patio. The restaurant is part of the Supple Group, based in Oshkosh.

The Granary Supper Club, N586 Military Rd., Sherwood, WI 54169; (920) 989-1233; granarysupperclub.com; Supper Club; $$. There aren't many places to get frogs' legs, so when they show up on a menu, you know this is a special place. Also, if a kid cleans his or her

More Than Just a Touch of Italy

Stefano Viglietti and his wife, Whitney, regularly travel back to his ancestral homeland of Italy to pick up additional culinary tricks. Always returning bursting with new ideas, he creates hearty, inventive dishes. The couple has put Sheboygan on the food map with their four eateries, all of which have won rave reviews and write-ups in major food magazines.

Field to Fork, 511 S. 8th St., Sheboygan, WI 53081; (920) 694-0322; fieldtoforkcafe.com; $–$$. Field to Fork cafe and grocery serves breakfast and lunch made with wholesome ingredients provided by local farmers. Three house-made soups and chili are served daily. On the first Friday of every month, Field to Fork hosts a Latin night with such exotic items as *boquerones en vinagre,* which are marinated white anchovies on crostini with salsa verde and slices of hard-boiled egg. This is where we go for our hearty-healthy, support-the-family-farm fix.

Il Ritrovo, 515 S. 8th St., Sheboygan, WI 53081; (920) 803-7516; ilritrovopizza.com; $$. The wood-fired Neapolitan-style pizzeria, with its wine bar, is a full Italian deli and a retail shop. We favor this place because the pizza here is unlike any other place we've discovered. It's not easy to find boscaiola, constructed with mixed mushrooms,

plate, The Granary gives 'em a free sundae. Adults go for the grilled ham steak, topped—of course—with a pineapple ring, or the pork chops served with applesauce, just the way Grandma would expect.

Harry's Restaurant, 128 N. Franklin St., Port Washington, WI 53074; 262-284-2861; Casual American; $. Check the menu closely here. Go for the option of homemade bread instead of the usual. We visit here regularly for early morning chow when roaming "The Port," once home to a major Lake Michigan fishing industry. You'll always get

rosemary, truffle cheese, smoked mozzarella, and pancetta, or a Calabrese style, with tomato, mozzarella, hot sopressata salami, and topped with a dash of basil.

Trattoria Stefano, 522 S. 8th St., Sheboygan, WI 53081; (920) 452-8455; trattoriastefano.com; $–$$. This is a special place for romantic anniversary dinners. Go for the *rigatoni alla bergamasca,* with sautéed Willow Creek Farm's Italian sausage; local shiitake, cremini, oyster, and button mushrooms; cave-aged pecorino cheese; a touch of cream; and Parmigiano-Reggiano cheese. For an occasional change of pace, switch to the osso buco alla Milanese, which is braised Strauss veal shank. You'll never go wrong with any dish at Stefano's. Cooking classes are regularly held here.

Duke of Devon, 739 Riverfront Dr., Sheboygan, WI 53081; (920) 458-7900; dukeofdevonpub.com; $–$$; The Duke of Devon is an English pub located on Sheboygan's historic riverfront. The Duke features gastropub food such as bangers and mash and cottage pies. Viglietti operates the Duke with his sister Emily; it opened in 2006 and quickly earned kudos for its beer selection and atmosphere. The curry chips, mussels, and clam strips are to die for, especially on hot summer Saturday afternoons, sitting out on the back deck overlooking the Sheboygan harbor.

perfectly done eggs just the way you want them, along with a side of Canadian bacon. Hash browns are crispy good, and hot java comes as a great pour.

HoBo's Korner Kitchen, 100 E. Main St., Belgium, WI 53004; (262) 285-3417; howdea.net/hobos-home.htm; Casual American; $–$$. For comfort food, this is a trucker's delight. HoBo's is a full-service truck stop, market, and restaurant located at exit 107 on I-43, just off the highway. The rule here is bluntly stated: "All-you-can-eat specials while supplies last." On Monday, there's the shrimp with french fries, coleslaw, and bread; Tuesday features broasted chicken with mashed potatoes; Wednesday's deal involves beef tips with mashed potatoes, a veggie, and bread; and Thursday is spaghetti day, with salad and slices of garlic bread. Breakfast is served all day.

Juice's Ghost Town, 990 County Hwy. Q, Grafton, WI 53024; (262) 376-9003; juicesghostown.com; Casual American; $$. Tackle the elk steak, one of the few places in the state where a diner can find such exotica. That's a typical Monday special at Juice's, while Tuesday portions out all-you-can-eat barbecued ribs. Or how  about a 22-ounce prime rib? Neighbors drop in to cheer for the local teams on the flat-screen televisions. Owner Mike (Juice) Gannon is the loudest cheerleader, and he serves up a goal-kicking baked French onion soup.

Lola's on the Lake, The Osthoff Resort, 101 Osthoff Ave., Elkhart Lake, WI 53020; (920) 876-5840; lolasonthelake.com; New American; $$-$$$. We enjoy the panoramic views of Elkhart Lake when we come in for dining at Lola's. The award-winning culinary team offers both a light menu and heartier fare. Steaks are hefty and delicious. We love the Hook's Blue Cheese Cake, served with tender greens tossed with buttermilk dressing. The dish is dazzled with red wine and poached pears, along with spiced pecans. Open to the public, Lola's main entrance is off South East Street in the resort complex. It is closed on Mon.

Morton's, N56 W6339 Center St., Cedarburg, WI 53012; (262) 377-4779; Burgers; $-$$. This is where we go for blues music and burgers or the Friday night fish fry when the legendary harmonica player Jim Liban often jams with guitar-riffing pals. For transparency's sake, Jim is the dad of our son-in-law Matt, a drummer. The place is crowded, noisy, and fun—just what one would expect from a corner bar that features lively jam sessions and lots of honest beer. And you can also get a veggie burger. Bring friends. Wear jeans. Shout and holler.

Mud Creek Coffee Cafe, 106 S. Military Rd. (State Highway 55), Stockbridge, WI 53088; (920) 439-1096; mudcreekcoffee.com; Casual American; $. The sign outside saying HIP RURAL catches the eye. The restaurant lives up to its claim, with deliciously fresh salads, panini, and all sorts of sandwiches and wraps with multigrain and gluten-free options. On Thursday night, there is a special Mexican menu with chicken quesadillas, nachos, burritos, and their own "almost famous" chili. Beverage-wise, folks here have everything, including mochas in numerous flavors, chai, teas, espresso, and coffee classics, with a nice selection of bottles of wine. There's a grand breakfast menu, too.

Pasquale's International Cafe, 305 Main St., De Pere, WI 54115; (920) 336-3330; pasqualesintlcafe.net; Italian; $$. Pasquale's is known for its authentic Chicago-style Italian beef, ravioli, pasta Alfredo, and antipasto. Pasquale's famous original baby-back ribs are for barbecue fans. For the Irish crowd, the restaurant also serves a darned good corned beef on rye. Local artist Cheryl Bowman has done a great job with her wall murals, done in a 1940s format.

Remington's River Inn, 130 S. Main St., Thiensville, WI 53092; (262) 238-2697; remingtonsriverinn.com; Traditional American; $–$$. Rarely will you see a place with as many stones as are placed into the arches and hallways of this comfortable, family place. The grilled shrimp brushed with sweet chile sauce, served with brown rice and fresh veggies is ace, as are the pork chops in a bourbon-maple syrup. With its back deck, it is a special summer place.

Robbins Restaurant, 1810 Omro Rd., Oshkosh, WI 54902; (920) 235-2840; robbinsrestaurant.com; Supper Club; $$. Since 1928, Robbins Restaurant has offered a taste of home cooking. The traditional favorites grace the menu, with chicken, chops, steaks, and seafood such as bacon-wrapped scallops among the tastiest items. It has several dining rooms, one with a fireplace, making it cozy for a winter visit. The restaurant is popular with visitors to the nearby EAA AirVenture Museum, which hosts AirVenture Oskosh at the end of every July. The event draws thousands of international visitors and hundreds of airplanes of every shape and size. Since the restaurant is so close to the airfield and the museum, many of the AirVenture participants enjoy eating at Robbins every year. If you want to talk airplanes and flight patterns, this is this place.

Roxy Supper Club, 571 N. Main St., Oshkosh, WI 54901; (920) 231-1980; roxysupperclub.com; Supper Club; $$–$$$. Look for the green awning over the front door. You can't miss it. Once inside, the extensive menu is quite impressive, with steaks, chicken, seafood, sandwiches, and soups. Since this is Wisconsin, the Cheese State, try a mozzarella log. Go for the stir-fry, a Roxy specialty with shrimp, scallops, beef tenderloin, or chicken, as well as a vegetarian option.

St. Brendan's Inn, 234 S. Washington St., Green Bay, WI 54301; (920) 884-8484; saintbrendansinn.com; Irish; $$. St. Brendan's offers traditional as well as contemporary Irish dishes. Specialties include grilled salmon, sautéed mussels, shepherd's pie, and Grandma Flanigan's Guinness Pot Roast. We're not sure who Grandma Flanigan was, but the pot roast is as good as it gets. The inn's dining room presents a European feel, with an Axminster wool carpet, eight stained-glass windows, and a bog snug (a sitting area with a fireplace). Owner Rip O'Dwanny also runs the **County Clare** (p. 83) guesthouse and restaurant in Milwaukee and the **52 Stafford** (p. 172) in Plymouth, WI. He earned the name "Rip" as a kid, "ripping" a baseball out of the field when he came up to bat.

Schreiner's Restaurant, 168 N. Pioneer Rd., Fond du Lac, WI 54935; (920) 922-0590; fdlchowder.com; Casual American; $–$$. Boneless short ribs, pork chop suey on rice, haddock fillet, liver, fried chicken, and hot beef with made-from-scratch gravy bring back your delightful pre-diet days. The restaurant features a breakfast quiche of the day, such as a sausage and cheddar variety. We like stopping here because it offers down-home cooking, with a fabulous French onion soup and smoothly wonderful New England clam chowder among our favorite selections. Desserts here draw folks from around eastern Wisconsin, particularly for the homemade apple pie and the hot mince pie with rum sauce. Now when was the last time you had that? Beer, wine, and cocktails are available.

Sideline Sports Bar & Restaurant, 1049 Lombardi Access, Green Bay, WI 54304; (920) 496-5857; Casual American; $–$$. There are sports, sports, and more sports at the Sideline Sports Bar. The place is loud and crazy on days when the Green Bay Packers play, conveniently located near the team's Lambeau Field. Not to miss anything, 33 televisions are tuned to games. You can order burgers in

GREEN BAY COOKING

Three Three Five Dining Studio, 335 N. Broadway, Green Bay, WI 54303; (920) 431-1111; threethreefive.com. Christopher Mangless, a Green Bay native and graduate of the Johnson & Wales culinary arts program in Denver, hosts this private dining studio. Mangless holds regular cooking classes for 15 to 30 students at a time, offering both demonstrations and hands-on opportunities. Be sure to bring your own apron or purchase one on-site. The studio is open to the public every Wed year-round, if no private event is booked. Mangless features local ingredients purchased from Green Bay's Broadway District Farmers' Market during the growing season. Each week, he offers a different menu with seasonal small plates and craft drinks.

three sizes, from a third-of-a-pound up through a one-pound monster. Or you can tackle a Sideline salad, wraps, or a chicken sandwich.

Texas Roadhouse, 4304 Gander Rd., Sheboygan, WI 53083; (920) 457-7427; texasroadhouse.com; Steak House; $$–$$$. Even if this is a chain, the Texas Roadhouse dishes out hand-cut steaks, flaky ribs, made-from-scratch sides, and fresh-baked rolls. The pulled pork is okay, too. Pairing well with brewskis is the unlimited supply of in-shell peanuts to nosh.

Trepanier's BackYard Grill & Bar, 838 E. Johnson St., Fond du Lac, WI 54935; (920) 924-9400; visitbackyard.com; Casual American; $$. Patty and Mark Trepanier, proprietors of the BackYard

Grill & Bar, used to own the popular Trepanier's Sunset Supper Club in Fond du Lac from 1981 to 1992. In 2004, the Trepaniers opened the BackYard Grill & Bar. Daughter Colleen helped to develop the family's "Casual Dining, Serious Food" concept. For lunch, walk in, sit down, and dig into a fresh croissant topped with eggs, baked with ham and spinach, and finished off with melted cheddar cheese. A side of pesto bistro sauce is a delightful accompaniment. The Trepaniers are always experimenting, looking for that perfect menu item. One winner has been the grilled swordfish topped with a fresh blueberry and mango salsa, complete with a truffle-infused balsamic glaze and choice of spuds.

Union Hotel and Restaurant, 200 N. Broadway, De Pere, WI 54115; (920) 336-6131; Traditional American; $$$. Portion amounts here are large enough to satisfy the Green Bay Packers defensive line. In fact, you'll find a lot of locals dining here after a football game. The Union Hotel has one of the most complete wine lists in the area, as well as stiff cocktails. Remember those fantastic relish trays in the days of yore? The Union Hotel serves them loaded with carrot sticks, peppers, and celery, along with liver pâté, ham salad, and bread and crackers. The building is about a century old, and the restaurant area is comfortably quiet, even as guests discuss tackles, conversions, and that oh-so-great handoff.

Waupaca Woods Restaurant, 815 W. Fulton St., Waupaca, WI 54981; (715) 258-7400; waupacawoodsrestaurant.com; Casual American; $$-$$$. The Woods is located behind the Waupaca Woods Mall, so there's no need to worry about parking. It offers a delicious round steak, ham, chicken, shrimp, and pork chops. A Woods breakfast is for hearty eaters, especially when two pieces of french toast and choice of bacon, ham, or sausage links or patties show up from the kitchen. Try the grilled kielbasa sausage, along with two fresh eggs served with hash browns or American fries.

Fishy in Port Washington

What is billed as the world's largest one-day outdoor fish fry was launched in 1965, with entertainment, games, and food, food, food. **Fish Day** is always held on the third Saturday in July (portfishday.com), providing a financial lifeline for nine civic organizations that run the fish-and-chips stands throughout the day. They use their proceeds for such civic purposes as the waterfront Rotary Park, a harbor walk, the Kiwanis Pavilion, and the marina's fish-cleaning stations. The menu has been the same since the beginning: deep-fried fish-and-chips, beer, and soda. It's fun to take the kids to watch the morning's grand parade, which steps off on Wisconsin Street at Walters Street and moves down St. Mary's Hill through the downtown area, before turning at Grand Avenue and ending at Milwaukee Street.

Plus there is the Fish Day Run and Walk, an arts and crafts fair, and custom car and hot rod show. The smoked fish eating contest has become a traditional attraction.

Wendt's on the Lake, N9699 Lakeshore Dr., Van Dyne, WI 54979; (920) 688-5231; wendtsonthelake.com; Seafood; $–$$. Located on US 45 between Fond du Lac and Oshkosh, Wendt's overlooks the west side of Lake Winnebago. At 137,700 acres, the lake is the country's largest within a single state. For more than 50 years, the Wendt family has proudly served award-winning lake perch, so their Friday night fish fry is the go-to destination for the locals. But Wendt's also serves their delicious perch throughout the week. In a rush, take-out is an option. The restaurant also serves wraps, sliders, pizza, and a grandiose prime rib on Saturday. Since the lake is such a great fishing spot, you'll find a lot of anglers here. Naturally, their fish stories are as great as Wendt's on the Lake meals.

Whispering Orchards & Cafe, W1650 County Rd. MM, Cleveland, WI 53015; (920) 693-8584; Casual American; $. Whispering Orchards has a fantastic country breakfast, with oversize apple pancakes and cheddar cheese omelets. Local artists exhibit their works on the wall of the red barn. Outside is a petting zoo, with a corn maze making for family fun in the autumn. Picnic tables on the patio are perfectly placed to capture the sinking sun in late spring or summer. The gift shop has homemade preserves, honey made by the orchard's bees, fresh apples and apple cider, and maple syrup.

Landmarks

Cafe Soeurette, 111 N. Main St., West Bend, WI 53095; (262) 338-2233; cafe-soeurette.com; New American; $$–$$. This delightful restaurant wins kudos from food critics, as well as applause from the locals. Dishes can be modified as gluten-free or vegetarian. Chef Jodi Janisse makes hot from-scratch soups, deli-style sandwiches, and homemade baked goods. Area farmers provide meats, cheeses, and preserves. Janisse also has a variety of pasta sauce for sale.

Chuck's Place, 406 N. Main St., Thiensville, WI 53092; (262) 242-9797; Casual American; $–$$. Locals lovingly call this "Chuck's Ducks" because you can get roasted duck here—a favorite treat—by calling ahead for takeout. The 6-ounce charbroiled tenderloin, two fried eggs, hash browns, and toast make for a hearty breakfast. Grabbing an old-fashioned burger for lunch or taking in a hot turkey sandwich with mashed potatoes, gravy, and cranberry for dinner are equally hearty. By the way, the Friday fish fry features a rainbow trout, either broiled or panfried.

52 Stafford, An Irish Inn, 52 Stafford St., Plymouth, WI 53073; (920) 893-0552; 52stafford.com; Irish; $-$$. This 1892 building was originally a hotel and is now listed on the National Register of Historic Places. Owner Rip O'Dwanny stays true to his heritage by serving Irish root soup and other traditional Gaelic dishes. He also presents fresh spinach salad, roasted chicken breast sandwiches, and Black Angus burgers for lunch. Dinner could mean the rack of lamb, roast duckling, and steamed salmon. Each Wednesday, fans pack into the pub room for live music with a Celtic bent. Be aware that the restaurant is closed Sun.

The Jail House Restaurant, 897 Pleasant Valley Rd., West Bend, WI 53095; (262) 675-9302; jailhousewi.com; Traditional American; $-$$. Seemingly out in the middle of a cornfield, the Jail House packs 'em in nightly for its prime rib, steak, or chicken. Every other night offers something topflight from the kitchen. You can meet friends for the Fish Fry Friday, knowing that the parking lot is jammed and adjacent roads lined with autos. Spending time at the bar over martinis, Pinot Grigio, or Fat Tire beer is a given. The half rack of ribs and choice of coconut, stuffed, or jumbo shrimp are Tuesday's specials. There are two levels in the building, which always seem to be full of delighted diners like us, driving in from Milwaukee, Germantown, Jackson, Cedarburg, and Grafton.

Machut's Supper Club, 3911 Lincoln Ave., Two Rivers, WI 54241; (920) 793-9432; machuts.com; Supper Club; $$-$$$. Norman and Lorraine Machut opened Machut's Supper Club in 1961, and it's still run by family members. Dinner entrees include a choice of rice, noodles, or a potato, along with a tossed salad. The soup and salad bar can be added for a small fee. Although steak is king here, many patrons favor the barbecued pork ribs. The menu is always a pleaser.

No No's, 3498 State Hwy. 33, Newburg, WI 53060; (262) 675-6960; nonosrestaurant.com; Traditional American; $–$$. Dating from its roadhouse days as the Triangle Inn in the 1930s, No No's offers great grub served in a neighborhood atmosphere. The decor today is golf themed, with its Back Nine sandwiches and burgers called "bogeys." Naturally, "birdies" are chicken, whether dished out as cordon bleu, Italiano, or baked. Steak Italiano is a signature dish, tenderloin smothered in tomatoes and mushrooms, and then topped with mozzarella. Wednesday is Blues Nite with live bands. During Lent on Tuesday, No No's serves up all-you-can-eat fried smelt, grouper, and peel-your-own shrimp. Be sure to make a reservation. Don't be fooled by No No's mailing address indicating West Bend.

The Port Hotel Restaurant and Inn, 101 E. Main St., Port Washington, WI 53074; (262) 284-9473; theporthotel.com; Traditional American; $$–$$$. Featuring steaks and seafood, the Port Hotel has a cozy, white tablecloth look that is not pretentious despite the folded napkins. It's the friendly, competent staff that sets the mood. We especially enjoy sitting under an umbrella on the outdoor patio in the summer. The hotel itself has a rich history, starting as The American House in 1857. After several subsequent owners and name changes, it morphed into the Port Hotel in 1973 and quickly became a special place for wedding receptions during the bride and groom season. So you may be sidestepping any number of bridal parties, but that's part of the fun, toasting the loving couples.

Simpson's, 222 S. Main St., Waupaca, WI 54981; (715) 258-2330; simpsonswaupaca.com; Traditional American; $$–$$$. Don't be scared away from Simpson's just because the place is said to be haunted. Supposedly, a ghostly family inhabits the dining room, or at least that's what the after-hours cleanup crew says. Actually, the spirits might merely want several of the pickled mushrooms served at the bar or a spread of grilled garlic on the warm, buttered bread when dinner comes. A Friday fish fry draws a lot of the neighbors, as do steak and other seafood. Simpson's is open daily for lunch and dinner, with karaoke on Thursday. There are 15 beers on tap, any one of which is perfect for the Friday beer-battered haddock. The original restaurant opened in 1932.

Specialty Markets, Stores & Producers

All That and a Bag O Chips, W75 N865 Tower Ave., Cedarburg, WI 53012; (262) 389-9103. Stacy Wilke and her husband, Steve, make tortilla chips in different flavors that are sold at the Cedarburg Piggly Wiggly and at area festivals. According to UrbanDictionary .com the company's name means "all that and more, or something cool." Production is done after hours at a local restaurant. The chips are gluten-free, except for the seasoning, and include lime and salt, cinnamon sugar, pepper supreme, and seasoning salt. Strawberry, apple harvest, and peppermint are seasonal touches.

Beerntsen's Confectionary, 108 N. 8th St., Manitowoc, WI 54220; (920) 684-9616; beerntsens.com. This is a must-stop every time we come to Manitowoc to visit the Wisconsin Maritime Museum with its vast array of Lake Michigan–related artifacts. But you'll have to find out for yourself how a World War II submarine ended up there. While pondering, stroll up the street from the lakeshore to Beernsten's and indulge in a chocolate fix. This old-timey malt shop opened in 1932 and still has its old wooden booths. Ohhhh, that peanut brittle and butter almond toffee. We'd be remiss if we didn't mention Beernsten's sponge candy, cordial cherries with their sweetly juicy insides, and Mint Melt Aways.

Blau's Saukville Meats, 501 E. Green Bay Ave., Saukville, WI 53080; (262) 284-0898; blaussaukvillemeats.com. We've been coming here for years, particularly for the bison burgers and steaks, along with organic chicken and deer, pork, or beef sausages. The bacon here is among the best. Numerous hunters bring their "trophies" here for prepping into grill-size portions of elk and other edible critters.

The Elegant Farmer, 1545 Main St. (Highways ES and J), Mukwonago, WI 53149; (262) 363-6770; elegantfarmer.com. Critics have long said that the pies made at The Elegant Farmer are the best in the nation. Pastry lovers agree wholeheartedly, especially when indulging in the apple pie, which is baked in a paper bag. You can also get jumbo fruit muffins, fruit crisps, breads, and giant-size cookies, along with popcorn and vegetables in season. Whenever you can't get to the main farm and store, you can often purchase a pie at numerous grocery stores throughout Wisconsin, Illinois, Iowa, and Michigan.

Ewig Brothers Fish Company, 121 S. Wisconsin St., Port Washington, WI 53074; (262) 284-2236; ewigsmokedfish.com. This smokehouse continues a multigeneration family tradition dating from the 1920s. Canadian whitefish is shipped in fresh, then brined and smoked with hardwoods—the flavor and textures that go so well on crackers. Ewig's also has smoked lake trout and Alaskan salmon, as well as a smoked fish spread and salmon fillets. Great Lakes perch are the perfect choice for a home fish fry with 8 to 10 fillets per pound. Orders are shipped via a two-day service.

Kelley Country Creamery, W5214 County Rd. B, Fond du Lac, WI; 54937, (920) 923-1715; kelleycountrycreamery .com. This farmstead has been in the Kelley family since 1861 and—wow—can they make ice cream! Of course, the fresh milk helps. Among the many flavors are acai blueberry ice cream, black raspberry cheesecake, and a seasonal kiwi

Farm Markets, Where Produce Rules

Cedarburg Farmers Market, Cedarburg Cultural Center, W62 N546 Washington Ave.; (262) 377-9620; cedarburg.org. Fri, 9 a.m. to 2 p.m., June to Oct.

Five Corners Farmer's Market, parking lot of Wayne's Drive-In, 1331 Covered Bridge Rd., Town of Cedarburg; (262) 377-4509; town.cedarburg.wi.us/cedarburg-government. Sat, 9 a.m. to 2 p.m., mid-June through mid-October.

Green Barn Farm Market, 2835 Locust Rd. (off of State Highway 44), Ripon; (920) 748 7749; greenbarnfarmmarket.com/barn.html. Farm is open daily during the growing season, as well as daily at its Ripon located on the corner of East Oshkosh and Stanton Streets.

Sheboygan Farmer's Market, 8th and Erie in downtown Sheboygan; (920) 457-7272 ext.11; visitsheboygancounty.com. Wed and Sat, 7 a.m. to 2 p.m., early June until Oct.

strawberry. The ice cream parlor attached to the farm serves up numerous sundae styles, as well. Kids really go for the mud sundae made with Oreos and gummi worms. The creamery also offers a wide variety of ice cream cakes.

Lakeshore Culinary Institute, 712 Riverfront Dr., Sheboygan, WI 53081; (920) 457-9050; lakeshoreculinaryinstitute.com. The Lakeshore Culinary Institute Dining Room of Lakeshore Technical College is open for dinner from 5 to 7:30 p.m., Wed through Fri when classes are in session. Dinner reservations are required for these truly fun meals prepared by the students. Diners can also sip cocktails, beer, and wine.

Schwai's Meat & Sausage, W62 N601 Washington Ave., Cedarburg, WI 53012; (262) 376-2060. Schwai's has some of the best braunschweiger this side of Berlin's Brandenburg Gate, and if you haven't had a Schwai's brat, you haven't had a brat. Tom Schwai's outlet in Cedarburg operates from a storefront that has been a meat market since around 1917. This is an old-time butcher shop, with all the spicy sausage scents one would expect emanating from links of many varieties that dangle from hooks almost everywhere. You can also purchase the company's products at its processing plant, W3940 County Hwy. H, Fredonia, WI 53021, (262) 692-2731. That site is more industrial, but its freezers are packed with just as many offerings.

Silver Creek Brewing Company, N57 W6172 Portland Rd., Cedarburg, WI 53012; (262) 375-4444; silvercreekbrewing.com. Established in 1999, Silver Creek Brewing Company was organized by members of a local homebrewers' club. They opened their brewpub in Cedarburg's historic grist mill in 2002 and have been brewing craft beers from the club's own recipes since 2004. Four year-round beers and four seasonals are brewed, plus a classic blonde root beer.

Slow Pokes Local Food, 1229 12th Ave., Grafton, WI 53024; (262) 375-5522; slowpokeslocalfood.com. This is where we go to get some of the best natural and organic produce, farm-raised meats, raw milk cheeses, and wellness books. The entire store offers only gluten-free items. For added value, classes are held upstairs, with a variety of topics, including how digestion affects the skin. Sit at one of the small window tables and sup a vegan soup or munch a dairy-free pizza. Owner Kathleen McGlone was faced with numerous health issues in her family and subsequently began studying nutrition and its connection to food allergies and various related diseases. McGlone is a wealth of info on what's good to eat and what's good for you.

GET IT FRESH HERE, WHERE FARM STANDS RULE

Nature's Natural Way Farm (Lubbert's Produce), N4883 Kelly Rd., Fond du Lac, WI 54937; (920) 517-6914; naturesnaturalwayfarm.com.

Nieman Orchards, 9932 Pioneer Rd., between Horns Corners and Grarville Roads; Cedarburg, WI 53012; (262) 377-4284; niemanorchards.com.

Witte's Vegetable Farm, 10006 Bridge Rd., Cedarburg, WI 53012; (262) 377-1423; wittesvegfarm.com. Stand hours: Mon through Sat, 8 a.m. to 8 p.m.; Sun and holidays, 8 a.m. to 6 p.m.

Susie Q Fish Market, 1810 East St., Two Rivers, WI 54241; (920) 793-5240; susieqfishmarket.com. The LeClair family has been fishing Lake Michigan from Two Rivers for more than 130 years. Their French-Canadian ancestors moved to this area on the shores of Lake Michigan in the mid-1800s from Quebec. The company now owns two trawlers (*Susie Q* and *Peter Paul*), one gill net boat (*Avis-J*), and a trap-net boat (*Jamie Ann*). The trawlers fish for smelt, the gill net boats go for chubs, and the trap-net boat fishes for delicious whitefish. Its smoked fish is top rated, especially with crackers and beer.

Tamara's the Cake Guru, 1529 Oregon St., Oshkosh, WI 54902; (920) 236-9144; cakeguru.com. Tamara Mugerauer has won the Cupcake Warrior Championship at the Wisconsin Restaurant Expo, snagging a gold medal and People's Choice Winner in the Creative Cake division, along with other awards. Each day, Tamara's puts out 12 to 15 varieties of tantalizing cupcakes. Her basic cake flavors are white, chocolate, and marble, with an extensive list of fruity styles, including raspberry.

Von Stiehl Winery, 115 Navarino St., Algoma, WI 54201; (920) 487-5208; vonstiehl.com. The winery is listed on the National Register of Historic Places, which makes it a truly fine "vintage" indeed. Von Stiehl presents 25 varieties of wines, from traditional grape wines to sweeter fruit wines made with Door County cherries. The Gold Medal–winning Cabernet Sauvignon is as fulfilling as the winery's brandy-fortified cherry wine. Von Stiehl hosts numerous events throughout the year, including June's Ladies' Fest & Stiletto Strut. For $35, guests enjoy a massage, two glasses of wine in a keepable Naughty Girl glass, plus lunch and a chocolate truffle. Adding to the fun is a shopping "faire" with specialty vendors, bands, and belly dance lessons. Among favorite wines poured that weekend are Naughty Girl red, Sassy Sangria, White Stiletto, Risqué Riesling, and many more. Hunky, more or less, "pool boys" are on hand to refill glasses.

Eastern Wisconsin—South of Milwaukee

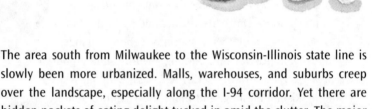

The area south from Milwaukee to the Wisconsin-Illinois state line is slowly been more urbanized. Malls, warehouses, and suburbs creep over the landscape, especially along the I-94 corridor. Yet there are hidden pockets of eating delight tucked in amid the clutter. The major cities here are Racine and Kenosha, each alongside Lake Michigan, which lends a special charm to their respective downtowns. Smart chefs are opening new restaurants throughout the region, knowing that their strategic locations can attract diners both from Milwaukee and Chicago.

Foodie Faves

Casa Capri, 2129 Birch Rd., Kenosha, WI 53140; (262) 551-7171; casacapri.com; Italian; $$. For more than 60 years, the Stella family has used original northern Italian recipes dating back to the early 1900s. The menu is augmented by steaks and seafood, but the restaurant's signature pasta dish is the baked stuffed rigatoni. The pasta is made fresh

Lake Geneva Retreats

The Grand Geneva Resort, 7020 Grand Geneva Way, Lake Geneva, WI 53147; (262) 248-8811; grandgeneva.com. The resort originated as a Playboy Club in the late 1960s, experienced tough times as the Americana, and was rescued by the Milwaukee-based Marcus Corporation and its hotel division in the late 1990s. Where Bunnies once cavorted, the Grand Geneva has morphed into a prime, full-service vacation retreat, complete with swimming pools, a ski hill, and other getaway amenities. Its **Ristoranté Brissago** has consistently won top awards for its Italian wine list and menu. Attention has certainly been paid to the details emphasized at the Brissago, where even the Parmigiano Reggiano comes from a small family-run cheese plant in Regia Amelia, Italy. Regular visitors favor the restaurant's special wine dinners, usually featuring noted Italian vintners. They've included Michel Chiarlo, scion of a seven-generation winemaking family from the Piedmont region.

You'll never go hungry at the Grand Geneva, a super resort experience with plenty of other dining options. Check out the the Geneva ChopHouse and its Sunday brunch, the Grand Cafe, Leinenkugel's Mountain Top Lodge, Links Bar & Grill, the Cafe Gelato, the Geneva Club Lounge, Smokey's Bar-B-Que House, and the Hungry Moose Food Court for a quick munch. Then it's back to the pool, the slopes, or to your room with a good novel.

The Abbey Resort, 269 Fontana Blvd., Fontana, WI 53125; (800) 709-1323; theabbeyresort.com. Guests at the Abbey can satisfy their caffeine needs at Cafe Latte, chow down the barbecue in the Waterfront restaurant and bar, and enjoy the white-tablecloth Fontana Grill, which offers small plates and a sweeping array of entrees, some being vegetarian or gluten-free. It's great fun relaxing poolside with snacks and drinks from Gazebo Grille. You can also kick back in The Helm, the resort's cocktail lounge. There are plenty of appetizers to sample, with live music every Friday and Saturday evening. See The Abbey Resort and Executive Chef Joshua North's recipe for **Gluten-Free Vegan Key Lime Pie** on p. 300.

daily. The spaghettini with anchovies is a foodie fix that can't be beat, while some diners enjoy the mostaccioli with broccoli and cauliflower, topped with Romano cheese. Casa Capri also has plenty of pizza options. However one spells it, the word here is always "yummmm!"

Chancery Pub & Restaurant, 207 Gas Light Dr., Racine, WI 53403; (262) 635-0533; thechancery.com; Casual American; $$. The Chancery is actually part of a small Wisconsin chain, and we miss the one in Milwaukee next to the old Schwartz bookstore, both 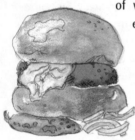 of which closed several years ago. The Chancery eventually edged across southern Wisconsin and into northern Illinois. This particular Chancery is adjacent to the Radisson Hotel, overlooking the harbor, with a nautical theme throughout. For value, try the fresh, made-to-order, one-third-pound burgers for only two bucks on Wednesday in the bar area.

Chef's Corner Bistro, N2430 Geneva St., Lake Geneva, WI 53191; (262) 245-6334; chefscornerbistro.com; German; $$–$$$. Here you can get Bavarian pork chops, a schnitzel sample, Hungarian beef goulash, and other Teutonic wonders. There are always plenty of specials, ranging from broiled Lake Superior whitefish to beef short rib sauerbraten. For an experiment, try the Chef's Surprise, specifying only meat or fish, then see what the kitchen comes up with. You'll discover the restaurant between Lake Geneva and Delavan, near William's Bay.

The Corner House, 1521 Washington Ave., Racine, WI 53403; (262) 637-1295; cornerhouseracine.com; Steak House; $$–$$$. If you need a meat fix, the Corner House is the place, especially for prime rib. Apparently, everyone in Racine has a story about this place from over the years, always a tale featuring slabs of beef in some version of thickness and cut. But you can also get oysters Rockefeller, if you wish.

Kringlevlle, Wisconsin

Racine claims the title as the most "Danish City in America," although its heritage has diluted over the generations. Yet thankfully, one touch of the past is still going strong, in the shape of a pastry. The *kringle* is a large, flat, oval sweet made from layers of buttery yeast dough, filled with fruit, pecans, or chocolate and topped with a sugary coating. A typical kringle measures about 14 inches long and 10 inches wide, weighing around a pound and a half. These bakeries are favorites, noted for those old-time delicacies, now considered Wisconsin's official pastry.

Bendtsen's Bakery, 3200 Washington Ave., Racine, WI 53405; (262) 633-0365; bendtsensbakery.com. Bendtsen's has been featured on the Food Network and in numerous publications. The first Bendtsen, Laurits, came to America and opened his bakery in 1934.

Larsen's Bakery, 3311 Washington Ave., Racine, WI 53405; (262) 633-4298; larsenskringle.com.

Lehmann's Bakery, 4900 Spring St., Mt. Pleasant, WI 53406; (262) 898-7810; lehmannsbakery.com.

O&H Danish Bakery, 1841 Douglas Ave., Racine, WI 53404, (262) 637-8895; 4006 Durand Ave., Racine, WI 53405, (262) 554-1311; 717 S. Sylvania Ave. in the Petro Travel Plaza at I-94 and State Highway 20, Sturtevant, WI 53177, (262) 898-1950; ohdanishbakery.com.

DeRango's Pizza Palace, 3840 Douglas Ave., Racine, WI 53140; (262) 639-4112; derangos.com; Italian; $–$$. Good, hearty Italian food is the forte of Domenico DeRango and his wife, Mirella. They came to the United States in 1959 from Calabria with their two children, Benny and Carmela. After a brief time working at a foundry, Dominic found his calling at his brother's restaurant and soon started his own place. Chicken parmigiana, lasagna, and other pasta dishes are on the menu, along with New York strip and sirloin. One of the best carryouts is the 16- by 32-inch party pizza.

Franks Diner, 508 58th St., Kenosha, WI 53140; (262) 657-1017; franksdinerkenosha.com; Casual American; $. Launched in 1926, the restaurant has been a Kenosha downtown eating landmark for several generations. Its motto is "Be nice or leave." If you hunger for a tasty cinnamon roll and good coffee, you'll love the diner the minute you walk in. Philly cheesesteak sandwich and chicken potpie are on the menu. As at grandma's house, the folks here admonish "Don't play with your food. Did you wash your hands? Eat your vegetables." Breakfast is wonderful, especially the "garbage plates" made up of five eggs, hash browns, green peppers, onions, and jalapeño peppers for zest. Add ham, bacon, Spam, or scratch-made hash for an extra kicker. A veggie platter is also offered. Don't worry about the crowds; you'll get a seat eventually. Any wait is worth it.

HobNob, 277 S. Sheridan Rd., Racine, WI 53403; (262) 552-8008; thehobnob.com; Supper Club; $$–$$$. Since 1954, the HobNob has retained the ambience of a classic Wisconsin supper club, with linen tablecloths, paintings on the walls, and signature ice cream drinks. Diners especially favor the Angus beef and seafood, as well as the decadently delicious Chocolate Grasshoppers, Pink Squirrels, and the Golden Cadillacs. Shame on us.

House of Gerhard, 3927 75th St., Kenosha, WI 53142; (262) 694-5212; houseofgerhard.com; German; $$. Gerhard Dillner came to the United States from his native Germany, and with his wife, Ruth, he opened his restaurant in 1964. Their family continues to serve really, really German cuisine, such as the *Kasseler Rippchen,* which is smoked pork loin with red cabbage, or the *Schweinehaxe,* a tender roasted pork shank on a bed of sauerkraut. The wurst is the best, being a platter of grilled bratwurst and knockwurst, served with sauerkraut, or order a cordon bleu schnitzel sandwich, made up of ham, swiss cheese, and hollandaise sauce atop a Gerhard schnitzel. This delicacy is served on a Bavarian pretzel roll, complemented with french fries.

Mangia Trattoria, 5717 Sheridan Rd., Kenosha, WI 53140; (262) 652-4285; kenoshamangia.com; Italian; $$–$$$$. Mangia has long been considered by food critics to be the best restaurant between Milwaukee and Chicago. Chef-Owner Tony Mantuano, nominated for a James Beard "Best Midwestern Chef" award, opened Mangia (Italian for "eat") in 1988. The rich foccacia bread is a specialty. The *spaghettini del pescatore,* with its full platter of shellfish, remains a top seller, as does the braised duck  and peas. A wide variety of wine is available, including a light red 2011 Dolcetto d'Alba from the Piemonte region, a high-end 2007 Vino Nobile di Montepulciano, and many other reds, whites, and sparking vintages in between. Mantuano and his sister Susan Mantuano-Tishuk present cooking classes during the year, so sign up early to be assured of a spot. Mantuano also owns the fabled Spiaggia restaurant on Chicago's Michigan Avenue.

Medusa Grill and Bistro, 501 Broad St., Lake Geneva, WI 53147; (262) 249-8644; medusagrillandbistro.com; Bistro; $$. The bistro has a small 12-table dining room and 10 bar chairs at "the counter." The creamy asparagus soup is worth a visit, as is the shrimp bisque. Follow up with grilled halibut. Be aware that a handwritten sign above the bar asserts, I LIKE THE MUSIC A BIT LOUD——CHEF GREG.

Sebastian's, 6025 Douglas Ave., Racine, WI 53402; (262) 681-5465; sebastiansfinefood.com; New American; $$$. Owners Patrice and Scott Sebastian use fresh, organically grown herbs and vegetables from their own garden, a greenery oasis adjacent to the restaurant. They also make more than 25 scratch-made sauces for their dinner and dessert menus. What is especially appealing is that the menu changes seasonally to take advantage of what's fresh at that particular time. Dedicated foodies have deemed Sebastian's as first-rate in every way.

Simple Cafe, 525 Broad St., Lake Geneva, WI 53147; (262) 248-3556; simplecafelakegeneva.com; Casual American; $. Settle into the Simple, where good food comes on large platters. Among the local purveyors are **Yuppie Hill Poultry** (p. 200), **River Valley Ranch** (p. 197), and Brook Farm. The Simple supports an environmentally sound process of building and producing, such as composting organic waste;  recycling metals, paper, glass, and plastics; and using rainwater for its gardens. Discarded lumber was used in the construction of the restaurant and its furniture. For an ace breakfast, try the eggs Sardou, poached eggs on a croissant with artichokes, fresh spinach, mozzarella, Parmesan cheese, and a Creole hollandaise holding this all together. A hefty chorizo black-bean breakfast burrito is another plus. For lunch, votes go for the Korean barbecue skirt steak, Asian slaw, kimchee, and Sriracha honey sesame mayo on corn tortillas. They also have a **Simple Cafe** (p. 80) at 2124 N. Farwell Ave.

Soon's Sushi Cafe, 2100 54th St., Kenosha, WI 53140; (262) 658-0220; soonssushicafe.com; Japanese; $$. The cafe is owned by Soon Noel and her husband, Robert. Before coming stateside, Soon operated her own restaurant on an island off Korea for about 17 years. This is a family-friendly place, noted for its California roll or the asparagus, avocado, and cucumber roll. The octopus roll is a fun

Racine's Top Two Little Bars

Waves Grill & Pub, 107 4th St. (corner of 4th and Lake) Racine, WI 53403; (262) 634-7668; wavespub.com; Traditional American; $$. Waves has a top-notch menu in an intimate space. You will appreciate the entrees that come with a starch side, including buttermilk mashed potatoes, mashed sweet potatoes, or jasmine rice. Scaloppine of chicken and the vegetarian wild mushroom ravioli with Boursin cream sauce and grilled vegetables are two marvelous options, depending on whether you like meat or not. By calling ahead, you can even arrange to have dishes for people with allergies to fish, nuts, gluten, dairy, or any other foods. The Waves makes sure you are looked after. **Yardarm Bar & Grill,** 930 Erie St., Racine, WI 53402; (262) 633-8270; yardarmbargrill.com; Casual American; $$. "Sand dollar" potatoes are a specialty of this joint, where the rooms look like the inside of a wooden ship. A wide selection of beers on tap where everyone soon knows your name.

option. Soon also has a wide range of tempura-style dishes and such edible exotics as deep-fried squid legs. Even the plain, old-fashioned chicken fried rice is a marvel.

Tickled Pink Coffee Shop and Bistro, 80 S. Walworth Ave., Williams Bay, WI 53191; (262) 245-9330; Bistro; $. Banana smoothies and sandwiches in a shop with frilly vintage hats and antique furniture make for a fun combination. There are clothes, accessories, jewelry, purses, candles, and bath products. The coffee bar at the back of the room serves **Colectivo** (p. 69) coffee and fruit drinks. This makes it easy to browse while waiting for a latte. Tickled Pink is primarily a girly place, but a guy can find plenty of eats while his significant other roams the aisles.

The Wine Knot Bar & Bistro, 5611 6th Ave., Kenosha, WI 53140; (262) 653-9580; wine-knot.com; Bistro; $–$$$. Wine flights, as well as a broad selection of bottles and glasses of classic reds and whites, are popular here. The Wine Knot claims to be Kenosha's only "official" wine bar. This downtown restaurant has a full menu with lamb chops, filet mignon, seafood, duck breast, and other selections that are some of the best in the area. Start a meal with a bowl of flavor-rich tomato basil soup or a steak and spinach salad. Most of the appetizers come as half plates with a full plate option. Live music is a regular feature, usually with a jazz touch.

Landmarks

Ray Radigan's, 11712 Sheridan Rd., Pleasant Prairie, WI 53158; (262) 694-0455; rayradigans.com; Steak House; $$–$$$. Founded in 1933, Radigan's is a converted farmhouse. The glowing red neon sign outside is a landmark in the community. When here, think steak and eat steak. Original owner Ray Radigan died several years ago, and his son, "Young Mike," now runs the restaurant. Mike gets whole sides of prime beef which he ages and cuts. The very, very hungry aim for the 28-ounce T-bone. A petite filet is perfect for less-hungry diners. For seafood lovers, the lobster Thermidor and the Texas Gulf shrimp rack up dining points in the plus column.

Specialty Markets, Stores & Producers

Jelly Belly Visitor Center, 10100 Jelly Belly Ln., Pleasant Prairie, WI 53158; (866) 868-7522; jellybelly.com. The store is open

Bag It Up & Let's Eat

Bristol Farmers Market, 19801 83rd St., Bristol, Wed, 2 to 6 p.m., May through Oct; (262) 857-2368.

Kenosha Farmers' Markets, Tues, Union Park, 45th Street and 8th Avenue; Wed, Columbus Park, 54th Street and 22nd Avenue; Thurs, Lincoln Park, 18th Avenue and 70th Street; Fri, Baker Park, 66th Street and Sheridan Road; Sat, Columbus Park, 54th Street and 22nd Avenue, June through Nov, 6 a.m. to 1 p.m.; (262) 605-6700; kenoshacvb.com/shopping/farmers-markets.

Kenosha HarborMarket, 56th Street and 2nd Avenue, Kenosha, Sat, 9 a.m. to 6 p.m., mid-May through mid-Oct; (262) 914-1252; kenoshacvb.com/shopping/farmers-markets/kenosha-harbormarket.

Lake Geneva Historic Horticultural Hall Farmers' Market, Horticultural Hall, 330 Broad St., Thurs, 8 a.m. to 1 p.m., May through Oct; (262) 745-9341.

West Racine Farmers Market, 3100 Washington Ave., West Racine, Wed, 1 to 5 p.m., early May through end of Oct; Fri, 8 a.m. to noon, mid-May through late Oct; (262) 886-3091; pinehill1912@yahoo.com.

daily from 9 a.m. to 5 p.m., with tours throughout the day. It's a great place to learn the secrets of making jelly beans. The retail store features Jelly Belly beans, confections, gifts, and a sample bar. Some 50 flavors of the confection are made here, with recipes provided to make your own sweets at home. Did you know that you could concoct the taste of a raspberry crème brûlée by combining their French vanilla, raspberry, and toasted marshmallow beans?

Kenosha HarborMarket, 514 56th St., Kenosha, WI 53140; (262) 914-1252; kenoshaharbormarketplace.com. This bustling outside market is held weekly on Kenosha's lakefront beginning in mid-May. A winter HarborMarket is inside Rhode Center for the Arts, 514 56th St. Patrons can find everything from African tiger melons, baklava, and Greek pizza to homemade ricotta plus bushels of fresh produce. There are several parking lots in the area, with parking allowed along both sides of 56th Street. The Kenosha trolley line trundles past the market, featuring several refurbished old-time carriers.

Linnea Bakery, 512 56th St., Kenosha, WI 53140; (262) 484-4203; linneabakery.com. In honor of their Swedish and Norwegian grandparents, Mark and Kim Rutkowski have created a mix of traditional and modern Scandinavian foods. The bakery serves breakfast and lunch and features Swedish, Norwegian, Finnish, Danish, and Icelandic breads and pastries. Linnea's soups and sandwiches are made from scratch. You can also purchase imported grocery products and Scandinavian gifts. Visitors need to try the *kanelbulle,* a pretzelesque cinnamon treat made daily. The coffee is Swedish dark roast, brewed at the bakery with cardamom.

Robin's Nest Cakery, 5607 7th Ave., Kenosha, WI 53140; (262) 652-1054; robinsnestcakery.com. This gourmet sweet shop features custom-made cakes, decadent cupcakes, and decorated sugar cookies. Also, decorating parties and cake-decorating classes are a favorite pastime during the winter.

Sandy's Popper Ice Cream, 5503 6th Ave., Kenosha, WI 53140; (262) 605-3202; sandyspopper.com. Oodles of bags packed with popcorn line the shelves, with candy and ice cream of all kinds temptingly within reach. The made-to-order sundaes, malts, and shakes make for great summertime splurging. Be aware of seasonally adjusted hours, so it's wise to call ahead.

Sweet Corn Lady & Daughters, Delavan; No phone; sweetcornlady.com/index.html. The SCL has been selling produce in the Delavan area since 1957. Look for the bright yellow farm stand on State Trunk Highway 50 at the corner of Inlet Shore Drive, a block west of Reed's Marine. There is also a truck selling produce on the courthouse square in Elkhorn during the summer. In addition to the corn, the stand displays tomatoes, peaches, muskmelons, beans, green peppers, watermelons, and other fruits and veggies. Folks in the know can hardly wait until the time comes for the farm's raspberries, new potatoes, plums, and nectarines.

Sweet House of Madness, 521 Broad St., Lake Geneva, WI 53147; (262) 248-2190; thesweethouseofmadness.com. Breads, rolls, and granola are made with panache at this made-from-scratch artisan bakery and pastry shop. Everything starts with simple ingredients: flour, sugar, Wisconsin butter, locally sourced eggs, highest-quality chocolate, and fresh, fresh fruit. A foodie can appreciate the Swedish apple cake, the pumpkin bread, an oatmeal raisin bar, or an Irish coffee truffle cupcake.

Tenuta's Delicatessen and Liquors, 3203 52nd St., Kenosha, WI 53144; (262) 657-9001; (262) 657-9001; tenutasdeli .com. Imported groceries, meats, oils, and cheese, along with Kenosha's largest selection of specialty beer, wine, and liquor, are the draw here. There is also a magnificent range of cigars. Pop in for meatballs and huge green olives whenever a craving for Italian exotica hits. There is a neat outdoor dining area when weather permits. The meatball "bombers," grilled panini sandwiches, and related Italian-style "fast food" are the best. Take home some of Tenuta's egg noodles, which come in numerous sizes, shapes, and styles. There are fettuccine, capellini, ravioli, gnocchi, and other varieties. Tenuta's has a long, distinguished history in Kenosha, opening in 1950.

Eastern Wisconsin—West of Milwaukee

Heading west out of Milwaukee toward Madison via I-94, State Highway 18, or any of the other roads is like heeding Horace Greeley's sage advice. Of course, in his 19th-century heyday, there wouldn't have been so many eateries to serve the hungry traveler. Now, however, one is almost tripping over quality restaurants serving the best in local produce and meats. You can't go wrong heading out toward the sunset.

Foodie Faves

Cafe Carpe, 18 S. Water St. West, Fort Atkinson, WI 53538; (920) 563-9391; cafecarpe.com; Casual American; $. This is a family-friendly cafe, bar, and music room situated in a century-plus building alongside the roiling Rock River. Bill Camplin and Kitty Welch have run the Carpe since 1985, always hosting top musical names from around the country. Among the many entertainers have been Larry Penn, Jim Schwall, and the Midwest Guitar Trio. The kitchen is small, but no

SWEETEST FEST

Chocolatefest, 681 Maryland Ave., Burlington, WI 53105; (262) 763-7185 (the phone is only staffed the week of the event); chocolatefest.com. Each Memorial Day weekend, Burlington hosts the sweetest festival in the state. The first fest was held in 1987, to help Nestlé celebrate its 20th anniversary as one of the town's major employers. Music, a carnival, a bike ride, and a parade are integral to the festivities. A 12,000-square-foot Chocolate Experience Tent features a range of activities from chef demonstrations to the popular Project Yum-Way, a candy-wrapper clothing design contest. Naturally, there is plenty of chocolate in almost every form imaginable.

problem: Come here for the music and ambience. The vegetarian and organic offerings emphasize locally grown produce. Look on the board for the day's specials, which could be a jambalaya or a stuffed pizza. The cafe has a nice selection of microbrews.

The Duck Inn Supper Club, N6214 State Hwy. 89, Delavan, WI 53115; (608) 883-6988; duckinndelavan.com; Supper Club; $$. Of course, delicious duck is prepared here in several ways, although the name dates from Prohibition days when the place was a speakeasy, one where patrons could "duck in" for a drink. Go for the cashew duck breast or roasted half duck served on wild rice. Extend a toast to the good old days with an old-fashioned, martini, or manhattan, noted as among the most savory around the region. There are three dining rooms in which to sit. Owners Jeff and Nora Karbash used naturally grown local produce as often as possible.

Frontier Dining Room, 2400 E. Geneva St., Lake Lawn Resort, Delavan, WI 53115; 262-728-7950; lakelawnresort.com; Traditional

American; $$–$$$. This is a fantastic breakfast place, with a monster buffet. The made-to-order omelets are worth every nibble. The room is also noted for its butternut squash soup and the chicken and dumpling soup. Be sure to sit by the window for a view of the grounds and Lake Geneva.

The Pub, 114 N. Main St., Oconomowoc, WI; 262-567-8850; aelredspub.com; Irish; $$. Since 2001, The Pub has served up Irish hospitality, just five minutes north of I-94, exit 282. Owners/ proprietors Aelred and Bernie Gannon hail from Sligo, Ireland, and really know how to make Auld Sod shepherd's pie and a thick, rich lamb stew. Artisan cheese from Ireland and Wisconsin is another plus. The menu regularly changes, yet the Guinness remains a fine pour, and an international wine list keeps guests coming back. Patrons are also drawn by the specials, which could be a scallop salad, duck confit, herb-stuffed trout, and even a scrumptious shrimp étouffée. Of course, there is the requisite corned beef and cabbage. At The Pub, it's easy to keep thinking green all year long.

Landmarks

Fireside Dinner Theatre, 1131 Janesville Ave., Fort Atkinson, WI 53538; (800) 477-9505; firesidetheatre.com; Supper Club; $$–$$$. The Fireside is one of the Midwest's most popular entertainment destinations and the only Actor's Equity dinner theater in Wisconsin. The Klopcic family has 50-some years of hospitality under their collective belts. The music presentations range from the fabled *Annie Get Your Gun* to the Sizzlin' '60s live band revue. The Friday fish fry with steamed Norwegian cod with peppercorn beurre blanc sauce gets a four-chef's-hat nod (out of five). It is always recommended to have a reservation.

Grill Junkies, 1288 Summit Ave., Oconomowoc, WI 53066; 262-567-7000; grilljunkies.com; Burgers; $. Yes, you can have a healthy burger; it just depends on the ingredients and prep.  Yet for meat lovers, the Kick-Ass burger is a mix of Angus brisket, chuck, and short-rib cuts. Top this with avocado, grilled red peppers, lettuce, tomato, and coleslaw for a tasty mix. Grill Junkies emphasize gluten-free breads and rolls, plus interesting sides such as pad thai noodles and Indian flatbread with curry.

Mullen's Dairy & Eatery, 212 W. Main St., Watertown, WI 53094; (920) 261-4278; mullensdairy.com; Casual American; $. Located in downtown Watertown since 1932, Mullen's is a family-oriented place with wide tables and comfy chairs—a dedicated sandwich and soup place. The best part is the selection of malts, shakes, or sundaes. Who thinks about the butterfat and who cares? Mullen's has earned a well-deserved listing as the "Cream of the Crop" in the Sundae Hall of Fame.

The Union House Restaurant, S42 W31320 State Hwy. 83, Genesee Depot, WI 53127; (262) 968-4281; theunionhouse .com; Traditional American; $$–$$$. Mushroom tarts, short ribs, and caramel cashew bread pudding, plus a broad wine list, make the Union House a pleasant stopover after a visit to Ten Chimneys. The museum house, about a mile or so to the west, was the once the home of the late, great theater couple, Alfred Lunt and Lynn Fontanne. Subsequently, a double cream, baked French brie with blackberry puree makes a perfect companion to a tour. The Union House dates to 1861, so there is a lot of history to experience. See Chef John Mollet's recipe for **Pecan-Crusted Chicken with Kentucky Bourbon Sauce** on p. 308.

HISTORIC BURGERS IN EASTERN WISCONSIN

These three eastern Wisconsin eateries serve burgers the old-fashioned way: thick, juicy, and downright good, better, best. For years, our road trips have included pausing at these must-stop-at places.

Wayne's Drive-In, 1331 Covered Bridge Rd., Cedarburg, WI 53012; waynesdrivein.com; $. This circular little restaurant attracts motorcycle riders, retirees favoring the 10 percent senior-citizen discount, kids, softball teams, and just about anyone else who appreciates a steak sandwich, hamburgers, and old cars. Wayne's hosts classic cruise night on Thursday, where autos dating prior to 1987 are encouraged to show off their grilles. Just for the heck of it, we often stop here for a cheeseburger or Big Wayne Burger fix, perching at one of the inside tables. Wayne's is found at the Five Corners intersection just north of the Cedarburg city limits.

Kiltie Drive-In, 36154 E. Wisconsin Ave., Oconomowoc, WI 53066; (262) 567-2648; $. Summer doesn't officially begin until the grill is

Specialty Stores, Markets & Producers

J. Lauber's Ice Cream Parlor, 2010 Church St., East Troy, WI 53120; (262) 642-3679; Ice Cream; $. With its four-page menu of ice cream offerings, including 20 flavors of malts, you can't go wrong. Peruse the extensive candy selection while listening to music on the old jukebox. This is truly a kid place.

NuGenesis Farm, N68 W33208 Hwy. K, Oconomowoc, WI 53066; (800) 969-3588; nugenesisfarm.org. NuGenesis and Turtle Creek Gardens are committed to growing healthful produce. Founded

fired up at the Kiltie Drive-In. High school kids still deliver a tray of heaping burgers, done the same way for the past several generations. The Kiltie has been around for at least 60 years, according to longtime regulars. Nobody cares if there isn't inside seating. The Kiltie is ready-made for a traditional car-cruising culture, especially for anyone digging the homemade root beer that is consistently vanilla frothy. Order a round of shakes, cheeseburgers, and the occasional onion rings through the old-fashioned squawk box. Look for the red neon sign announcing the drive-in and you won't be led astray.

Kewpee's, 520 Wisconsin Ave., Racine, WI 53403; (262) 634-9601; kewpee.com; $. Sit at the counter and order a cheeseburger with all the trimmings, along with french fries and homemade root beer or a malt thick enough for an elephant to sit on. This is the way fast food should taste. The Kewpee's chain started in the 1920s, and it's where we go for a real burger, one with soul and a bit of fun history on the side. Tiny vintage Kewpee dolls are displayed throughout the restaurant.

in 2010 by three-time cancer survivor Kathy Bero, NuGenesis helps prevent disease, support your body through a chronic illness, and prevent recurrence through the food you eat. Food as medicine classes are regularly held here, taught by registered dietitians and chefs who want to keep you heart-healthy. The farm is a showcase for organic growing methods and outdoor, hands-on learning for kids and grownups.

River Valley Ranch & Kitchens, 39900 60th St., Burlington, WI 53105; (262) 539-3555; rivervalleykitchens.com. This is a prime place for securing the freshest mushrooms, along with onions, squash, and other veggies in season. The store is open 7 days a week, 364 days a year (closed Christmas Day). It's easy to find since the complex of

FARM STANDS FOR HARVEST FUN

Brightonwoods Orchard, 1072 288th Ave., Burlington, WI 53105; (262) 878-3000; brightonwoodsorchard.com.

Brower's Produce, W490 State Rd. 20, East Troy, Wisconsin 53120; (262) 642-5244.

fields, barns, mushroom growing houses, and the store are just 8 miles east of the beautiful resort area around Geneva Lake, located right off State Trunk Highway 50 and County Road P. You can also find products from the Ranch at Chicago- and Milwaukee-area farmers' markets, including Milwaukee's winter market at the Mitchell Park Horticultural Conservatory, better known locally as "The Domes." In 1976, Bill Rose and his son Eric founded the mushroom farm in the Fox River Valley, and in 1997, Eric established a commercial kitchen, turning out flavorful sauces, dips, salsas, and pickled veggies.

River's Edge Meat Market, 521 S. Main St. (State Highway 26), Jefferson, WI 53549; (920) 674-6466; riversedgemarket.com. This market is worth a stop for quality meats and locally grown produce, plus cheeses and luscious pastries. Folks here make their own rubs and marinades that are sold over the counter. The attached Edge Restaurant & Bakery features a full menu, with barbecued pulled pork a bestseller.

Rushing Waters Fisheries, N301 County Rd. H, Palmyra, WI 53156; (262) 495-2089; rushingwaters.net. Rushing Waters president Peter Fritsch often hosts spring morel mushroom hunts, as well as lunches in the Trout House and tours at his 80-acre farm. The surrounding woods carpet the rolling hills in the picturesque Kettle Moraine State Forest. In addition to fishing on-site, you can also order online or catch up with the gang at area farmers' markets.

Farm Markets for Plenty o' Goodies

Burlington Farmers' Market, at the corner of Washington and Pine Streets, Thurs, 3 to 7 p.m, May through Oct; (262) 210-6360; burlingtonwifarmersmarket.com.

East Troy Farmers' Market, at Wild Flour Bakery & Cafe, across from Frank's Piggly Wiggly, Fri, 3 to 7 p.m., late May through early Oct; (262) 642-3770; easttroywi.org/drupal2/east-troy-farmers-market.

Jefferson Farmers' Market, behind Jefferson City Hall at the corner of West Dodge Street and South Gardner Avenue, Thurs, 11 a.m. to 6 p.m., spring through early autumn; (920) 674-7700; jeffersonwis.com/Farmers%20Market.htm.

Kewaskum Farmers' Market, American Legion parking lot, 1538 Fond du Lac Ave., Thurs, 8 a.m. to 3 p.m., early June through mid-Oct; (262) 626-3350.

Lake Country Farmers' Market, County Road C and Highway K, Stone Bank, Thurs, 3 to 6 p.m., June 6 through Sept 26; (262) 966-1800.

Oconomowoc Summer Farmers' Market, South Municipal Parking Lot behind 175 E. Wisconsin Ave., Sat, 7:30 a.m. to noon, mid-May through late October; (262) 567-2666; oconomowoc.org/calendar/summer-farmers-market.

Sturtevant Farmers' Market, Fountain Banquet Hall, 8505 Durand Ave., Mon, late May through late Oct; (262) 260-8224; ladyglory96@yahoo.com.

Waukesha Farmers' Market, Riverfront Plaza off Barstow (between Barstow and Broadway, south of the Fox River), Sat, 8 a.m. to noon, early May to late Oct; (262) 547-2354; waukeshafarmersmarket.com.

StoneBank Baking Company, W335 N6805 Stone Bank Rd., Oconomowoc, WI 53066; (262) 966-2200; shop.stonebankbaking .com. The bakery specializes in sponge doughs, all-natural ingredients, and made-from-scratch items. Often when we stop in at our nearby Fresh Market grocery store, we buy a bag of StoneBank's heart-healthy snacks, including the mint chocolate chip or the strawberry chocolate walnut cookies. They are baked without chemicals, preservatives, or trans fats, with minimal cholesterol and saturated fat and no added sodium.

Sweet Mullets Brewing Company, N58 W39800 Industrial Rd., Oconomowoc, WI 53066; (262) 456-2843; sweetmulletsbrewing .com. The brewmeister here creates award-winning beverages,  and the gang produces several really exotic beers, such as a jalapeño light-bodied ale; the Pumpkinstein, with roasted pumpkin and pumpkin-pie spices; and a full-bodied Rye Bob, made with 43 percent rye. Cheese pairings, beer and cheddar flights, fish tacos, and small plates are among the menu items.

Yuppie Hill Poultry, W1384 Potter Rd., Burlington WI 53105; (262) 210-0264; yuppiehillpoultry.com. Lynn Lein began farming with her father in 1999 and started raising chickens for eggs. Soon she was providing eggs for area restaurants and farmers' markets around Southeastern Wisconsin. The original main barn, which once housed 2,500 hens, now houses a cafe that serves delicacies such as smoked chicken and Chippewa wild rice soup. In 2008, she built a new barn on the north side of the property.

Central Wisconsin

Where to start and end the counties that make up the wide swath of central Wisconsin is open to geographical interpretation. So for conversation's sake, let's talk about enumerating food favorites from the Wisconsin-Illinois state line on the south to State Highway 29 on the north, which is sometimes called the "relief of tension" line. Those in the tourism world say that since most of the state's hectic urban centers are below that demarcation, life is slower and more vacation-like above that. Be that as it may, regardless of how the state is divided, there are plenty of food choices. So let's now tackle Wisconsin's midstate with its organic farms, dairies, outdoor markets, high-end restaurants, and great pub grub. While on your journey around the region, be sure to eat plenty of Wisconsin cheese and count the cows. For the record, there are approximately 1,260,000 dairy cows in Wisconsin, the average number of dairy cows per Wisconsin farm is 98, and a happy Wisconsin dairy cow averages 6.7 gallons of milk per day or 206 gallons of milk per month.

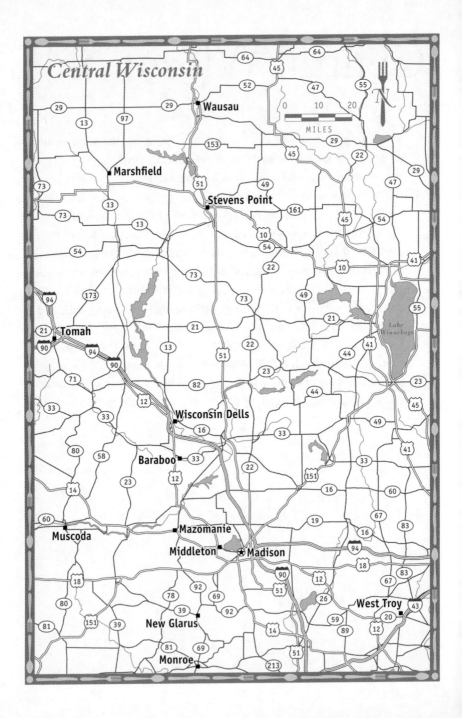

Madison

Madison is the capital of Wisconsin and the county seat of Dane County, with a 2011 estimated population of 236,901, making it the second-largest city in Wisconsin after Milwaukee. These folks love to eat. For a partial listing of the city's eateries, check in with Greater Madison Convention and Visitors Bureau (CVB), 615 E. Washington Ave., Madison, WI 53703 (608-255-2537 or 800-373-6376; visitmadison.com/restaurants/all-restaurants). The CVB's informational website breaks out the array of eating options as waterfront, outdoor, sweet treat, breakfast and brunch, world flavor, and farm to table, along with food events and tours, plus breweries, wineries, and spirits.

Foodie Faves

Alchemy Cafe, 1980 Atwood Ave., Madison, WI 53704; (608) 204-7644; alchemycafe.net; New American; $–$$. Chef Matthia Melchizedek makes culinary magic with whopping, thick-cut onion rings prepared in a house-made beer batter with herb buttermilk, árbol chile, and citrus barbecue sauces. His sweet potato fries are also to die for, twice fried and served with tarragon mayo and organic blackberry jam. These sides are among the most creative in a city where ingenuity in the kitchen is taken for granted. Hamburgers can be a dime a dozen, so how about trying an Alchemy buffalo melt, with patties from a farm

Ice Cream, We All Scream for Ice Cream

The **University of Wisconsin's Babcock Ice Cream** is served in the **Babcock Hall Dairy Store,** Union South, or the UW Memorial Union. There's nothing like enjoying a hearty dish or cone of ice cream while lolling lakeside at the student Union Terrace. At Babcock, the world-famous ice cream comes in a variety of flavors, with our favorites being chocolate turtle or a simple vanilla. You can also order a toasted On Swissconsin ham and cheese on rye bread or a Wisconsin Swing, with turkey, bacon, and cheddar and Monterey Jack cheeses, with chives and lettuce. Coffee is done up by Madison's Ancora Coffee Roasters, whose Dark Thunder packs a punch. On Football Saturday, the cafe is open until 5:30 p.m. The Dairy Store is located at 1605 Linden Dr., Madison, WI 53703 (608-262-3045; babcockhalldairystore.wisc.edu).

Built in 1951, the plant is the oldest university dairy building in the country and is named after Stephen Moulton Babcock, a hard-working research professor in the agricultural chemistry department. Moulton invented the initial reliable butterfat content milk test in 1890, which was a great boost for the Dairy State's cow crowd. Guided tours for 10 or more folks include a stop on the second-story observation deck that overlooks the plant. Tours are free, but if you want a taste sample, there is a small fee. Or you can opt for a self-guided tour. The hall is the home of the Department of Food Sciences, which is part of the university's College of Agricultural and Life Sciences. The butterfat content ranges from 12 percent for regular ice cream to 17 percent for super-premium ice cream. It's all due to contented cows. Milk is secured from the university's own cows and purchased from several local farms.

in Cambridge, Wisconsin, just up the road from the State Capitol. Add roasted shallots, fresh melted Wisconsin mozzarella, tomato, and thyme on a freshly baked roll—and don't forget the garlic mayo. Locally grown produce is used for the salads, the peanut butter is made in house, and the ample supply of vegan and vegetarian dishes are well marked on the menu. For a bonus, there's free live music nightly, whether bluegrass, funk, folk, or jam rock. Noted Wisconsin musicians also show up, such as guitarist Jim Schwall hosting the Madison Songwriters' Guild Song Showdown and open mike.

The Blue Marlin, 101 N. Hamilton St., Madison, WI 53703; (608) 255-2255; thebluemarlin.net; Seafood; $$–$$$. All streets lead to The Blue Marlin, a historic commercial building at the intersection of East Washington, North Hamilton, Mifflin, and North Pinckney Streets in downtown Madison. Parking is close at hand on the street or in nearby parking structures. The Blue Marlin remains a favorite fine-dining outlet in the state capital. The cornmeal-crusted trout, poached sea scallops, and seared prawns are always at the top of our eating-out wish list. The comprehensive wine list covers some 80 labels. Reservations are suggested because space is limited, especially for the highly valued outdoor seating in the summer.

Brasserie V, 1923 Monroe St., Madison, WI 53711; (608) 255-8500; brasseriev.com; Bistro; $–$$. The kitchen in this neighborhood eatery and taproom is orchestrated by Chef Rob Grisham, whose European-inspired brasserie offers more than 150 beers and features a menu with many Wisconsin cheeses. Lunch and dinner are served daily, with only a light menu on Sunday. Chalkboards above the dark wood bar announce the regularly changing specials, yet the dinner menu always features a 12-ounce steak, plus frites. The Jacobson Brothers' duck sausages with carrot-maple puree is a culinary gift and particularly flavorful. The Brasserie V pitches Wisconsin producers, which include **Potter's Crackers** (p. 225), Bleu Mont Dairy, Hook's

Order and Then Sit Back

EatStreet makes Madison food delivery fast and convenient. This is a free, online ordering service that connects diners with their favorite local restaurants. EatStreet sends the order to the restaurant, which you can either pick up or have delivered. Among the participating restaurants are Pizza di Rome, Taco Shop, Cheba Hut, and Gumby's Pizza. Five percent of the profits go to Madison charities such as Habitat for Humanity, the Dane County Humane Society, and similar organizations. Contact the folks here at customer.service@eatstreet.com or call (866) 654-8777.

Cheese, Garden To Be, and Harmony Valley Farms, among others. Linger over desserts? The Pinkoko French dark chocolate confections are sweet-tooth favorites. Live music includes the mellow singing of Nick Moran and Megan Hamm or that of another performer.

The Coopers Tavern, 20 W. Mifflin St., Madison, WI 53703; (608) 256-1600; thecooperstavern.com; New American; $–$$. Chef Tim Larsen comes up with great presentations, often reflecting proprietor Peter McElvanna's Gaelic heritage. One is a Sconnie, or Scotch egg (a hard-boiled egg wrapped in a fried Knoche's Market brat patty), served with house pickles and husky mustard. For another appetizer, try the roast beef rockets, with jalapeños, cheese curds, and mashed potatoes. Comfort foods include mac 'n' cheese with a twist, topped with roasted pork belly from Fox Valley Farms and Guinness stout. The restaurant is downtown on Capitol Square.

Edo Japanese Restaurant, 532 S. Park St., Madison, WI 53715; (608) 268-0247; edojapanesewi.com; Japanese; $–$$. Edo's offers appetizers, sushi, teriyaki, and other traditional Japanese foods.

Underground Goes Above ground with Good grub

Forequarter, 708 E. Johnson St., Madison, WI 53703; (608) 609-4717; undergroundfoodcollective.org/forequarter; $–$$. This is a collective of classically trained and learn-as-you-go chefs who prepare handcrafted meats. There is no set food fare because, as they say here, "We don't believe in set menus because what tastes good varies from season to season and from year to year." The collective's classes and cooking demos earn rave reviews. The folks here also operate the **Underground Food Collective,** 931 E. Main St., Madison, WI 53703 (608-338-1527), and the **Underground Butcher,** 811 Williamson St., Madison, WI 53703 (608-338-3421). The collective sells products wholesale, focusing on restaurants and markets, as well as through its community supported agriculture (CSA) consumer clients. The collective partners with vendors such as Just Coffee, Sylvan Meadows for lamb and beef, **Driftless Organics** (p. 289), Cherokee Bison Farms, Fountain Prairie Farms for its prized Highland cattle, and Snug Haven Farm for spinach and other greens. The group has even taken its guerrilla philosophies to New York City to showcase its talents. The collective also participates in the Bike the Barns annual cycling adventure through central Wisconsin's lush farm country. The proceeds benefit low-income families, helping them purchase local, fresh produce. Forequarter sponsors "A Celebration of the Pre-Industrial Pig," with times and dates about a fabulous down-home pork-based meal spread via word-of-mouth and social networking.

Daily takeout and delivery is popular with University of Wisconsin students living in the area.

Graze Gastropub, 1 S. Pinckney St., Madison, WI 53703; (608) 251-2700; grazemadison.com; Bistro; $$. Graze is L'Etoile's (p. 216) adjacent "brother" for more casual dining, featuring 12 Wisconsin craft beers, along with an expanded wine list. Graze's light menu includes oysters on the half shell and charcuterie after midnight. Graze presents grass-fed beef, acorn- and whey-fed hogs, artesian trout, and cave-aged cheeses. Among their providers are Blue Valley Gardens, Blue Mounds, Jones Valley Farm in Spring Green, and Fountain Prairie Farm in Fall River. See Graze's recipe for **Grilled New York Strip Steak with Sungold Tomatoes, Fava Beans, Fresh Mozzarella & Basil Vinaigrette** on p. 302.

The Great Dane Pub & Brewing Co., 123 E. Doty St. Madison, WI 53703; (608) 284-0000; greatdanepub.com; Casual American: $. Founded in 1994, The Great Dane is proud of its mahogany bar and numerous beers, ales, and lagers. Each season also features a specialty brew. The bar emphasizes hearty pours and having fun, with its billiards lounge, beer garden, lounge, gift shop, and pool hall. You won't be barking up the wrong tree at the Great Dane if hunting for quality brews. Look for Peck's pilsner, Crop Circle wheat, Devil's Lake red lager, and its stout. The place also has a great whiskey collection. Great Dane also has two other brewpubs in Madison on Midvale Boulevard at Price Place (608-661-9400), or eastside, located on Cottage Grove Road at Jupiter Drive (608-442-1333). Two other facilities are located outside Madison: 2980 Cahill Main, Fitchburg, WI 53711 (608-442-9000), and 2305 Sherman St., Wausau, WI 54401 (715-845-3000).

Ha Long Bay, 1353 Williamson St., Madison, WI 53703; (608) 255-2868; hlbmadison.com; Asian; $–$$. Named after the picturesque bay in Vietnam, this family-owned restaurant has earned five stars from hungry reviewers. The noodle dishes are appropriately tasty and the Thai curries appropriately hot. Go for the fried squid, tossed with salt, pepper, onion, and hot pepper and presented on bed of lettuce. The chicken with shiitake mushrooms, garlic, and ginger is considered among the best in town. All the lunch specials come with steamed rice and a choice of cucumber salad or the soup du jour. Vegetarians go for the deep-fried tofu dipped in a house sesame sauce.

Harmony Bar & Grill, 2201 Atwood Ave., Madison, WI 53704; (608) 249-4333; Casual American; $. The Harmony has a great and well-earned reputation as Madison's dumpiest bar with the best food. We often drop in here whenever visiting Mad City, whether for a cheeseburger, barbecued pork, or veggie burger. The longtime regulars, all of whom are characters, prop up their elbows on the long wooden bar. The Harmony has regular live entertainment, as well as a fabulous jukebox selection of jazz, blues, classic rock, and classic country. This is a cash-only joint, as is any good, old-fashioned dive with panache.

Inka Heritage, 602 S. Park St., Madison, WI 53715; (608) 310-4282; inkaheritagerestaurant.com; Peruvian; $$–$$$. Demonstrating the diversity of Peru and its mix of cultures, Inka offers a wide range of interesting items such as *jalea,* a melange of shrimp, calamari, crab legs, black mussels, tilapia, and yucca, along with a smooth Creole sauce. The *tacu tacu* is a rice and bean pancake that has been grilled and then served with bite-size beef tenderloin, onion, tomatoes, and plenty of fresh cliantro. The Inka serves a wide range of Spanish, Chilean, and Argentinian wines. Executive Chef Esmeralda Bascones was born in Lima and is well-known around Madison for her delicious designer pastries.

Ironworks Cafe, 149 Waubesa St., Madison, WI 53704; (608) 241-1574; goodmancenter.org/services/ironworks-cafe; Sandwich Shop; $. At the Ironworks Cafe, students learn to use fresh, local food made with seasonal ingredients and pick up management and business skills. The cafe partners with East High School's alternative education program, with professional restaurateurs acting as mentors. The facility features classical music in the background, so eating here is really a mellow experience. Be aware that the Ironworks is open only from 7 a.m. to 3:30 p.m., Tues through Fri, with a weekend brunch on Sat and Sun from 9 a.m. to 3 p.m. It's best to call ahead to be  sure the kitchen is up and running because of the kids' school schedules. Entrees change almost weekly, but smoked trout crostini is always a favorite. Vegetarian options are always available. The blueberry scones made here are also marvels.

Marigold Kitchen, 118 S. Pinckney St., Madison, WI 53703; (608) 661-5559; marigoldkitchen.com; Casual American; $–$$. In their marketing info, the Marigold crew insists, "Don't just sit there, being hungry. Stop by for creative healthy food prepared by friendly folk." The perking **Colectivo** (p. 69) coffee lures a crowd every morning, taking in a newspaper to read before heading to the office or to the university. Chef Kristy Schwinn's breakfasts are masterpieces, especially her sandwich made with a fried organic egg, cheddar-spiked Boursin, and applewood-smoked bacon, with tomato and green onion on toasted ciabatta. The Marigold is only a block off Capitol Square, making it a convenient stop for any early morning business meetings. Daily specials for lunch might include an organic gazpacho or a ham, red bean, and collard greens soup.

Nostrano, 111 S. Hamilton St., Madison, WI 53703; (608) 395-3295; nostranomadison.com; New American; $$. For lunch, a whitefish sandwich always seems so satisfying, yet the fennel sausage is another temptation. For dinner, go for the grilled guinea hen or the rabbit boudin. Sometimes, it's just nice to sit still, converse with your significant other or friend and down a draught Hoppy Feet from Clown Shoes Brewery in Ipswich, Massachusetts, or sip a martini made with St. George Botanivore gin, with its touches of Cocchi Americano, an Italian aperitif wine. The Nostrano staff is always coming up with such new and exciting drinks and can even suggest a beverage that goes well with the restaurant's grilled octopus. You can be assured of a memorable meal here.

The Old Fashioned Tavern & Restaurant, 23 N. Pinckney St., Madison, WI 53703; (608) 310-4545; theoldfashioned .com; $$; Casual American; $–$$. Madisonites flock to The Old Fashioned for happy hour specials. Founded in 2005, the place has a timeless feel. Grilled eggplant, portobello mushroom, roasted red pepper and zucchini, with goat cheese and black olive tapenade on toasted country bread add a contemporary culinary touch. Grass-fed beef burgers are staples. Remember to add the fried onions, slices of smoked bacon, aged cheddar, garlic sauce, and a soft-cooked egg. The toasted roll has been lovingly buttered. The Old Fashioned loves the local touch, with **Ruef's Meat Market** (p. 246) supplying *Landjaeger* sausages, and beef hot dogs from Baranek's Farm served on a bun from **Clasen's European Bakery** (p. 219). For "wild times," the restaurant holds a karaoke night on Wednesday.

Pat O'Malley's Jet Room Restaurant, 3606 Corben Ct., Madison, WI 53704; (608) 268-5010; jetroomrestaurant.com; Casual American; $–$$. Located at the Madison airport, this is one of the city's secret gems. Capitalizing on the site, menu items have an airline theme. For instance, The Pilot is an omelet made with applewood-smoked bacon, American cheese, fresh mushrooms, and sour cream. The

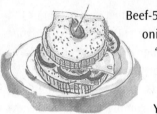

Beef-52 is made of thinly sliced roast beef, sautéed onions, and swiss cheese on grilled marble rye. "This sandwich has never bombed," asserted one of the waitstaff with all seriousness. The Jet Room is open only for breakfast and lunch. Yes, there is a real Pat O'Malley, who ran the O'Malley Farm Cafe in Waunakee for about two decades before taking a year off to sell real estate. He bounded back into the restaurant world when the airport became an option. This is a no-frills eatery, yet one with fun views of planes taking on and off. The restaurant is on the far north side of Truax Field.

A Pig in a Fur Coat, 940 Williamson St., Madison, WI 53703; (608) 316-3300; apiginafurcoat.com; Bistro; $–$$. Despite the quirky name, Pig has a fantastically varied menu, with the unfamiliar blended with the tried and true. Giving it a buzz, duck fat fries, rabbit *rillettes,* and pork belly paired with butternut squash fit in perfectly with the smoked sardines, smoked salmon, and 30-day dry-aged strip. The bread pudding deserves a mention, with its white chocolate, cherries, pecan, and caramel gelato. Local produce and providers are emphasized, with Jade Mountain Coffee & Tea, True Coffee Roasters, Underground Meats, and Jordandal Farms among them. The interior is sleek, polished, and a fine backdrop for the food displays that fly out of the kitchen. The restaurant's title is a play on a Kazakhstan dish called "fish in a fur coat," discovered when the owner's sister worked in the Peace Corps.

Quivey's Grove, 6261 Nesbitt Rd., Madison, WI 53719; (608) 273-4900; quiveysgrove.com; Traditional American; $$–$$$. Back in the 1850s, this complex of buildings was one of the top livery stables in the region. The Stone House restaurant and the Stable Grill there harken back to that era with a fieldstone look. The menu items are named after various historical Wisconsin figures, such as the Beef Barstow, a center-cut boneless rib eye steak, pan-seared and served on

Dairyland Cheese Potatoes, with roasted mushrooms and onions in red wine sauce. This dish at the Stone House honors William Barstow, the governor who resigned when the Wisconsin Supreme Court invalidated his 1856 election because of voting irregularities; he went on to become a Union general during the Civil War. The Stable Grill recognizes one of Madison's suburbs with its Monona Meatloaf and the nearby village of Lodi with the Lodi Sausage Sampler.

Sardine, 617 Williamson St., Madison, WI 53703; (608) 441-1600; **sardinemadison.com; Bistro; $$–$$$.** A diner can't go wrong when starting out with a platter of oysters, warm goat cheese, and crostini with a petite arugula salad, or fried smelt with a goodly portion of pickled cabbage and dazzled with tartar sauce. There isn't a real Moroccan sardine on the menu, but the grilled Norwegian salmon, French lentils, sautéed spinach, portobello mushrooms, tomatoes, and beurre blanc would please even King Oscar. We regularly drive in to Madison for one the Sardine's Monday ethnic dinners. Get there early for the hors d'oeuvres and then enjoy a Greek or Tuscan dinner with the appropriate wines. Servings are family style, a good way to meet one's elbowmates at the table, who may include a university researcher, a doctor, a farmer, and an electrical engineer. The bistro is on the west shore of Lake Monona in Machinery Row, a complex of old factories, a brewery, and other historic commercial properties.

Smoky's Club, 3005 University Ave., Madison, WI 53705; (608) 233-2120; **smokysclub.com; Steak House; $$–$$$.** Take no notice of that stuffed shark hanging above the bar because you come here for steak and martinis. This is old-world eating and drinking, complete with a traditional relish tray that features marinated herring. The chefs here proudly serve cuts they boast are as thick as "two fists atop each other." Smoky's Martini Club claims more than 1,500 members and over a hundred different

WHEN IN WISCONSIN, SAY CHEESE

When one says "cheese" in Madison, the Dairy State's capital, everyone smiles. Rightly so. Madison is surrounded by numerous internationally acclaimed cheese producers within a short drive of Capitol Square. Nearby Green County alone has some 13 cheese plants, each barely a 45-minute drive from the governor's office, even when driving within the speed limit.

This is a city that prides itself on knowing and rewarding good cheese. After all, Madison is the home site of the World Cheese Competition, attracting more than 2,000 entries from 20 countries. The annual Wisconsin Original Cheese Festival at Madison's Monona Terrace always draws attendees from around the state, just to sample product made by dozens of Wisconsin's best cheesemakers. For information on cheese, as well as other dairy products, the gang at the Wisconsin Milk Marketing Board are truly in the know. You can contact them at 8418 Excelsior Dr., Madison, WI 53717 (608-203-7235; eatwisconsincheese.com).

kinds of martinis. Soups are made from scratch, and beets are hand-pickled. Janet and Leonard "Smoky" Schmock opened their restaurant in 1953, now run by their sons Larry and Tom. Some of their staffers have worked here more than a quarter of century, so they know their stuff. So when craving steak in Mad City, Smoky's is the place to go.

Taj Indian Restaurant, 1256 S. Park St., Madison, WI 53715; (608) 268-0772; thetajindianrestaurant.com; Indian; $–$$. The mulligatawny soup with lentils and spiced vegetables topped with cilantro help get dinner started. For seafood lovers, basic shrimp dishes include curried, vindaloo, saag, *jalfraize,* mushroom, and masala styles. Regulars often opt for a tandoori or Taj's mixed grill with chicken, chicken tikka, lamb, and *reshmi* kebabs and tandoori shrimp, dished up with fresh onions and a plethora of green peppers. For testimonials, there are numerous framed awards and happy customer letters covering the entryway walls.

Landmarks

Ella's Deli and Ice Cream Parlor, 2902 E. Washington Ave., Madison, WI 53704; (608) 241-5291; ellasdeli.com; Sandwich Shop; $–$$. We've enjoyed Ella's for years, even when it was first located on State Street. The original place opened in the early 1960s as a deli and grocery. Now located on the city's east side since 1976, Ella's has all sorts of kitschy indoor displays featuring animated jugglers, flying acrobats, wizards, and a Beatles diorama among other attractions that keep kids distracted while waiting for their food. Ella's also features a 1927 carousel on the front lawn. When its protective tarps come down after a winter hiatus, area residents know that spring officially is here. And the food? Ella's house-made chicken matzo-ball noodle soup and the chili are winners. Try the Sizzler, with pastrami, aged swiss cheese, sauerkraut, and grilled rye bread, or a jumbo platter of tongue, corned beef, cheese, tomato, and more pastrami. The Wisconsin Five Cheese Burger is also dynamite. Bagels come as plain, whole wheat, cinnamon raisin, or onion. For exotica, you might want to have a jelly and peanut butter omelet.

Harvest Restaurant, 21 N. Pinckney St., Madison, WI 53703; (608) 255-6075; harvest-restaurant.com; New American; $$$. Harvest is praised for its ever-evolving menu using Wisconsin's organic, local foods. Harvest Restaurant has been featured in *Gourmet* magazine as one of the country's best farm-to-table restaurants. Dishes such as grilled fresh asparagus, complemented with farro, spinach, and a house-made ricotta cheese are as fine-tuned as the major entrees, such as house-made tagliatelle pasta with pork sausage, arugula, garlic, and chile flakes. The restaurant is located in the heart of the city with a view of the State Capitol. Cheese is big at Harvest, with Edelweiss Creamery, Hidden Springs, Roelli, and Seymour Dairy among the 16 or so Wisconsin cheesemakers on the menu. A make-your-own cheese plate is a must-eat, with the bartender helping with wine and beer complements. There's no dress code at the Harvest where the motto is, "We will never tell you what to wear. Come as you are."

Jamerica Caribbean Restaurant, 1236 Williamson St., Madison, WI 53703; (608) 251-6234; jamericarestaurant.com; Caribbean; $–$$. Located across from the **Willy Street Co-op** (p. 226), Jamerica is tiny and casual but you can count on authentic Caribbean cuisine. Of course, there are the traditional fried plantains and jerk chicken. You can also get pepper-pot callaloo soup, dumplings with fritters, and Mango Rundown Catfish. You can find Red Stripe beer, ginger beer, mango nectar, and Ting soda in the cooler at the back of the restaurant. Owner Martin Deacon was born and raised in Port Antonio on the northeastern coast of Jamaica, some 60 miles from Kingston. Deacon always seems to be cheerful and as sunny as the skies over his native island.

L'Etoile, 1 S. Pinckney St., Madison, WI 53703; (608) 251-0500; letoile-restaurant.com; French; $$–$$$$. Since 1976, L'Etoile ("The Star") has delighted area gourmets who love the dishes prepared by Executive Chef Tory Miller, a James Beard "Best Chef Midwest" winner. He partners in the restaurant with his longtime friend Dianne Christensen. Their menu changes seasonally, with most of the ingredients being locally sourced, even from its root cellar produce in the winter. In the spring, Miller might serve roasted Blue Valley Gardens asparagus, with Korean barbecued pork belly, shallots, radish, and kimchee vinaigrette.

Special dinners at L'Etoile are out-of-this-world wonderful, including tributes to such regional cuisines as those from Spain or Provence. Wine dinners and tastings are regularly scheduled. *Gourmet* magazine called L'Etoile one of the country's top 50 restaurants. When we want a Madison exceptional dining experience, one with tablecloths and candles, L'Etoile is where we head. Stop in for more casual fare at L'Etoile's adjacent gastropub, **Graze** (see p. 208). See Executive Chef Tory Miller's recipe for **Grilled New York Strip Steak with Sungold Tomatoes, Fava Beans, Fresh Mozzarella & Basil Vinaigrette** on p. 302.

Monty's Blue Plate Diner, 2089 Atwood Ave., Madison, WI 53704; (608) 244-8505; montysblueplatediner.com; Casual American; $–$$. This is a neighborhood gathering spot, which keeps Monty's busy, especially since breakfast is served throughout the day. Sweet potato hash is made with peppers, onions, and zucchini and spices, grilled and then served with two eggs any style. You can also substitute tofu scramble for a vegan breakfast. For a surprise lunch treat, try the meatless meat loaf. We won't divulge the ingredients. You'll just have to stop here and try it. There are many gluten-free menu items, and you can still indulge in the fabulous hot fudge brownie sundae, a delight made with Sassy Cow Creamery ice cream. You won't feel too, too guilty afterward. Well, okay, maybe just a bit.

Specialty Shops, Markets & Producers

Bavaria Sausage, Inc., 6317 Nesbitt Rd., Fitchburg, WI 53719; (608) 836-7100; bavariasausage.com. With its exterior Teutonic façade, you know you've come to the right *Wursthaus*. The shop is in a western Madison suburb, but claims a Madison area clientele. Everything sold here is *wunderbar,* simply wonderful. Authenticity is the watchword, with *Aufschnitt* (cold cuts), salami, *Sulze, Schinken* (ham), and *Wurstsalat*. If that's not enough to get into a Teutonic mood, head home with bags of *Landjaeger*, summer sausage, wild game sausage, and steak jerky. The dedicated shopper can also find mustards, chocolate, cheese, kraut, and bratwurst. This is a family-run operation, with meaty products without fillers, additives, artificial coloring, Liquid Smoke, or MSG. Look for the weisswurst, a traditional Bavarian sausage crafted from minced veal and pork. The sausage, a favorite served around Oktoberfest, is usually flavored with parsley, lemon, and complementary taste treats that shall remain close to the sausagemaker's vest.

Brennan's Market, 5533 University Ave., Madison, WI 53705; (608) 233-2777; and 8210 Watts Rd., Madison, WI 53719; (608) 833-2893; brennansmarket.com. Back in 1942, Frank Brennan opened a fruit stand in Green County and began selling local cheese for sale. His son Skip now runs the five-store company and uses many of the same

 suppliers as did his dad. Brennan's focuses on Wisconsin artisanals, spreads, and even those famous squeaky cheese curds. The firm's headquarters are in Swiss-founded New Glarus, about 45 minutes south of Madison and in the heart of Wisconsin's cheese country. For lovers of all things exotic, Brennan's emphasizes flavored cheddars such as horseradish, blue cheese, maple syrup, and even one with a touch of Chilean Merlot. Brennan worked with Jeff Wideman, master cheesemaker at Maple Leaf Cheese in Monroe, to create a cranberry cheddar. The combination of these two top Wisconsin products is a customer favorite.

Capital Brewery, 7734 Terrace Ave., Middleton, WI 53562; (608) 836-7100; capital-brewery.com. Wisconsin Amber, a rich malty lager with a slight hop zing, is the flagship beer at Capital. On the other hand, the lightly hopped Lake House is one of Capital's several seasonals, best sipped on a hot summer afternoon. These are just two of the wide selection of Capital's thirst-quenching offerings. The brewery, which opened more than 25 years ago, was one of the first in the country to produce craft beers. Its *Biergarten,* which is open from spring through October, is among the best places in Madison to hunker down and do some serious beverage tasting. Brews from other outlets and a selection of wines are options. Pet lovers like the fact that dogs are welcomed on the patio; just be sure that Fido is leashed. Free live music is regularly booked on Thursday and Friday. The brewery doesn't have a kitchen, but you can bring in your own food or call a local restaurant for deliveries. A hall is available for inclement weather and winter sipping. We're glad that Capital makes beer drinking so easy.

Clasen's European Bakery, 7610 Donna Dr., Middleton, WI 53562; (608) 831-2032; clasensbakery.com. Baked goods almost seem to fly off the shelf on any given morning, so come early to this landmark Madison bakery. Known for its croissants, Clasen's has the traditional flaky butter style, but also a ham and cheese, spinach and feta, turkey and cheddar, boysenberry, chocolate, or almond. Food authors such as Madison writer Mary Bergin regularly drop by for book signings. Particularly chewy and good are the farmers sourdough, alpine six-grain, and French country cracked wheat breads. You'll never go wrong with the sweet pastries. For instance, Clasen's Easter egg tortes are made of yellow cake, layered with vanilla buttercream and raspberry preserves, and then coated in rich dark chocolate—what a way to celebrate a holiday—or for overall decadence, go for the Black Forest torte, a chocolate cake, brushed with kirsch, and then layered with cherries and vanilla buttercream. Take home a bag of macaroons. Clasen's has been around for more than 50 years.

Fraboni's Italian Specialties, 822 Regent St., Madison, WI 53715; (608) 256-0546. Fraboni's has been a Madison fixture since 1971, for anyone in need of olive oil, with Sicilian Partana, Cucina Viva, Lucini, Santa Chiava, and Raineri among the several dozen extra-virgin varieties. Among the organics are San Giuliano Alghero Organic, Paesano, and Iliada Kalamata Organic. Fraboni's also has

unfiltered and pure oils, plus vinegar, pasta in dozens of shapes, and tomato products. Julius Caesar might have been a deli regular at Fraboni's if he had known about the 11 varieties of homemade submarine sandwiches. Another Fraboni's location is at 108 Owen Rd., Monona, WI 53716 (608-222-6632).

Fromagination Cheese Store, 12 S. Carroll St., Madison, WI 53703; (608) 255-2430; fromagination.com. Madison's premier artisan cheese store bursts with cheese, cheese, and cheese, and includes many Wisconsin brands favored by owner Ken Monteleone. Across the street from the State Capitol, Fromagination is happily ensconced in a building built in the early 1900s and renovated with reclaimed slate floors and brightly painted walls. For breakfast and lunch, customers flock around tables made from rescued Wisconsin barn wood. As a green space, with recycled and found objects put to work again, such as clocks from the old Capitol building dating from 1917, the store exudes a laid-back charm. Cheese-savvy locals, students, and ever-present tourists mingle over lunches of **Nueske's** (p. 245) smoked ham with **Roth Käse** (p. 246) fontina, lettuce, grainy mustard, and Natural Acres honey, plus a side of cornichons. Fromagination's signature side salad consists of fresh baby greens, juicy grape tomatoes, roasted red pepper, and grated SarVecchio cheese from Sartori Foods in Plymouth, Wisconsin. Monteleone also sells a wide selection of other state products, from reserves and jellies to Madison-made **Potter's Crackers** (p. 225) and various Wisconsin sausages.

Gotham Bagels, 112 E. Mifflin St., Madison, WI 53703; (608) 467-7642; gothambagels.com. Chef Scott Prentiss and Owner Joe Gaglio believe that New York–style "bagels are it." Whether sitting in or taking out, start with the basic hand-rolled, fresh-from-the-oven bagel with the smoked salmon and cream cheese. They'll bag up a New York dozen (13 bagels) for carryout. Lots of drop-in customers go for the value-added options, such as build-your-own servings of bagels and add-ons that can feed up to 12 to 15 hungry people. This hefty sack of bagels includes three 1-pound portions of turkey, chicken, egg, and tuna salads, plus eggplant crisps or kosher salami, along with arugula, tomato, red onion, pickles, mayo, and that ubiquitous yellow deli mustard. Gotham also has a wide variety of regular sandwiches and salads, each with a New York name such as Spanish Harlem shredded pork, Dyker Heights corned beef, and Brooklyn chopped salad.

Greenbush Bakery, 1305 Regent St., Madison, WI 53715; (608) 257-1151. This has been a certified kosher kitchen since 1998, serving some of the best glazed cake doughnuts and apple fritters in the world. Rarely can anyone walk out of this store without at least a raspberry-filled chocolate or a pumpkin variety, and toss in a sour cream for good measure. You won't find a loaf of bread here, just doughnuts and more doughnuts. Since this hideaway is so popular, morning is a mad rush for an easy, on-the-go breakfast.

Madison Sourdough Co., 916 Williamson St., Madison, WI 53705; (608) 442-8009; madisonsourdough.com. Bakers begin their labor of love around 1 a.m. According to the company, it takes a 36-hour cycle from start to finish to produce a loaf of its bread. The hops and malt beer bread, a sesame fennel baguette, classic white sourdough, and caraway rye are among the top sellers. The store's cafe, with its wooden tables and comfortable antique-looking chairs, serves

Sweet Home, Madison

DB Infusion Chocolates, 550 N. Midvale Blvd., Madison, WI 53705; (608) 233-1600; infusionchocolates.com. Oh, that heavenly perfume of fresh chocolate. Founder/former owner David Bacco studied at the French Culinary School in Chicago where he learned the techniques of creating marvelous chocolate creations. After working at several Madison-area restaurants, he opened his own store in 2008, a few blocks from **The Great Dane Pub & Brewing Co.** (p. 208). Subsequently, we can enjoy two vices between a short walk. You can even sip cups of flavored chocolate; at last count there were four. Bacco now lives in Southern California, bringing his love of sweets to the foodies on the coast.

Gail Ambrosius Chocolatier, 2086 Atwood Ave., Madison, WI 53704; (608) 249-3500; gailambrosius.com. Why is Madison so lucky to have so many chocolate manufacturers? Among them, Gail Ambrosius stands tall. *Dessert Professional* magazine has named the company one of the top 10 chocolatiers in North America. This designation is well deserved. To find the shop, look for the bright orange awnings. Ambrosius herself grew up on a Wisconsin dairy farm, one of 10 kids. Her mom made a marvelous chocolate pudding, so Ambrosius named one of her chocolates Lucille's Vanilla after her mom, Lucille. Ambrosius studied with the Valrhona and Cluizel chocolatiers in France to hone her craft and regularly visits her

breakfast and lunch. Guests can perch there and enjoy pancakes, roast beef sandwiches, and veggie burgers. At 2:30 p.m., the shop offers an afternoon menu to pair with the store's beer and wine selections, taking orders until 4:30 p.m. Executive Chef Molly Maciejewski cures and smokes her own hams and salmon and concocts sweet and loving preserves and jazzy pickled vegetables. Partnering suppliers are local, including Lonesome Stone Milling in Lone Rock and Kickapoo Coffee from Viroqua.

cacao bean producers in Costa Rica. She and her staff of 10 produce several thousand chocolates every day. For an interesting side note, some of the paper used in the shop is made from discarded bean shells and fallen cacao leaves. You can also purchase Ambrosius's chocolates at stores around Madison and nearby communities, as well as in Chicago.

Maurie's Fine Chocolates of Madison, 1637 Monroe St., Madison, WI 53711; (608) 255-9092; mauriesfinechocolates.com. Maurie's has a wide assortment of truffles, all handcrafted by resident chocolatier Cher Diamond and staff. If decadence is your game, you must indulge yourself with the balsamic-infused Avalon Truffle or the lemon cardamom Lucy Truffle. Also try the English toffee, salt caramel, and terrapins made with toasted pecans, chocolate, and caramel. Everything is made in-house. The shop opened in 1993, with Diamond being a second-generation chocolatier who named her business after her dad, Maurie.

Metcalfe's Market, 726 N. Midvale Blvd., Madison, WI 53705; (608) 238-7612; shopmetcalfes.com. Long a Madison staple, Metcalfe's is located in Hilldale Mall, just off traffic-heavy University Avenue near Lucia Crest Park. Owners Tim and Kevin Metcalfe promote cheese samplings as integral to their operations, especially encouraging cheeses such as cumin, sajji BBQ, and tandoori Goudas by Huma Siddiqui's White Jasmine. This Madison-based, Pakistani-influenced spice and tea company partnered with Meister Cheese Company in Muscoda, Wisconsin, to come up with these tongue-tingling varieties. Metcalfe's has a large deli area, offering the usual sandwiches and related items. Tomatoes, greens, melons, and other produce are mostly grown at nearby farms. For one of the best deals in town, Saturday is Metcalfe's double-coupon day. The company's other two stores are Metcalfe's West Towne, 7455 Mineral Point Rd., Madison, WI 53717 (608-829-3500), and Metcalfe's Wauwatosa, 6700 W. State St., Wauwatosa, WI 53213 (414-259-8560).

One Barrel Brewing Co., 2001 Atwood Ave., Madison, WI 53704; (608) 630-9286; onebarrelbrewing.com. Owner/ manager/brewer Peter Gentry started making beer in his home and subsequently opened this brewpub. One Barrel is Madison's first so-called nanobrewery, making only a single barrel of beer at a time. Labels include Strong Ale, Penguin Pale Ale, and The Commuter Session Beer. Among its promotions is the Thursday Bike Night, where your first beer is $1 when you show your helmet. The bartenders are friendly and fast, even when the place crams up, which it often does, especially on UW football days. Guest beers are often on tap. Decor is Madison hip, with lots of exposed brick. Food on hand includes premade Framonbi's pizza, soft pretzels, and cheese plates.

People's Bakery, 2810 E. Washington Ave., Madison, WI 53704; (608) 245-0404; peoplesbakerymadison.com. We were turned on to this little gem by a Grant County farm friend who makes regular pilgrimages here for baklava and gyros. Emphasizing Lebanese and other Middle Eastern baked items, you can load up on hummus and falafel. Discovering the taste bud wonders of *moohamara,* a blend of roasted red peppers, pomegranate, and walnuts, was a grand culinary experience. The store is owned by Nabil Elghadban, who peeks up behind the pastry counter with a broad smile. People's has earned numerous foodie awards from Madison "Best Of" and other surveys.

Potter's Crackers, 100 S. Baldwin St., Ste. 303, Madison WI 53703; (608) 663-5005; potterscrackers.com. The company was launched by Peter Potter Weber and his mom, Nancy Potter, in 2006. Pete is a food science graduate of the University of Wisconsin, and Nancy had owned the New Glarus Bakery for 25 years. They figured the award-winning cheese industry in Wisconsin needed the perfect cracker. Subsequently, they turn out whole-grain, handmade crackers made with Wisconsin milled whole-wheat flour and local milk and butter. Small, local farms in central Wisconsin provide the ingredients. Among them are Great River Milling, Sassy Cow Creamery, Keewaydin Farms, West Star Farms, and Sandhill Cranberry. These aren't typical grocery store crackers. Certified organic, Potter's presents fun varieties such as caramelized onion, hazelnut graham, rosemary, and caraway rye. Seasonals might be a cheddar mustard and a rhubarb graham. They also offer gluten-free and vegan varieties. The crackers are sold in dozens of fine food outlets around Wisconsin and elsewhere in the country.

Steve's Wine, Beer, Spirits, 3618 University Ave., Madison, WI 53705; (608) 233-6193; stevesknows.com. Shop founder, the late Steve Varese, opened his cozy shop in 1956, quitting his job as conductor with the Milwaukee Railroad to initially run his store in the converted living room of the family home. He once emphasized that he catered to customers who didn't purchase their beers and wines from grocery stores, but who wanted a more sociable shopping presence. Varese died in 2007, yet Steve's keeps that same friendly feeling under the management of partners Randy Wautlet, Wayne Crokus, Karen Eigenberger, and Joe Varese; Crokus and Varese run the original store in Shorewood Hills. The facility includes a deli-style cheese room and a wine and spirits room. Steve's knowledgeable crew also can put together gift baskets, each with bottles of refreshing beverage augmented by generous cut-and-wrap cheese selections.

Patrons regularly ask to include fresh Madison-made chocolate from **Gail Ambrosius Chocolatier** (p. 222) and David Bacco Chocolats.

Willy Street Co-op, 1221 Williamson St., Madison, WI 53703; (608) 251-6776; and 6825 University Ave., Middleton, WI 53562; (608) 284-7800; willystreet.coop. Despite its current size after several expansion moves, the current Willy Street Co-op retains its early '70s feel, even though the co-op now has more than 20,000 members and 160-plus staff. It remains a cornerstone of the Madison community, self-proclaiming "fairly priced goods and supporting local and organic suppliers." And that means Wisconsin cheese with some 240 cheeses stocked at the co-op. About 70 percent are Wisconsin brands, made by more than 30 different state cheesemakers. Among state brands are Bleu Mont Bandage Wrap Aged Cheddar from pasture-grazed cows, Otter Creek Pesto Cheddar, Next Generation raw milk Caribbean cheddar, and Uplands Pleasant Ridge Reserve. The store also has a sushi bar, a rentable community room, a courtyard for plant sales and sitting with a fruit smoothie and good novel, a kids' play area, and even a rain garden to the rear of the store. The co-op makes its own soup at an off-site kitchen, which is then brought to the deli and served either at inside tables or patio seating.

Elsewhere in Central Wisconsin

Yes, there is life outside the state capital, with numerous restaurants we've discovered over the years on our travels through Wisconsin's heartland. You can find steaks, burgers, fish, and exotic fusions throughout the entire central region of the Dairy State. We like searching out places that have fabulous scenic views from the dining-room windows, cozy decks for summer evening relaxing, and husky breakfasts in small-town diners.

Foodie Faves

Back When Cafe, 606 3rd St., Wausau, WI 54403; (715) 848-5668; backwhencafe.com; Traditional American; $$. Chef Jolene Lucci emphasizes fresh, organic ingredients as much as possible and is a strong advocate of the Slow Food movement. The cafe is situated in a century-old building, one of the oldest in downtown Wausau's historic River District. It is open Tues through Sat for dinner only. Look for the explosion of seasonal flowers out front as Wisconsin's winter fades away. Locals say this is a great date locale, as well as a fine place for meeting up with friends and enjoying a quiet meal done with classy flair.

227

Baumgartner's Cheese Store and Tavern, 1023 16th Ave., Monroe, WI 53566; (608) 325-6157; baumgartnercheese.com; Casual American; $. Baumgartner's Cheese Store and Tavern opened in 1931 and calls itself Wisconsin's oldest cheese store. Good things just don't change. The cheese displays are in coolers inside the front door on the right. After perusing and purchasing, meander to the rear where the long, long, long bar is a grand place to hang out on a rainy Saturday afternoon. Above the bar is an extensive mural depicting a battle of the

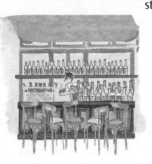

steins. You have to study the artwork for awhile to really figure out the theme. Several beers help. There are several tables along the left side where old cronies discuss the day's events. A giant world map is stuck with pins from all the international visitors who have wandered into Baumgartner's over the years. Be sure to add your home locale. The world's second-best chili, after mom's, is worth a bowl and taking a jar back home. They are famous for their limburger cheese sandwiches with a slice of raw onion on dark rye. Be sure to slather on a generous portion of the old-fashioned stone-ground horseradish mustard for the final glory. A jar is conveniently placed on each table. While you can get braunschweiger, corned beef, shaved turkey, and related sandwiches during the day, only cheese sandwiches and chili are served after 8 p.m.

Bernard's Country Inn, 701 2nd St. North, Stevens Point, WI 54481; (715) 344-3365; bernardscountryinn.com; Supper Club; $$-$$$. Bernard's has been on the Stevens Point dining scene since opening in 1973. Escargots bourguignonne and duck à l'orange are prominent in the extensive menu, with most entrees being served with the option of potato dumplings, spaetzle, or home-fried potatoes. Mouthwatering schnitzels and sauerbraten are testimonials to the skills of Bernard Kurzawa, its Berlin-born proprietor. This award-winning restaurant is closed both Sun and Mon.

Christian's Bistro, 3066 Village Park Dr., Plover, WI 54467; (715) 344-3100; christiansbistro.com; Bistro; $$–$$$. Located only a couple of blocks from Worzella Pines Park on Lake Pacawa, this bistro serves an interesting array of foods, including a marvelous chocolate truffle espresso cream torte for dessert. The best way to get here is via Plover Road off I-39; turn south on Village Park Drive. You can watch the kitchen staff in action through the open viewing space. See Chef Christian Czerwonka's recipe for **Potato & Beer Soup with Bistro Flatbreads** on p. 313.

The Dining Room at 209 Main, 209 N. Main St., Monticello, WI 53570; (608) 938-2200; 209main.com; Bistro; $$–$$$. Even the appetizers here are special. After all, this is a four star–rated restaurant run by master chef Wave Kasprzak. Indulge yourself with his Southwestern spiced salmon cakes, a dazzler with a smoked tomato remoulade and three-pepper escabèche, which is a basic Mediterranean dish of a poached or pickled fish. Meals are done here with flair, with a favorite being the grilled tenderloin filet with its Worcestershire glaze. Dinners include a house salad with fresh herb vinaigrette. Almost every ingredient here is fresh and locally produced, when possible. Regular cooking classes attract participants from around the region, with the bar open for cocktails in case a bit of refueling is helpful during such a session. The Dining Room is in the heart of Wisconsin's cow and cheese country with its Swiss heritage.

Father Fats Public House, 945 Clark St., Stevens Point, WI 54481; (715) 544-4054; fatherfats.com; Bistro; $$–$$$. Specializing in small plates, the trendy menu changes daily, so check out facebook .com/fatherfats for the latest updates. For instance, you might get a soup of the day, followed by chipotle-Parmesan oysters, scallops and halibut cheeks, baby back ribs, potato chip–crusted fresh swordfish, and pork belly *carnitas*. Father Fats has become a regional draw, with visitors driving in from Eau Claire, Wausau, and elsewhere around central Wisconsin for a strawberry-basil-balsamic martini with house-infused rosemary Hendrick's gin and one of the daily bruschettas. Folks are encouraged to settle in and enjoy a real food experience. The dining room is hip, with lots of fronting windows for viewing the street scene.

Flannery's Wilhelm Tell Supper Club, 114 2nd St., New Glarus, WI 53574; (608) 527-2618; flannerysnewglarus.com; Supper Club; $$. Even with their Irish heritage, it doesn't seem a stretch that Mike and Ruth Flannery run a Swiss supper club with a sports bar touch. Be assured there is plenty of fondue and swiss cheese, cheddar cheese and grilled cheese sandwiches, plus chicken parmigiana. The smoothly mellow old-fashioneds set the tone here, deserving a four-star rating. The prime rib is great, too.

Glarner Stube, 518 1st St., New Glarus, WI 53574; (608) 527-2216; glarnerstube.com; Swiss; $–$$. The Stube is located in a century-plus building that over the years has housed a cigar factory, then a pool hall, followed by a bowling alley, and finally a bar and restaurant beginning in the early 1950s. Capture the shop's Swiss heritage with a *Kalberwurst,* a mild veal sausage, or the *Schublig,* a spiced beef sausage made by the nearby **Ruef's Meat Market** (p. 246). You can also get steaks, chops, chicken, shrimp, and Swiss meatballs, which seem to be almost the size of bowling balls, or at least a tennis ball, made with a blend of veal, pork, and beef and finally covered in a tomato-mushroom gravy. Plenty of upscale beers, at least eight from the **New Glarus Brewing Company** (p. 243), are proudly poured from an array of fancy tappers at the copper-topped bar. You can get a platter of house-cured meats when seated at the bar during the winter, making a perfect companion for a Spotted Cow or Fat Squirrel brew from New Glarus Brewing.

Gus's Drive-In, 3131 Main St., East Troy, WI 53120; (262) 642-2929; gussdrivein.com; Burgers; $. With traditional drive-up fare,

Gus's is a great stop in a prime location. Close to the Alpine Valley Resort and minutes from Lake Geneva, this drive-in is found on easy and scenic tour through the Kettle Moraine State Forest. And on Saturday, just follow the sound of rumbling and thundering engines to Gus's during its Cruise Nights. Car lovers love the display of classics, hot rods, and rad rods every weekend.

The Kitchen Table, 118 E. 3rd St., Marshfield, WI 54449; (715) 387-2601; Casual American; $–$$. For comfort food, eating here is like eating at home. Yes, that is Hungarian goulash being served to those customers over there. That's why The Kitchen Table is so great. A wide selection of omelets is available each morning, along with cinnamon rolls served with a slice of orange. The grilled meat loaf and cheese sandwich is worth pulling off the freeway for. Another lure is the Hawaiian open-faced sandwich made with grilled ham, fresh pineapple, and swiss cheese. The little restaurant, which serves plenty of honest coffee, holds a number of four- and six-top tables for families or clusters of codgers, plus a bar fronted by several stools for solitary dining.

Log Cabin Family Restaurant, 1215 8th St., Baraboo, WI 53913; (608) 356-8034; logcabin-baraboo.com; Casual American; $–$$. We regularly eat here when visiting the nearby Circus World Museum, a national historic site once the winter quarters of the old Ringling Bros. circus. The Log Cabin, which actually does have a log cabin ambience, is family friendly and perfect for dining on a budget. Takeout is also available. The strawberry-banana pancakes and the pecan pancakes are renowned among vacationers touring the area. There's no clowning around with the homemade pies, warmed and dolloped with ice cream. Every ringmaster and acrobat in the family should be pleased with the fare here.

WISCONSIN DELLS,
WATER PARK CAPITAL OF THE WORLD

The Dells, or *les dalles* from the French for "river gorges," has been a vacation getaway since the 1800s. Among its mind-numbing number of attractions, the city became known for its water parks. Among them are Noah's Ark with its Surfing Safari surf machine, Wilderness Resort's spraying fountains, and Kalahari Resort, proud of having Wisconsin's first swim-up bar. All that splashing around certainly leads to hearty appetites. After drying off, head for the following:

Alamo Smokehouse, 951 Stand Rock Rd., Wisconsin Dells, WI 53965; (608) 253-7233; dellsalamo.com; Barbecue; $$. Located in downtown Dells at the bridge, the decor is rustic Western. The menu is a mix of barbecue and Tex-Mex, with all the smoking done on-site. Try the roasted corn chowder or barbecue brisket pizza. For dessert, there is a plethora of chocolate treats.

Buffalo Phil's Pizza & Grille, 150 Gasser Rd., Wisconsin Dells, WI 53965; (608) 254-7300; buffalophilsgrille.com; Pizza; $–$$. The pizza, rotisserie chicken, pasta, and the rest of your meal are delivered by miniature toy trains that run throughout the restaurant.

Moosejaw Pizza & Dells Brewing Co., 110 Wisconsin Dells Pkwy. South, Wisconsin Dells, WI 53965; (608) 254-1122; dellsmoosejaw .com; Casual American; $–$$$. The on-site brewery bottles two popular ales, Rustic Red and Honey Ale, which you can purchase in six-packs at the restaurant. The restaurant has many suggestions for pairing your food with one of their beers. For instance, a Blonde Bock goes with anything barbecued or a red meat entree. At Moosejaw, the bock is perfect with a pork sandwich, ribs, New York strip, or one of its specialty pizzas. A fruit beer, such as Apple Ale or Raspberry Cream Ale, is a nice complement to a house salad or an after-dinner ice cream sundae.

Paul Bunyan's Cook Shanty, 411 State Hwy. 13, Wisconsin Dells, WI 53965; (608) 254-8717; paulbunyans.com; Breakfast; $–$$. One almost expects Paul Bunyan and his blue ox, Babe, to be waiting on tables here, with its Northwoods-log look, lumbering artifacts, checkered tablecloths, and famous buttermilk doughnuts. No reservations are required in this 450-seat restaurant. Vacationers crowd here for the all-you-can-eat stacks of breakfast pancakes that come with sausage links, scrambled eggs, smoked ham, fried Wisconsin potatoes, and orange juice. There is also an extensive lunch and dinner menu. Another outlet is located at 8653 State Hwy. 51 North, Minocqua, WI 54548 (715-356-6270).

Port Huron Brewing Co., 805 Business Park Rd., Wisconsin Dells, WI 53965; (608) 253-0340; porthuronbeer.com. Friday and Saturday afternoon tastings are held in the brewery's Engine House Tap Room, which is outfitted with a 24-foot-long handmade bar top. The brewery's first batch rolled out in 2011, with beer in kegs available since 2012. Among its selections are the Hefeweizen, brewed in the tradition of German wheat beers, and the oatmeal stout, with oodles of roasted and caramel malts making for a muscular black beer that is still creamy and smooth.

Thunder Valley Inn, W15344 Waubeek Rd., Wisconsin Dells, WI 53965; (608) 254-4145; thundervalleyinn.com; Casual American, $$. You'll get beef pot roast with sauteed onions, hand-peeled mashed potatoes with gravy, fresh vegetables, a salad with homemade dressing, and freshly baked wheat/rye bread with strawberry rhubarb jam, plus dessert! Old-timey fiddling, piano, and accordion music, along with loads of jokes, are integral to the program. The Inn hosts a farmers' market on Sunday morning during the summer.

Milty-Wilty, W7411 State Hwy. 21/73, Wautoma, WI 54982; (920) 787-2300; Burgers; $. This drive-in has been serving custard for more than six decades. As such, for a state that prizes a classic drive-in experience, the Milty-Wilty is the stuff of legend. Burgers are done just the right way, and custard is appropriately smooth. Seek a giant neon sign with an ice-cream cone, and ye shall find satisfaction. The Milty-Wilty is open only from late spring through early autumn.

Mitchell's Hilltop Pub & Grill, 4901 Main St., Stevens Point, WI 54481; (715) 341-3037; hilltoppubandgrill.com; Casual American; $$. There are not many restaurants where you can enter by going through a vintage beer vat. For part of the experience, look over the old-time photos of long-ago Stevens Point that adorn the walls. Specials on Friday are particularly "fishy," with lake perch, walleye, or cod served up with a baked potato, traditional french fries, crosscut fries, potato salad, or fresh fruit. The place jumps whenever a group of motorcycle riders pulls in for lunch. You can hunker down at the bar, in a booth, or at a table. Sitting outside under a striped umbrella with a tequila barbecue burger and a locally brewed Point beer makes a pleasant summer day even better.

New Glarus Hotel Restaurant, 100 6th Ave., New Glarus, WI 53574; (608) 527-5244 or (800) 727-9477; newglarushotel.com; Swiss; $$. The hotel is a landmark in this town founded by Swiss immigrants in the mid-1800s, and its restaurant features a wide range of traditional Swiss specialties, including *Geschnetzeltes,* which are thin slices of lightly browned veal served with a white wine sauce. Another is the piccata schnitzel, a dish from the Italian-Swiss canton of Ticino that consists of pork tenderloin fillets dipped in a cheese batter, then panfried in fresh butter and covered with sautéed mushrooms. Again, harkening to Switzerland's Italian heritage, the Ticino Pizzeria

Restaurant is under the balcony of the hotel, with a Monday evening all-you-can-eat spaghetti and meatballs dinner. Many of the locals come to the hotel for the Friday and Saturday dances, featuring such noted band names as the Zweifel Brothers and Steve Meisner.

The Old Feed Mill Restaurant, 114 Cramer St., Mazomanie, WI 53560; (608) 795-4909; oldfeedmill.com; Casual American; $–$$. Among the faves are baked mac 'n' cheese and a roasted chicken, marinated in apple cider and served with garlic mashed potatoes and veggies of the season. When you tie on the feed bag at the Old Feed Mill, make sure that one entree is the full rack of barbecue pork back ribs. A pot roast special for four is a good deal, served family style. There is a well-stocked Sunday brunch buffet and a Friday night fish fry, both Wisconsin traditions. What's best, the bread and pasta are made from organic stone-milled flour ground on-site by miller David Moreno. Visitors can watch the process from safely behind a glass partition. The restored mill is on the National Register of Historic Places.

Prime Quarter Steak House, 1900 Humes Rd. (US 14 East), Janesville, WI 53545; (608) 752-1881; primequarter.com; Steak House; $$–$$$. Patrons can grill their own steaks, or have the chef prepare the entree. The Prime Quarter chain, headquartered in Madison, has four restaurants in Wisconsin. Each place offers USDA prime beef, large baked potatoes, and an unlimited salad bar with about two dozen items. If you can survive the 40-ounce steak in less than 1 hour and 15 minutes, including a trip to the salad bar, a baked potato, and Texas toast, you become a member of the restaurant's Beefeater's Club. Winners receive a medallion that can be redeemed for a regular Prime Quarter dinner on a subsequent visit.

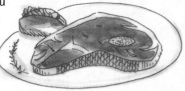

Richard's Restaurant & Bar, 5305 N. 32nd Ave., Wausau, WI 54401; (715) 675-7070; richardssupperclub.com; Supper Club; $$. Richard's offers a range of fried chicken, fillets, jumbo shrimp, and prime rib. The Friday fish fry has plenty of offerings, such as haddock, either broiled, breaded, or beer-battered, plus perch, bluegill, walleye, poorman's lobster (halibut), and shrimp. The all-you-can-eat wings for $5 on Thursday packs in a crowd, so be prepared to wait unless you arrive early. There are 13 homemade sauces to select from, if you want to lather up your wings. Look for Richard's near the large white water tower.

The Speakeasy Lounge and Restaurant, 19 N. High St., Janesville, WI 53548; (608) 531-0012; gospeakeasylounge .com; Traditional American; $$. Once known as the Bennison & Lane Baking Company, a producer of commercial baking products, and home to other businesses over the years, this building retains a venerable feel. The Speakeasy opened in 2004 and quickly became a featured Janesville restaurant. For a decadent treat, try the deep-fried cheese curds and fresh-cut french fries, as well as the brick-oven pizzas using dough made fresh each day. There aren't many places in the state with a Friday fish fry of hand-breaded cod loins, accompanied by potato pancakes. The loins are the thick, rich meat located above the fish's spine. Homemade cheesecake is truly light and airy, among the variable pastries depending on what local materials are available in season. The Library tearoom is adjacent to the lounge, as is the Leona & Eddie shop with its tea-related and kitchen items.

Taj Mahal, 2624 Humes Rd., Janesville, WI 53545; (608) 754-8355; thetajmahaljanesville.com; Indian; $$. The Taj has a great buffet, offering up a range of Indian items, from chicken tikka masala to all sorts of curry. A basket of fresh, hot naan bread is delivered to each table. But you can also order other breads, such as *chapati*, whole wheat roti, deep-fried *poori*, and a multilayer *paratha*. The spinach *aloo*, a ragout of potatoes, spinach, light cream, cinnamon, and other spices, makes for a wonderful dish. Not to mention the lamb *shahikorma*, lamb cooked in cream with herbs and cashews. Tune in for the Bollywood videos playing on the television. For subcontinent fare, the Taj is tops.

Turner Hall, 1217 17th Ave., Monroe, WI 53566; (608) 325-3461; **turnerhallofmonroe.org; Swiss; $–$$.** Monroe's historic Turner Hall derives its name from the German word for "gymnast," which is *Turner*. The first *Turnhalle* was built by Swiss immigrants in 1868 on the same site as the current facility. Women's rights advocate Susan B. Anthony and John F. Kennedy are among a long list of well-known visitors. The hall still hosts receptions, wakes, bowling competitions, concerts, dances, and concerts by noted Swiss musicians. The Rathskeller Restaurant is always bustling, particularly packed for the Friday night fish fry. Numerous Swiss-themed dishes are on the menu, most featuring potatoes and cheese. Turner Hall's rösti, a popular potato dish, is among the best between Monroe and Zurich.

Wedges, 2006 N. County Rd. E, Janesville, WI 53545; (608) 757-1444; **Traditional American; $–$$.** Lunch and dinner are served seven days a week with regular specials, including a traditional Saturday-night prime rib dinner. There is usually enough served for carry-home leftovers. Music lovers stopping over on Thursday can experience the limelight with karaoke. Live music is regularly scheduled on the weekends. Sports lovers appreciate the televisions. Takeout is available.

Basil Restaurant, 2106 Schofield Ave., Weston, WI 54476; (715) 298-0677; basilweston.com; Asian; $$. Flavors from South and Southeast Asia mingled with those of Europe come as a surprise, something you might not expect for central Wisconsin. Basil is noted for its curries, with kudos earned for the pho and the spring rolls. Even the grilled salmon served over mixed greens gets a happy nod. Since owner Jim Daly is Irish, he even has an Irish stew on the menu, although his wife, Tee, is Thai, making for a great international combo.

Blue Spoon Cafe, 550 Water St., Prairie du Sac, WI 53578; (608) 643-0837; bluespooncafe.com; Bistro; $–$$. It's casual and fun here, augmented by a large wine list. While visiting, sample the artichoke and olive bruschetta or the olive and tomato bruschetta, both of which are equally marvelous. Among the fun items for breakfast are the custard pancakes, made with Wisconsin-made Culver's custard for a rich, creamy batter. Pancakes with wild rice and pecans sound too healthful to eat, but go ahead anyway. For kids of all ages having lunch, consider the peanut butter–caramelized onion-pickle burger. Be careful of the Firehouse Chili. It's so hot . . . it's so good. Wine tastings are held monthly throughout the year, usually starting around 6 p.m. and featuring major Oregon, Washington, Chile, Argentina, New Zealand, and other vintners.

The Del-Bar, 800 Wisconsin Dells Pkwy., Lake Delton, WI 53940; (608) 253-1861; del-bar.com; Supper Club; $$–$$$. The Del-Bar dates back to 1943 when it was opened by Jim and Alice Wimmer, whose family remains owners. You'll find the Del-Bar to be one of the best places in the region for its cuts of meat, from rib eye to filets, and for great panfried walleye, as well.

Ed Thompson's Tee Pee Supper Club, 812 Superior Ave., Tomah, WI 54660; (608) 372-0888; teepeesupperclub.com; Supper Club; $$–$$$. Tee Pee is noted for its range of daily specials, including Monday's blackened prime rib, Tuesday's beef tenderloin and shrimp, and on down the line. The full soup and salad bar at Sunday brunch, from 10 a.m. to 2 p.m, is a good deal. The omelets are remarkable. Since the lounge is open on Sunday, guests often start off with a Bloody Mary or screwdriver. If you are in Tomah and need a lunch stop, experience Tee Pee's potato cheese soup or a prime rib sandwich. Thus fueled, you can then be on your way.

House of Embers, 935 Wisconsin Dells Pkwy., Wisconsin Dells, WI 53965; (608) 253-6411; houseofembers.com; Supper Club; $$–$$$. When rambling through the Dells in the winter, we enjoy stopping at the House of Embers and opting for a table near the fireplace. Talk cozy. Then talk hearty central Wisconsin fare: steaks, seafood, and all the other dishes that have made this a favorite of visitors since it opened in 1959. The restaurant's critically acclaimed and happily devoured ribs are consistent crowd pleasers. The cinnamon rolls, dressings, sauces, and desserts are made in-house. At night, the glowing neon HOUSE OF EMBERS sign is a pleasant beacon, especially after hours of travel.

Roxbury Tavern, 8901 County Hwy. Y, Sauk City, WI 53583; (608) 634-8434; roxburytavern.com; Pub Grub/Sandwiches/Pizza/ Gumbo; $. Don't let the mailing address fool you, the Roxbury Tavern is actually in the crossroads community of Roxbury, which is close enough for government work. The tavern's economy of scale is small-batch, hand-done food. Parties of eight or more can be accommodated but give a couple of days' notice if you are bringing in a traveling circus. Each menu item is a gem. For top consideration, indulge in the shrimp

Creole, integral to the Roxbury's Friday night fish presentation. The Creole consists of a third of a pound of grilled shrimp with a rip-roaring tomato sauce over rice, and jalapeño cornbread. Breakfast on Sunday morning could include the Tree Hugger, consisting of two granola cakes. An ATM is on-site. As a fund-raiser for area senior services, the tavern holds its traditional piano burning on Father's Day, when an actual piano topped by a foil-wrapped turkey is set ablaze.

Wedl's Hamburger Stand and Ice Cream Parlor, 200 E. Racine St., Jefferson, WI 53549; (920) 674-3637; Burgers; $. For years, this has been one of our most fun places to stop for a bag o' burgers, turned out seasonally from an 8-by-8-foot hut just off Jefferson's main street. Watching the special technique of making the burgers is part of the fun. A ball of meat is dropped onto an iron griddle, which has a layer of melted lard or fat. The glob is smashed flat with a spatula, fried quickly, flipped, and served. Long considered one of the best places in the state for a hamburger, Wedl's has been around for several generations under different names. You may have to stand in line for a few minutes, but the wait is worth it. While it's okay to eat inside for a more varied fare and for the ice cream, the summertime rush of eating a freshly fried burger outside is the big draw. The stand and ice cream parlor close at the beginning of November and reopen around St. Patrick's Day in March.

Specialty Stores, Markets & Producers

ÆppelTreow Winery & Distillery, 1072 288th Ave., Burlington, WI 53105; (262) 878-5345; aeppeltreow.com. The winery uses its own apples and pears for its various styles of wines, including sparkling and dessert wines. An on-site distillery is used for creating its

Brown Dog whiskey and a pear brandy. We particularly enjoy the Barn Swallow hard cider. The folks here work with Mark Johnston of L'eft Bank Wine Company, a major distributor of wines and spirits throughout Wisconsin.

Black Earth Meats, 1345 Mills St., Black Earth, WI 53515; (608) 767-3940; blackearthmeats.com. The butchers here provide fresh meat to restaurants and retailers in the upper Midwest, as well as to customers through its retail store in Black Earth and via the Internet. The company is a certified USDA organic facility praised for its humane handling of their pastured animals, which are grass-fed. How can anyone go wrong with Black Earth's Box-O-Meat, one that is chock-full—or should we say "chuck-full"—of various cuts?

Carr Valley Cheese Company, S3797 County G, La Valle, WI 53941; (608) 986-2781; carrvalleycheese.com. Carr Valley Cheese is one of America's finest specialty cheese plants, with classics such as aged cheddar cheese and award-winning originals such as Cocoa Cardona and Gran Canaria. The company was launched in 1902 and quickly garnered a reputation for great dairy products. Certified master cheesemaker Sid Cook has captured more top national and international awards than any other cheesemaker in North America. As a fourth-generation cheesemaker, he received his own cheesemaking license at the tender age of 16. Cook still uses only locally produced cow, goat, and sheep milks. Carr Valley's Black Sheep Truffle is an enjoyable treat, alongside Cook's suggested bottle of a Barolo, an amazing red wine from Italy's Piedmont region. The Carr Valley Cheese Store (2831 Parmenter St., Middleton, WI 53562, 608-824-2277), offers more than 100 of his company's products. There are also outlets in Mauston, Wisconsin Dells, Mazomanie, and at his plant in Fennimore. Look for the giant mouse outside the latter, eating a huge hunk of cheese. Actually, the fake rodent is only a float sculpture used in area parades. Cheese lovers take classes at the Carr Valley Cheese retail outlet at 807 Phillips Blvd., Sauk City, WI 53583 (608-643-3441), about a 30-minute drive north of Madison.

Chalet Cheese Co-op, N4848 County Rd. N, Monroe, WI 53566; (608) 325-4343. Chalet produces pungent limburger, along with other award-winning varieties such as baby swiss and several versions of brick. The plant is just north of Monroe, the state's cheesemaking capital and home to more than a dozen cheese plants.

Cress Spring Bakery, 4035 Ryan Rd., Blue Mounds, WI 53517; (608) 767-3875; cressspringbakery.com. Cress Spring Bakery creates great crafted breads, made with natural leavening and baked in a wood-fired brick oven. For their bread, they grind their grain provided by area farmers. The rye is particularly chewy and good, especially with braunschweiger, raw onion, and heavy German mustard along with a **Capital Brewery** (p. 218) pilsner brewed in nearby Madison. It's a taste marriage made in heaven. The bakery was built in 1996 by owner Jeff Ford, who is fond of quoting from Rumi, a 13th-century Persian poet. One of Ford's favorites: "There is a basket of fresh bread on your head, yet you go door to door asking for crusts. Knock on the inner door, no other."

Holland's Family Cheese, Holland's Family Farm, N13851 Gorman Ave., Thorp, WI 54771; (715) 669-5230; hollandsfamilycheese .com. Rolf and Marieke Penterman are first-generation dairy farmers who moved from the Netherlands to Wisconsin in 2002, following Rolf's brother Sander who came in 1999. The family now owns 480 acres with more than 800 milk cows, along with some thousand or so beef cattle. Wanting to learn more about cheese, Marieke resturned to Holland where she worked on a *boerenkaas,* a farmhouse cheese plant. In 2006, she produced her initial batch of Gouda. In 2013, her Marieke Gouda, delicately aged from six to nine months, captured the Mature

Grand Champion of the US Championship Cheese Contest. As confirmed Gouda lovers, we agree that the honor was well deserved. You can get this marvel at Holland's retail outlet in Thorp, in stores around the country, and online.

The Main Grain Bakery, 1009 1st St., Stevens Point, WI 54481; (715) 630-1486; themaingrainbakery.com. "Bready or not, here we crumb," is oft-repeated with grins at the Main Grain. Local, organic ingredients are used as much as possible. All of the community-oriented bakery's discarded organic material, from excess dough to eggshells, is composted and brought to the University of Wisconsin–Stevens Point campus garden. Instead of selling day-old items, the bakery donates leftover products to the Salvation Army and other charities. Among the more interesting items is the Firecracker, a roll filled with cayenne pepper flakes; white aged sharp cheddar and whole coarse cornmeal ease the peppery heat and result in a rich yellow crust. These are usually sold on Wednesday, alternating weekly with the sesame sticks. The Stinger bread, concocted with roasted garlic, crushed black peppercorns, and Parmesan cheese, is an adventurous eat. Don't ask how many muffins the bakers have made over the years. Everyone has lost count.

New Glarus Brewing Company, 2400 State Hwy. 69, New Glarus, WI 53564; (608) 527-5850; newglarusbrewing.com. The brewery produces six beers year-round: Spotted Cow, Two Women, Raspberry Tart, Moon Man, Black Top, and Serendipity. It also brews six seasonal beers, such as the crispy Totally Naked lager and a hale 'n' hearty coffee stout. The company was founded by Deb Carey, who remains president, while husband Dan is master brewer and co-owner of the farm. He apprenticed in Munich, so he knows his beer. The company has a small gift shop where all the brews are for sale. Plus

EAT CHEESE, THIS IS WISCONSIN

Green County's cheese factories are noted for their numerous types of wonderful cheese, offering both traditional flavors and interesting new versions on an ancient theme. For an extensive listing of the county's many plants, check with Green County Tourism, 1016 16th Ave., Monroe, WI 53566 (888-222-9111; greencounty.org/cheese.iml). Many plants offer tours where you can watch the cheesemaking process from behind large glass windows. The factories are also convenient locales where you can pick up a pound or three of Havarti, gruyère, fontina, Edam, and Gouda.

National Historic Cheesemaking Center, 2108 6th Ave., Monroe, WI 53566; (608) 325-4636; nationalhistoriccheese makingcenter.org. Located in Monroe's old railroad depot, the Center is easy to find: Outside are two upturned copper cheese vats. The facility is located on Monroe's south side, just off State Highway 69 at 21st Street. Once you wander through the front door and pay the small admission fee, you learn the backstory of cheesemaking during the late 1800s and early 1900s in south-central Wisconsin. Your tour also includes a 15-minute video explaining the process of cheesemaking and how it is done today. The historic Imobersteg Cheese Factory has been moved to the site and can also be toured. Often a retired cheesemaker is on hand to answer questions, and special events are held regularly throughout the year. Many of these include servings of grilled cheese sandwiches.

there are tours and a tasting room with samples for a small fee. Many of the state's greatest bars serve New Glarus offerings.

Nueske's Company Store, 1390 E. Grand Ave., Wittenberg, WI 54499; (800) 392-2266; nueskes.com. The Nueske family came to Wisconsin in 1887, bringing with them their skills in smoking, spicing, and curing meat. In 1933, R.C. Nueske decided to market his smoked bacon, sausage, turkeys, and hams, and his emphasis on quality has continued. Nueske's meats can also be found at numerous restaurants throughout Wisconsin.

Red Eye Brewing Company, 612 Washington St., Wausau, WI 54403; (715) 843-7334; redeyebrewing.com. As the gang says here, "Raise a glass and a fork." The brewery makes a Belgian wheat, an American-style IPA, a Belgian Dubbel, and a smooth peach wheat. The attached restaurant sources local produce, herbs, and meat; even the pizza oven is fired by locally grown and sawed hardwoods. No fryers are used in the kitchen, which encourages a menu of healthy items. The buns here are made from the  same malt used in brewing the beer. Nothing goes to waste: Even the spent grain is returned to farmers for feed. The ribs are wonderfully fall-off-the-bone tender, especially when lathered in Red Eye's own barbecue sauce. Red Eye, in the heritage Grand Theater on 4th Street, is a 2-block walk from Wausau's Performing Arts Foundation, so it's a perfect stop après-Allegro Regional Dance Theater performances.

Rolling Pin Bake Shop, 2935 S. Fish Hatchery Rd., Fitchburg, WI 53711; (608) 270-9611; rollingpinbakeshop.com. Scones, pecan rolls, cinnamon buns, Danish, and chocolate croissants are just a few of the breakfast pastries produced by the gang headed by owners Tanya Laiter and Bill McKnight. The shop opened in 2001, evolving into a full-menu cafe serving breakfast and lunch. Wedding cakes are specialties, romantically and passionately made, of course. Biscuits and gravy and the Rolling Pin omelet are among the top early-morning dining options, with Cuban pork or turkey apple sandwiches perfect for lunch.

Roth Käse USA, 1325 7th Ave., Monroe, WI 53566; (608) 328-2122; rothkase.com. Although the original Roth cheese company was started in Switzerland in 1863, it opened its first big plant in the States in 1991. Monroe in Green County was selected because of its Swiss heritage, proximity to major urban markets, and wonderful grasslands making for contented neigborhood cows. Their fresh milk is collected from family farms within a 60-mile drive. This means that within 48 hours, the milk is used to create glorious craft cheeses that have won numerous international awards.

Ruef's Meat Market, 538 1st St., New Glarus, WI 53574; (608) 527-2554; ruefsmeatmarket.com. The Ruef family has been making sausages in New Glarus for more than half a century, chuckling that they have "the Wurst store in town." Their building has been a meat market since the 1920s. *Landjaeger, Farmerwurst, Schublig,* a garlicky cervelas,  smoked pork brats, *Mettwurst,* natural casing wieners, ring bologna, summer sausage, *Kalberwurst,* and a variety of bratwurst pack the cold-display cases and hang from racks behind the counter. The perfume of richly smoked meats is a draw for passersby. Wisconsin cheeses are featured, including limburger.

Wollersheim Winery, 7876 State Rd. 188, Prairie du Sac, WI 53578; (800) 847-9463; wollersheim.com. In 1972, Robert and JoAnn Wollersheim purchased their hillside land, which was perfect for vineyards. As a young man in 1984, Philippe Coquard came to the winery on an agricultural exchange program from the Beaujolais region of France. He was a lucky find, with degrees in winemaking, viticulture, and wine marketing. He became Wollersheim's winemaker and married the Wollersheim's oldest daughter, Julie. The Coquards now run the award-winning winery, which turns out around 220,000 gallons of wines each year. The offerings include a Domaine Reserve, ports, and even alcohol-free sparkling white grape juice. Tours and tastings make any visit especially rewarding. A wine garden is open daily from spring through fall.

Where to Get It Fresh

Throughout Central Wisconsin, farmers' markets abound during the growing and harvest season, presenting a wide range of delicious, healthy foods. You can find rainbow trout, cheese, garlic, swiss chard, squash, and hundreds of other items, each ready for the kitchen. Here are where some culinary discoveries are still "on-the-hoof."

Berlin Farmers & Artists Market, 192 E. Huron St., Berlin, WI 54923; (920) 979-7005; facebook.com/berlin.wi.farmersmarket. The market is located in Nathan Strong Park (East Side Park) and is open Tues from 4 to 7 p.m. June through Sept.

Capitol View Farmers Market, Madison, WI 53718; (608) 218-4732; capitolviewfarmersmarket.com. Located on the south side of Sharpsburg Drive, starting at the corner of North Star Drive. Wed from 3:30 to 7 p.m., June through Oct.

Columbus Farmers' Market, 409 N. Ludington St., Columbus, WI 53925; (920) 623-3425. Sun from 9 a.m. to 1 p.m., May through Oct. Adjacent to the Amtrak station.

Farm Stands and Pick Yer Own

Chet's Blueberry Farm, 525 County Rd. J, Custer, WI 54423; (715) 340-4989. The picking season begins approximately in the middle of July and lasts until the middle of Aug. Portable toilets available.

Clem's Orchard, N4663 County Rd. M, Montello, WI 53949; (608) 589-5235; garden_goddesss@hotmail.com. Owners Willard and Joann Hamilton have apples, beans, beets, sweet corn, cucumbers, eggplant, peppers, summer squash, and tomatoes, with honey from the hives on the farm. Open: Mid-July to mid-Sept.

Moseley Roadside Market, 5009 County Highway O, Warrens, WI 54666; (608) 378-4477; grant@moseleysmarket.com. Look for fresh baked goodies, preserves, beans, blueberries, sweet corn, cranberries, flowers, melons, onions, pumpkins, and raspberries. Open from mid-July until the end of Sept.

Rainbow Ridges Farms Bed & Breakfast, N5732 Hauser Rd., Onalaska, WI 54650; (608) 783-8181; rainbowridgefarms .com. Noted for clover and wildflower honey, as well as eggs and seasonal vegetables.

Turners Fresh Market and Greenhouse, E208 State Hwy. 54, Waupaca, WI 549981; (715) 258-3355; turners@ turnersfreshmarket.com. Open May 1 through Oct 31.

Dane County Farmers' Market, Capitol Square, Madison, WI 53715; (608) 455-1999; dcfm.org. Wed from 8:30 a.m. to 2 p.m., and Sat from 6 a.m. to 2 p.m., late Apr to early Nov.

DeForest Area Farmers' Market, Market St., DeForest, WI 53532; (608) 846-2922; deforestarea.com. Tues from 3 to 6 p.m., May through Oct.

Farmers' Market of Wausau, 400 River Dr., Wausau, WI 54403; (715) 443-6647. Wed and Sat starting at 7 a.m., early May through mid-Nov.

Janesville Farmers' Market, 100–200 N. Main St., Janesville, WI 53545; (608) 289-9292; janesvillefarmersmarket.com; Sat from 8 a.m. to 1 p.m., May to Oct.

Kronenwetter Farmers' Market, 2390 Terrebonne Dr., Kronenwetter, WI 54455; (715) 693-4200, ext. 3; kronenwetter.org. Most Sun from 9 a.m. to 1 p.m., mid-June to mid-Oct.

Mazomanie Village Market, 117 Brodhead St., Mazomanie, WI 53560; (608) 643-8445. Sat starting at 8 a.m., early May through late Oct.

Mount Horeb Farmers' Market, 110 N. 2nd St., Mount Horeb, WI 53572; (608) 437-2787. Downtown at Heritage Park under the water tower, at the Old School House. Thurs from 3 to 6:30 p.m., late spring through Oct.

Oregon Farmers' Market, 787 N. Main St., Oregon, WI 53575; (608) 873-9443. At Bill's Food Center parking lot. Tues from 2 to 6 p.m., early May through late Oct.

Waunakee Farmers' Market, 301 S. Century Ave., Waunakee, WI 53597; (920) 229-4153. At the Waun-A-Bowl. Wed from 3 to 6 p.m., early May through late Oct.

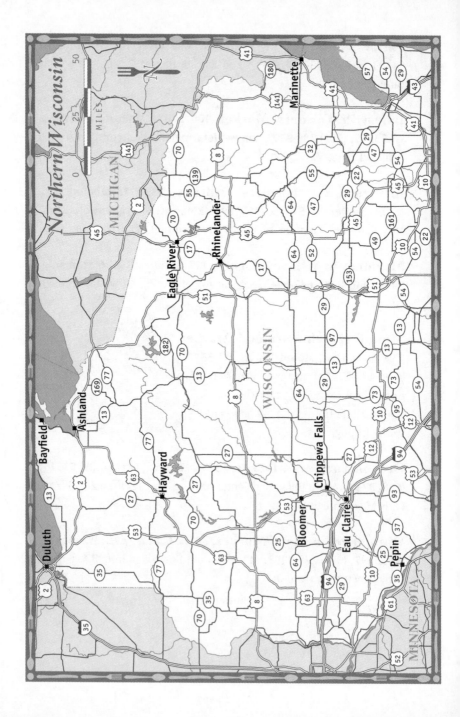

Northern Wisconsin

Look for the trees, an arbor that stretches from horizon to horizon, from sandy lakefront to rock-ribbed hillside. Look for the flopping perch and elusive walleye. The glorious sunrises and sky-bursting sunsets. The sleek canoes and powerful bass boats. The rustic log cabins and modern resorts. The old-fashioned supper clubs with their '50s look and 21st-century menus. The fanciful art galleries and rip-roaring-fun dinner theaters.

That sums up a getaway to Wisconsin's North County, a potpourri of hot-hot chili, hefty rib eyes, strong martinis, and taverns with mounted moose heads whose eyes follow you everywhere. The state's vacation paradise rims the Lake Superior shoreline southward to mid-Cheese Country. Some of Dairyland's best eateries are amid the pine forests, in the small towns and decently sized cities that are large enough to boast of having several coffeehouses, plenty of non-franchise burger joints, and numerous mom-and-pop restaurants proud of using fresh ingredients secured from local producers. Made-from-scratch dishes abound, prepared by talented chefs who know the traditional as well as the trendy. All this is combined with a hometown work ethic that means that the waitstaff actually smiles and the diner owner says hello.

Welcome to Northern Wisconsin. Pass the relish tray, please, and let's have dessert.

Angler's Haven Resort, 15437 County Rd. KK, Hayward, WI 54843; (715) 634-2757; anglershavenresort.com; Pizza; $–$$. Tucked along the banks of fish-rich Lac Courte Oreilles, the Haven presents pizza, pizza, and more pizza. The Bleu Cheese, with white garlic-herb sauce, Gorgonzola cheese, bacon, spinach, and green onions, is one of the more exotic. For spicy, chow down slices of the Firehouse, concocted with a hot red sauce and cheeses, Italian sausage, pepperoni, sweet bell peppers, tomatoes, jalapeños, and roasted garlic. Hand-done thin or thick crusts are available. Since most everyone here is a fishing fanatic, many of the pizza varieties have some sort of outdoor title: the Angler, the Tacklebox, and so on. Another section of the menu is set aside for "Bait & Tackle," with Beach Side Brats, Musky Bread, and Northern Nachos, along with the stock-in-trade buffalo wings and related pub grub. The "Bobbers" are a full pound of lightly seasoned roasted baby potatoes, optionally served with a dollop of sour cream thick with chives. In 2009, the bar at Angler's Haven was inducted as the first officially Honorary Leinie Lodge, named for **Leinenkugel** (p. 128) beer, which has been brewed in nearby Chippewa Falls since 1887.

Black Cat Coffeehouse, 211 Chappie Ave., Ashland, WI 54806; (715) 682-3680; blackcatashland.com; Casual American; $. The culinary philosophy at the Black Cat is that "simple-better food means better health." As such, everything in the kitchen is based on organic foods as much as possible, using local providers. On the list of producers are the next-door Ashland Baking Company, Tetzners Dairy, Hermit Creek, Great Oak, Deep Roots, River Road, Spirit Creek, Northwind Farms, Northern Nectar Honey, 6th Street Market, Bayfield Apple Company, Blue Vista Orchard, and White Winter Winery. So you can't go wrong with any of the offerings on this menu, which is mostly vegetarian. However, there is a bacon-lettuce-tomato sandwich for the carnivore crowd. The coffee at the Cat is a real caffeine kicker, using organic, fair-traded brands. Coffees are provided by Alakef Coffee Roasters in Duluth, as well as award-winning regional roasters such as Anodyne Coffee from Milwaukee, Peace Coffee from Minneapolis, and Kickapoo Coffee from Viroqua, Wisconsin.

Bohemian Ovens Restaurant & Bakery, 905 Martin Rd., Bloomer, WI 54724; (715) 568-3676; bohemianovens.com; Bakery Cafe; $–$$. The bakery is owned and operated by Mike and Sally Hable, who use a specially built brick oven that weighs 15,000 pounds. It uses burning hardwood that heats the bricks to 525°F, baking up to 40 loaves of bread at a time. Some of the taste treats include an Asiago, black pepper, and garlic variety, as well as a sourdough rye, gluten-free rice bread, and cranberry walnut, all with that wonderful aroma of freshness. The Hables also make a dynamite pie with hand-rolled crusts. Ohhhhh, that strawberry rhubarb! Now to the cakes: sheet cakes, round cakes, cupcakes, and cheesecakes in numerous flavors. True to its Bohemian name, the breakfast *kolaches* are fantastic additions, made with a sweet dough, filled with fruit, and baked prior to being sprinkled with confectioners' sugar. Different soups are made every day for lunch, including a rare nettle and the creamiest dill you probably have ever had. Pizza on Saturday night is on your own: The restaurant provides the hand-rolled 10-inch crusts, and you can add as many toppings as you want. The staff then takes your concoction and bakes it up in that aforementioned mega-oven.

Bogus Creek Cafe & Bakery, N2049 Spring St., Stockholm, WI 54769; (715) 442-5017; boguscreekcafe.com; Casual American; $–$$. For breakfast, indulge yourself with Swedish pancakes slathered with freshly whipped cream and laden with lingonberries. The Bogus Creek is famous for its hash, with the french toast running a close second. For lunch, there are fresh turkey clubs, tuna melts, loads of greens in the salads, and shrimp pico de pasta, among an extensive listing of other tasty items. Soups are homemade, just as they should be. There is a hefty wine and beer list, as well. Since this doubles as bakery, the aroma of freshly baked pastries and artisan breads make for a hard-to-resist lure. As they say at Bogus Creek, "Our food is real." This cozy getaway also features ice cream and a full espresso bar, as well as free Wi-Fi in the courtyard, a gluten-free menu, and an ATM in the bakery section. While here, say howdy to Bogus, the resident dog.

Cafe Mexicana, 421 S. Main St., Rice Lake, WI 54868; (715) 736-1184; Mexican; $. Noted for its large portions, the Cafe Mexicana features traditional south-of-the-border items, with the chicken quesadillas and fajitas prepared with heart and soul. The poblanos are as good as anywhere found along the Rio Grande. The salsa packs a punch, with makes it especially good with chips and beer.

The Crimson Cup, 424 Lincoln St., Rhinelander, WI, 54501; (715) 362-8994; Sandwich Shop; $. Walk up the steps into this glorious old white house and discover one of the best lunches you could find in the North Country. Panini and sandwiches certainly make the grade, as does the homemade soup. Peruse the gift selection, with loads of scarves, ornaments, and other gifty items for sale. Parking can be a hassle, but don't let that keep you away from the Crimson Cup's neat little outback dining patio in the summer.

Delta Diner, 14385 County Hwy. H, Mason, WI 54856; (715) 372-6666; deltadiner.com; Casual American; $–$$. If you are a first timer seeking out the Delta Diner, good luck, because Mason is only the mailing address and the restaurant is actually in the nearby crossroads of Delta. The diner gang proudly says that they are in the center of nowhere. Actually, the diner is not really that remote, being only a few miles from Iron River, so all the locals flock here. Just go with the traffic flow. After Labor Day, the place is closed Tues and Wed. Burgers served only on Mon, but year-round, from 11 a.m. to 7 p.m.

Fireside Supper Club, 6012 County Hwy. K, Rhinelander, WI 54501; (715) 369-4717; firesidesupperclub.com; Supper Club; $$. The club overlooks Town Line Lake, which offers a great vista. The Fireside has been owned by Earl and Margo Morey since 1989. They know their steaks, serving USDA-choice or higher graded meats, plus prime rib, fish fry, and ribs. You can get it all at the Fireside, which, by the way, also has an excellent bar scene. Remember that the Fireside is closed Sun.

Flat Pennies Ice Cream, W6442 State Hwy. 35, Bay City, WI 54723; (715) 594-3555; flatpennies.com; Casual American; $. This unique drive-in on Wisconsin's Great River Road is located adjacent to an old SooLine railroad car for dining and tour information. Bring Fido and use one of the "hitching posts" for your pet to sit near your table as you chow down one of the restaurant's fabled peanut butter sandwiches. They are made with a choice of jelly, chocolate, pretzel, honey, banana, and marshmallows. Due to its close proximity to the railroad, train engineers regularly stop their trains at Flat Pennies to sample the soft-serve ice cream. What is it about locomotives and chocolate- and cherry-dipped cones on a steamy summer afternoon?

Friendship House, 2260 Lincoln St., Rhinelander, WI 54501; (715) 362-5765; friendshiphouserhinelander.com; Casual American; $-$$. With a name like Friendship House, you can be assured of a warm welcome, good service, and great home-style cooking. Drop in for a breakfast omelet or pancakes, a hot turkey sandwich for lunch, or barbecued ribs at dinner, with plenty of alluring specials. This is a kid- and family-friendly caravansary, exactly what its name implies. What's best, the prices are reasonable and the food is plentiful, especially the chicken and dumpling soup served in bowls that seem as big as vats.

Harbor Restaurant & Bar, N673 825th St., Hager City, WI 54014; (715) 792-2417; harborbar.net; Caribbean; $-$$. Located on the Mississippi River across from Red Wing, Minnesota, boaters can find the Harbor at Mississippi River mile marker 791. You may think you've landed in the Caribbean when sitting down for the Jamaican jerk cooking found here, with all the top-secret seasonings made in-house. The menu is chicken friendly, offering jerk chicken, a lip-smacking blackened chicken, Cajun chicken, Caribbean chicken served with pineapple, a traditional fried chicken, and the ever-popular grilled chicken. Wraps, burgers, steaks, seafood, and stir-fries round out the food selections. Three generations of the Smith family have operated the restaurant and bar, expanding the marina and making other renovations. But the site has long hosted a tavern, the first incarnation dating back to the late 1890s.

Harbor View Cafe, 314 1st St., Pepin, WI 54759; (715) 442-3893; harborviewpepin.com; Bistro; $$-$$$. The cafe doesn't accept credit cards or reservations, so remember to take cash or a check when you have a hankering for braised chicken with chipotles on linguine. The restaurant is located on the banks of Lake Pepin, a widening of the Mississippi River. The menu is on a chalkboard, with a listing of entrees hinting at a Norwegian heritage with a Mediterranean touch. That is, you might find codfish cakes and Norwegian meatballs with a thick sour cream–cardamom sauce, along with pasta. The kitchen's mantra is "When in doubt, add more garlic." The cafe is closed Tues and Wed, with limited spring and fall hours.

James Sheeley House Restaurant and Saloon, 236 W. River St., Chippewa Falls, WI 54729; (715) 726-0561; jamessheeley house.com; Traditional American; $$. The Italianate-styled James Sheeley House was originally a boardinghouse and now serves cashew-crusted walleye and shrimp scampi in its incarnation as a restaurant. The slow-roasted prime rib is ace, of course sided with a baked potato. The Sheeley House burger also packs a wallop, a hefty critter made from a half pound of locally sourced grilled ground sirloin and served with a heap of french fries. Tuesday is Fresh Salmon Night, with Saturday billed as Sirloin Dinner Night. The building overlooks the Chippewa River on Business Highway 29.

Mickey-Lu Bar-B-Q, 1710 Marinette Ave., Marinette, WI 54143; (715) 735-7721; Burgers; $. This is a two-generational throwback with a jukebox well racked with oldies. The vintage decor is real, since Mickey-Lu has been around since 1942. Burgers are prepared on a charcoal grill, prettied up in a grand finale with a dollop of butter in the middle of the patty. As a matter of fact, the diner still grinds its own meat. The malt machine is around the corner from the grill, with a menu posted on a board to the left of the counter seats. Don't expect anything as fancy as fries on the side; only chips are added. For the record, *USA Today* once rated this place as among America's top 50 great burger joints.

Northwoods Brewpub and Grill, 3560 Oakwood Mall Dr., Eau Claire, WI 54701; (715) 552-0510; northwoodsbrewpub.com; Casual American; $–$$. This is Eau Claire's first brewpub, producing a far-ranging menu of beers, with the first batch being served in 1997. Among the brewskis listed are Kelly's Stout, White Weasel Light Ale, Half Moon Gold, and another nine regulars, plus several seasonals such as an Oktoberfest lager. The restaurant has a rustically timbered Northwoods ambience. All you need are the Three Bears to stroll out of the woods and join you at the dinner table. In addition to such entrees

as walleye and rib eye, you can go for the grilled chicken breasts smothered in swiss cheese, sautéed portobello mushrooms, and onions. For an out-of-the-ordinary sandwich, indulge in a Dockside Duck Burger with lean duck mixed and grilled with ground beef, or the Great Frontier Burger, made of bison meat. Both are served with a choice of fried chips, beer fries, or coleslaw. For a stupendous finale to a meal, the restaurant serves **Norske Nook** (p. 265) pies from nearby Osseo. Five stars go to the Friday breakfast special of corned beef hash with two eggs the way you like them, along with homemade white or whole wheat toast.

The Pub Restaurant and Wine Bar, 641 Main St., La Pointe, WI 54850; (715) 747-6322; madisland.com; Seafood/Steaks; $$–$$$. The Inn on Madeline Island has been a popular vacation site since 1983, plus hosting weddings, family reunions, and other larger gatherings. The Pub is an integral part of the complex. No matter where you sit in the restaurant, you'll get a great view of Lake Superior just outside the windows. The kitchen here can also prepare take-out meals for a picnic or charter excursion out on the lake's gray-green waters. Madeline Island, on the south shore of Lake Superior, is part of the Apostle Islands National Lakeshore. Although The Pub is closed in the winter, restaurants are open in Bayfield. The Inn is just across the channel from the village of Bayfield, linked by a ferry in the summer and iceboats in the winter. Or, if the ice is thick enough, you can carefully drive over a plowed roadway. See their recipe for **Pub Mussels** on p. 301.

Red Cedar Lodge, E4620 County Rd. C, Downsville, WI 54735; (715) 664-8354; red-cedar-lodge.com; Supper Club; $$. This used to be The Creamery Restaurant, which closed in 2010. The site was renovated and reopened with its new name in 2012 by entrepreneurial sisters Dawn and Melissa (Mel) Schroeder. The fare is low-key, yet wow-tasty and extremely nutritious, with Wednesday being pizza and burger night and Thursday featuring ribs and chicken. The blue cheese–crusted New York rib eye steak is another guaranteed taste-bud pleaser. At the pub side, you can order a grilled chicken sandwich, several varieties of pizza, and a range of burgers. The inn is super cozy, with expansive windows of the grounds and surrounding woods.

Rhinelander Cafe & Pub, 33 N. Brown St., Rhinelander, WI 54501; (715) 362-2918; rhinelandercafeandpub.com; Traditional American; $$. The cafe is both a casual breakfast and lunch getaway and a fine-dining facility. Foods are made from scratch, including breads and pies. Just watch out for the cheesecake if counting calories. For an evening meal, sample the fresh Lake Superior whitefish when it's available. The fish comes either planked, broiled, or panfried. Ask and ye shall receive. Naturally, there are plenty of house specialties. Don't step back from the roast Long Island duckling with orange sauce, or the veal Oscar. Locals know that the center-cut pork chops are among the best in the region and that dedicated diners call the spaghetti with meat sauce "the best pasta around."

Riverstone Restaurant, 219 N. Railroad St., Eagle River, WI 54521; (715) 479-8467; riverstonerestaurant.com; Supper Club; $$$. The Riverstone is called the North Country's most wine-friendly restaurant. Who is to argue, looking over the vintage listings. The vegetarian soup made with wild rice is appropriately creamy, with the addition of carrots, celery, onion, and sweet corn. Oh, those Wisconsin ingredients! You can also pig out with the roasted barbecue pulled pork served on a pretzel roll, complemented with coleslaw and blastaway fries. The cheeseburgers all use champion Wisconsin cheese, and you can add **Nueske's** (p. 245) applewood-smoked bacon for another cholesterol jumpstart. Speaking of cheese, the butternut squash ravioli is served with a dollop of Sid Hook's **Carr Valley Cheese Company**'s (p. 241) gorgeous blue in a velvety smooth sauce, along with spinach. And was there a mention of the veal pot roast with a root-vegetable mash that is a scrumptious blend of parsnips, potatoes, rutabaga, and carrots? How down and earthy can you get after this? Breads are house-made, as well.

The Shack Smokehouse & Grille, 3301 Belknap St., Superior, WI 54880; (715) 392-9836; Casual American; $$–$$$. This is a northshore Lake Superior club serving a 6-pound burger whopper called The Shackamanjaro. If you can eat this monster in 45 minutes and still sit up straight, it's free and your name goes up on the wall. Did we mention that the 'Jaro comes laden with a pound of bacon and 20 pickles all packed between two thick-crust pizza shells. If perhaps you are still hungrgy, follow that with the Chowaf, a chocolate waffle with ice cream and cookie crumbs dipped  in a chocolate ganache. The restaurant was remodeled in 2012, stepping back from its former life as a white-tablecloth, fine-dining establishment into one with a more casual atmosphere. If you knew the old Shack, check out the new look and fare. Just keep your health insurance card close at hand.

Skipper's Family Restaurant, 812 E. 1st St., Merrill, WI 54452; (715) 536-9914; Casual American; $–$$. Relaxing, charming, and comfortable are three adjectives that capture the essence of Skipper's. Crepes are available Saturday, as well as cinnamon buns the size of Clydesdale hooves. The restaurant is on State Highway 64, also known as 1st Street, and only a block from the scenic Wisconsin River, where it meets the smaller flowage of the Prairie River. Look for Skipper's in the white turn-of-the-20th-century building on the corner and follow your nose to a table. This is a great spot for lunch between exploring the nearby Prairie Dells Scenic Area and the Merrill Memorial Forest Wildlife Area, ambling along the Ice Age Trail or taking in the parks in the community. The abundance of such green space has earned Merrill the title of "City of Parks."

Wild Rice Restaurant, 84860 Old San Rd., Bayfield, WI 54814; (715) 779-9881; wildricerestaurant.com; New American; $$$. There's passion at the Wild Rice. After all, the folks here say that "cooking is like love. It should be entered into with abandon or not at all." This philosophy shows throughout, whether with a creamy wild rice soup complemented with smoked duck and Bayfield sugar pears in season, or the roasted Lake Superior whitefish and grilled lake trout. The restaurant changes its starches and veggies on a regular basis, depending what is locally available. The building itself is a contemporary marvel, designed by noted architect David Salmela of Duluth who worked closely with owner Mary Rice. Her artistic eye and the culinary talents of Executive Chef Jim Webster have placed Wild Rice on the Northwood's culinary map. Randy Anderson is Wild Rice's quintessentially gracious and knowledgeable maître d'. The restaurant is off State Highway 13 on the shores of Lake Superior, a few miles north of Big Top Chautauqua, a critically acclaimed musical venue that is a Bayfield summertime landmark.

Landmarks

Anchor Bar, 413 Tower Ave., Superior, WI 54880; (715) 394-9747; anchorbar.freeservers.com; Burgers; $. This bar is another go-to tavern in northern Wisconsin. Anchor Bar serves up huge burgers and fries amid a nautical theme. One of the artifacts is a life preserver from the ill-fated ore carrier *Edmund Fitzgerald,* which sank in stormy Lake Superior on November 10, 1975. Longshoremen, students, doctors, families, and others from all walks of life congregate in the cramped quarters, in a space that makes for elbow-rubbing conversation about the lake, fishing, politics, and the general state of life. Reviewers number the Anchor among the country's greatest burger bars. They include a cashew burger, made with real cashews and swiss cheese, and the Galleybuster triple burger. Anchors can barely get "aweigh" with that gastronomic battleship.

Bent's Camp, Lodge, Bar & Restaurant, 6882 S. Helen Creek Rd., Land O' Lakes, WI 54540; (715) 547-3487; bents-camp .com; Supper Club; $–$$. Dating from 1906, Bent's has the appropriate look of a bygone era, with its rustic decor including birch bark, held in place by cedar-bark strips, lining the ceiling and walls. Photos from the early days of Bent's Camp are everywhere, including on the menu. Almost everything has a homemade touch, from the

vegetables grown on-site to the handmade pizza. Steaks and roast duck are specialties, with nightly specials. Pork chops, ribs, and yellowfin tuna earn raves from ravenous visitors, in from a day of fishing. Speaking of fins, Bent's Friday fish fry attracts a big crowd. Breakfast is served Saturday and Sunday with a Bloody Mary bar available starting at the wee hour of 8 a.m. Early every August, Bent's hosts its Northwoodstock festival, with live music all day and lots of food and beer. This self-proclaimed "hippie hoe down" is good for laughs, plenty of hamburgers, and several rounds of brew.

The Chanticleer Inn, 1458 E. Dollar Lake Rd., Eagle River, WI 54521; (715) 479-4486; chanticleerinn.com; Supper Club; $$–$$$. The Inn overlooks the blue-green waters of Lake Voyager that is often dotted by small watercraft. In the winter, watch the deer crossing the ice. The Inn's extensive menu ranges from burgers to lobster. The Friday fish fry is worth a stop. You also can go for a light sandwich menu or, what the heck, enjoy the famous walleye platter with the

German potato pancakes. It's been said that this dish will help you row faster when the motor on your boat clunks out. In the summer, the Beer Garden is a casual must-stop, whether you come by boat, car, bike, or foot. There is free docking. There are charbroiled brats, hot dogs, burgers, rib sandwiches, grilled chicken sandwiches, and even Caesar salads that are mounded with lettuce and add-ons. The Chanticleer also has a full-service lounge overlooking the Beer Garden and the lake.

Fanny Hill Dinner Theatre, 3919 Crescent Ave., Eau Claire, WI 54703; (800) 292-8026; fannyhill.com; Supper Club; $$. The all-you-can-eat Sunday brunch and follow-up matinee is a highlight, with meal seating starting at 11:30 a.m. Performances are also available from Thursday through Saturday with seating beginning at 5:45 p.m. Fanny Hill was launched in 1978 and subsequently has produced more than 7,500 theatrical dinner experiences, mostly comedies and musicals. Performances have included *Elvis: The Essence of the King,* with the hip-shaking George Thomas performing to cheers and shouts; the farcical *Don't Dress for Dinner;* and Neil Simon's *Barefoot in the Park.* Meals are served in the Riverview Grille, with a range of items including coconut curried mussels, burgers, beef Stroganoff, bacon-wrapped filets, and scallops. The lemon berry mascarpone makes for a grand finale and applause for your meal. The dinner theater is popular with motor-coach tours.

Greunke's Restaurant, 17 Rittenhouse Ave., Bayfield, WI 54814; (715) 779-5480; greunkesinn.com; Casual American; $$. Centrally located in downtown Bayfield, the inn is a short stroll to Lake Superior, where you can watch the Madeline Island Ferry or take in the town shops. The restaurant itself has a 1940s feel, with all the Coca-Cola memorabilia and the old soda fountain. You have to try the whitefish livers, or take in a fish boil during the summer season. The attached

PICKLED EGGS AND BEER

Moccasin Bar, 15820 N. US 63, Hayward, WI 54843; (715) 634-4211; $. Hayward is the self-proclaimed "Muskie Capital of the World" and home of the National Freshwater Fishing Hall of Fame. The Moccasin is said to be one of the best Up North bars in Wisconsin. Put your Kia or Automobili Lamborghini just beyond the designated "Biggest, Rustiest, Loudest, Ugliest Truck in Town Parking Only" slots and saunter in for the time of your life. But don't expect much in the way of food; this is a beer dive, with all the chipmunks playing cards, along with record-setting stuffed fish and other demised critters lining the walls. Eat your quota of pickled eggs and quaff cheap beer, then move on with memories of all those glass eyes staring back at you, both from the other customers and from the mounted deer heads.

First Street Inn, a lodging facility for more than 130 years, now has 12 homey rooms. For a bedtime snack, try a pepperoni and onion from Sgt. Pepperoni's Pizza To Go; the pizza parlor is located 21 N. 1st St. (715-779-0153).

Herschleb's, 640 S. 16th St., Wisconsin Rapids, WI 54494; (715) 423-1760; Ice Cream/Yogurt; $-$$. Launched in 1939, Herschleb's remains a working ice-cream manufacturing facility in the same building as its 40-seat restaurant. The ice cream is shipped out to stores in quart, half-gallon, and one- or three-gallon containers. Herschleb's is a favorite stopover whenever in Wisconsin Rapids. Its sundaes are the talk of the town, part of a rite of passage for the city's ice cream lovers.

LaGrander's Drive In, 18143 County Hwy. X, Chippewa Falls, WI 54729; (715) 723-0672; Casual American; $. LaGrander's is an old-fashioned carhop joint located across from the Lake Wissota beach.

PIES AT THEIR BEST

Since opening in 1973, the landmark **Norske Nook** (norskenook .com) has become world famous for its Norwegian-style home cooking and scratch-made pies. The main bakery/restaurant is adjacent to a coffeehouse and Scandinavian gift shop where you can get Norwegian cookbooks, kitchen apparel, pies to go, and coffee mugs. For breakfast, king-size pancakes can be filled with Scandinavian lingonberries or blackberries, blueberries, or raspberries. The Ultimate Potato Pancake is topped with bacon, two eggs, and enough hollandaise sauce to fuel the crew of a Viking longboat. The Norwegian salmon wrap is a crowd-pleaser. This is made with a grilled fillet within a roll of buttered *lefse* dough and topped with a lemon slice, along with garnishes of lettuce and dollop of sour cream. Standard American fare is also offered, such as shrimp baskets, burgers, and sirloin steak. Wednesday is Pie Day, featuring a different flavor of pie accompanied by a cup of coffee. Kids, age 10 and under, eat free from every Saturday from 4 p.m. to close.

Norske Nook Restaurant & Bakery has four locations: 13804 7th St., Osseo, WI 54758 (715-597-3069); 2900 Pioneer Ave., Rice Lake, WI 54868 (715-234-1733); State Highway 27 South, Hayward, WI 54843 (715-634-4928); and 3560 Oakwood Mall Dr., Eau Claire, WI 54701 (715-552-0510). Each location is open seven days a week. For a fun fact, Norske Nook has competed six times at the National Pie Championship in Florida and captured at least 30 blue ribbons, along with dozens of other awards. Winners have included the apple cream cheese, baked strawberry, chocolate peanut butter, sugar-free peach, and blueberry crunch.

It's family-run, opened in 1978 by Bob LaGrander. His famous house-battered cheese curds come from LaGrander's Dairy, owned by Bob's brother. But the real deal at LaGranders is the ice cream. Made on-site, the most popular flavor is called Sinful, a well-deserved name for the real honey, chocolate chunks, and chocolate-covered peanuts folded in.

Rittenhouse Inn, 301 Rittenhouse Ave., Bayfield, WI 54814; (800) 779-2129; rittenhouseinn.com; Traditional American; $$$. Only the best and freshest ingredients are used in the Rittenhouse dishes, a true landmark in a region long known for its berries, vegetables, mushrooms, and fish. The Rittenhouse, which opened in 1975, is more than just a local favorite; it's internationally known through articles in *Bon Appétit, Gourmet, Midwest Living,* and the *New York Times.* Guests at the inn are offered a complimentary continental-plus breakfast of coffee, tea, or juice, and a fruit course. The basket of freshly baked muffins and pastries empties fast when slathered with a homemade Rittenhouse jam or jelly. Then it's on to homemade cinnamon-swirled french toast topped with berries and fresh whipped cream. The restaurant is open to the public for each meal, so you can enjoy your steel-cut oatmeal even if not overnighting it at the inn. Dinner menus change daily, depending on what's new in the larder.

Specialty Stores, Markets & Producers

Ashland Bakery, 212 Chapple Ave., Ashland, WI 54806; (715) 682-6010; ashlandbakingco.com. Every item in the display case is 100 percent scratch-made. Specialty breads are their forte. For instance, on any given Monday, you might get a jalapeño cheddar and a honey wheat, while on Tuesday, multigrain sourdough and a marble rye are presented in grand style. The deli counter has a wide range of items, from tabouli to numerous pesto varieties. The dessert case explodes with croissants, brownies, shortbread, chocolate tiramisu, and related delights. The company's breads are also found in outlets throughout  the state, as well as in numerous restaurants in Wisconsin such as the **Delta Diner** (p. 254) in Delta, the Ideal Market and Rivers Eatery in Cable, the Pinehurst Inn in Bayfield.

Joe's Cheese House, 1905 Dunlap Ave., Marinette, WI, 54143; (715) 735-6922. Locals have been coming to Joe's for their aged cheddar or aged swiss for more than three decades. You can sample before you buy, which may be a challenge because you won't want to stop with just a perfunctory nibble here and there. Many of Wisconsin's award-winning cheeses, as well as high-quality imports, are peddled here. Joe's can ship cheese and sausage to almost anywhere on earth.

Joe's Pasty Shop, 123 Randall Ave., Rhinelander, WI 54501-3757; (715) 369-1224; ilovepasties.com; $. This small house has been converted into a commercial kitchen, with picnic tables inside the porch for year-round eating. The deck has a couple of other tables for perching when the weather is good. Frozen pasties are also available for later devouring at home. If you aren't aware of what a real pasty tastes like, Joe's makes for a marvelous introduction to this quick, hearty meal that was once the the lunch-box favorite of Cornish miners. An authentic pasty, pronounced "PASS-tee," is usually made with ground beef and potatoes, onions, and rutabagas that are seasoned and wrapped in a crust. That being said, don't confuse this meat pie with the teeny-tiny bit of fabric draping a burlesque entertainer's upper regions or gluelike mashed potatoes, both of which are spelled the same way but respectively pronounced "PASTE-tee" and "PAST-ee." The meat used here is grass-fed beef or pork from Futility Farms in Gilman, Wisconsin. Subsequently, there are no hormones, steroids, or antibiotics to harm your gastrointestinal system. As an option, experience Joe's whole wheat pastry crust, constructed from white flour, canola oil, and sea salt. Joe's is a proud participant in Travel Green Wisconsin, which promotes reusing, recycling, and reducing waste. Joe's was launched in 1946 and remains in the same family. It was taken over in the early 2000s by Larry Lapachin and his wife, Jessica, whose great-uncle Joe and grandfather Frank Barbera started the pasty shop.

Legacy Chocolates, 632 S. Broadway St., Menomonie, WI 54751; (715) 231-2580; legacychocolates.com. Legacy opened its first store in Menomonie on Earth Day in 2002 and now sells its fresh, handmade works of chocolate art through hotel gift shops and other retailers. Staying true to its mission of being environmentally aware, the chocolate is made from the Criollo cocoa bean produced by small-scale, sustainable farmers in Venezuela. The Mayan sipping chocolate is particularly pleasing on the palate, especially during Wisconsin's cold winter nights. Truffles, sauce, and barks are also on the plus side for diehard chocolate connoisseurs.

Marchant's Foods, 1367 County Trunk DK, Brussels, WI 54204; (920) 825-1244; marchantsfoods.com. Marchant's presents an extensive array of bakery products. You want buns? They have fresh buns, plus cookies, bread, and desserts. Mornings bring out the doughnuts and sweet rolls. Marchant's also specializes in homemade Belgian pies, made of a soft dough crust with a fruit filling and a creamy cheese topping. The store's meat counter carries quality pork, beef, hams, and sausages, with its in-house smoking for their own sausages, bologna, hams, and bacon. Capitalizing on recipes handed down from the town's earliest Belgian settlers, *trippe* is a popular purchase. These are much like brats, but made with cooked cabbage. Marchant's also has a hot deli, so you can order fresh broasted chicken and barbecued ribs. When in season, the produce department works

Brewing in the North Woods

Valkyrie Brewing Company, 234 W. Dallas St., Dallas, WI 54733; (715) 837-1824; valkyriebrewery.com. Talk about manly brews: Dragon Blade lager, War Hammer porter, Big Swede imperial stout, and Night Wolf, a German-style *schwarz* or "black" beer. The initial batch from this family-owned microbrewery was produced in 1994, making it the first microbrewery in northwest Wisconsin. The brewery's taproom is open on Thurs, Fri, and Sat afternoon in the summer, with tours available on Sat. Each Oktoberfest in early October, the brewery goes for producing a record-size bratwurst, a delicacy made by Louie's Finer Meats. The 2012 brat was an amazing 135 feet long, beating out the 2011 mark of 131 feet.

Black Husky Brewing, W5951 Steffen Ln., Pembine, WI 54156; (715) 324-5152; blackhuskybrewing.com. The Black Husky is one of Wisconsin's only nanobreweries, making only small batches of beer for a dedicated audience. The company's headquarters is actually a real log cabin brewery tucked in the woods of northeastern Wisconsin. Tim and Toni Eichinger kick-started their operation in 2009, with their dog Howler as the inspiration for the black husky on its label. The beer is sold in Green Bay, Milwaukee, Shawano, Eagle River, Two Rivers, and woodsy hot spots such as Annie's Trading Post on Keys Lake in Florence and the Four Seasons Island Resort, Pembine. Among its selections, most of which have a dog theme, Black Husky brews Twelve-Dog imperial stout and Sparkly Eyes, an ale that philosopher/brew dude Eichinger claims "gives the disinclination to attack others." It was developed by Eichinger so, as he is quoted, "you too can adopt the peaceful ways of the Warrior Monk on your journey to being a Jedi of the New Earth Army." On that note, please pour another.

with local growers who provide Door County cherries, sweet corn, and apples. One of Marchant's snack-size fruit cups or small vegetable trays makes for a light snack or a heart-healthy lunch.

Silver Spring Foods, 2424 Alpine Rd., Eau Claire, WI 54703; (800) 826-7322; silverspringfoods.com. The facility, a subsidiary of Huntsinger Farms, specializes in horseradish, mustard, and other specialty sauces. The jalapeño mustard is strong enough to make a jumping bean jump twice as high, and don't try the extra-hot horseradish unless you want to really test your taste buds. The facility has been making horseradish since 1929. So you know the product has to be good, as well as nose-cleansing. For your scientific backgrounding, horseradish is a plant that comes from the mustard family and is considered one of the five bitter herbs for the Jewish Passover. Silver Spring does make kosher products and ships its goods around the country. The folks here will tell you that the word "horseradish" first appeared in print in 1597, found in John Gerarde's famous book on herbs called *The Herball,* or, *Generall Historie of Plantes.*

Where to Get It Fresh

Here are a few places where you can go in the North Country for flowers, honey, fruit, vegetables, eggs, maple syrup, fresh baked goods, beef, and loads of other locally produced items.

Catawba Farmers' Market, W9241 State Hwy. 8, Catawba, WI 54515; (715) 474-6713. Sat from 10 a.m. to 1 p.m., early July through mid-Sept.

Cornucopia Farmers' Market, Town Beach Park, Cornucopia, WI, 54827; (715) 742-3551. Thurs from 3 to 6 p.m., mid-June through Sept.

Farm Stands and Pick on the Go, Where the Selection Is Always Amazing

Bashaw Valley Farm and Greenhouse, W7402 Fox Trail Rd., Shell Lake, WI 54871; (715) 468-2591. Bashaw's is another great certified organic farm where you can pick or select from the already-picked in the farm stand. Lots of farm animals to observe.

Blue Vista Farm, 34045 S. County J, Bayfield, WI 54814; (715) 779-5400. Emphasizes organic apples, blueberries, pumpkins, raspberries, and pumpkin.

Don's Berry Patch, 29420 Engoe Rd, Washburn, WI 54891; (715) 373-2053. Great for stawberries.

Helene's Hilltop Orchard, N1189 Quarter Rd., Merrill, WI 54452; (715) 536-1207. There are both an indoor market and an uncovered outdoor market for baked goods, cherries, sweet corn, and cider made on premise.

Highland Valley Farm, 87080 Valley Rd, Bayfield, WI 54814; (715) 779-5446. Highland Valley uses integrated pest management practices for protecting its blueberries, red raspberries, and other crops instead of pesticides.

Saxon Harbor Berry Farm and Farm Market, 15556 N. State Highway 122, Saxon, WI 54559; (715) 893-2397. You can't go wrong with the apples, blackberries, blueberries, pumpkins, and raspberries from here.

Eau Claire Downtown Farmers' Market, 300 Riverfront Ter. (corner of Madison Street and Riverfront Terrace, next to the Madison Street bridge), Eau Claire, WI 54703; (715) 834-5697; ecdowntownfarmersmarket.com. Sat from 7:30 a.m. to 1 p.m., May; Wed and Sat from 7:30 a.m. to 1 p.m., and Thurs from 1 to 5 p.m., June through Oct.

Hudson Farmers' Market, 777 Carmichael Rd., Hudson, WI 54016; (612) 203-9030; hudsonfarmersmarketcarmichael.com. Sat from 8 a.m. to noon, mid-July through Oct.

Jeremy's Market, Garfield Avenue at the Zorn Arena North Sidewalk at the University of Wisconsin–Eau Claire, Eau Claire, WI 54701; (715) 836-4803; wisconline.com. Thurs from 7:30 to 11:30 a.m., end of Aug through end of Oct.

Menomonie Farmers' Market, 620 17th St. (Dunn County Fairgrounds), Menomonie, WI 54751; (715) 265-4271 ext. 1348; travelwisconsin.com. Wed from noon to 6 p.m., and Sat from 8 a.m. to 1 p.m., mid-May through Oct.

New Richmond Farmers' Market, 1100 Heritage Dr. (Heritage Center parking lot), New Richmond, WI 54017; (715) 246-3276. Daily from 7:30 a.m. until sold out, June through Oct.

Phillips Farmers' Market, corner of Maple and Avon Streets, Phillips, WI 54555; (715) 339-6516; pricecountywi.net/.../farmers-markets-local. Sat from 9 a.m. to noon, and Tues from 3 to 5:30 p.m., mid-July through Oct.

Rusk County Farmers' Market, State Highway 8 and West 4th Street North, at C53 Cloverland Rd., Ladysmith, WI 54848; (715) 532-3791; ruskcountywi.com/events.php. Sat from 8:30 a.m. to noon, and Wed from 3 to 6 p.m., early July through late Oct.

Western Wisconsin

The Great River Road, or in more plebeian terms, State Highway 35, runs along Wisconsin's western border. It skirts wildlife preserves, edges along state parks, overlooks locks and dams, and passes through numerous small towns and crossroads communities. Eagles, ducks, geese, and innumerable other birds flock here. The woods are full of deer and smaller critters. The towns are hospitable, delightful, and picturesque. Prehistoric people built animal mounds on the bluffs overlooking the river, linking the spirit world with the reality of life. Later, along came the Sac and Fox, among other native nations, followed by French explorers, Cornish miners, and Norwegian farmers. This bundle of ethnic energy contributes to the region today, where the traveler can find just about any kind of food desired.

Inland is the Driftless Area, where the unglaciated landscape rolls like a bunched-up carpet. Corn and soybean fields abound, with their gold and green the colors of the Green Bay Packers football team. The open acreages are interspersed with towering silos, red barns, and herds of Holsteins, the state's staple animal.

This is Western Wisconsin, once the frontier of America, and now its heartland.

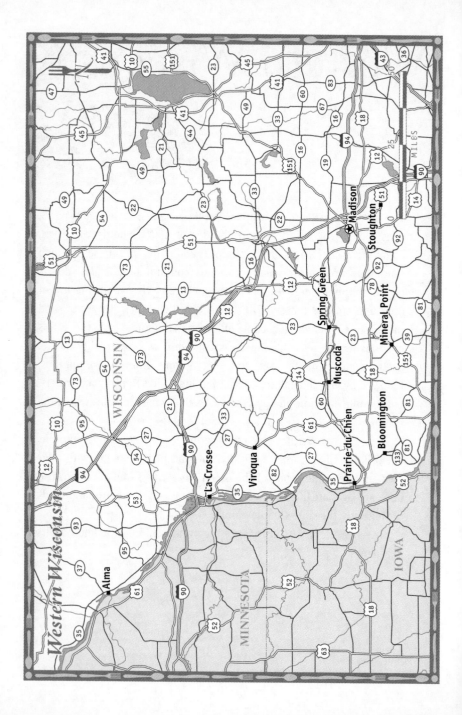

Western Wisconsin

MINNESOTA

WISCONSIN

IOWA

Madison
Stoughton
Spring Green
Mineral Point
Muscoda
Bloomington
Prairie du Chien
La Crosse
Viroqua
Alma

MILES

Foodie Faves

Beedle's Bar and Restaurant, W24966 State Rd. 54/93, Centerville, WI 54630; (608) 539-2251; beedlesbar.com; Bistro; $–$$. Owners Brad and Annie Beedle couldn't take the big city any more, so they moved to Centerville from St. Paul, along with their kids, Max and Jack. The family purchased the restaurant in 2006 and set about making it a comfort-food hideaway, with an expansive selection of hand-cut, in-house aged steaks, plus pastas and seafood. The long, low white-painted restaurant is cozy inside, where guests are quickly made welcome. Belly up to the bar. The challenge is to not eat too many beer-battered onion rings.

Buzzard Billy's Flying Carp Cafe, 222 Pearl St., La Crosse, WI 54601; (608) 796-2277; buzzardbillys.com; Cajun; $$. You probably never knew you'd ever eat Gator Fingers, at least those listed on Billy's menu. Rest easy, these items are not really digits at all, but farm-raised alligator tail sliced into thin strips, hand breaded, and deep-fried. This goodie is served with a Creole honey mustard dipping sauce. You can then top out with the restaurant's signature dish, which is a cup or bowl of gumbo. The blend of Gulf shrimp, crawfish tails, and andouille sausage in a highly seasoned roux-based broth is served here over rice. If really hungry, you could dive into the Bayou Platter, consisting of one blackened chicken breast, a half order of red beans and rice, a cup of chicken and sausage gumbo, and hush puppies. La Crosse is home to the second facility in the Buzzard Billy's franchise, opening in 1997 in what was formerly an 1860s brick hotel. The restaurant is located on Pearl Street downtown, merely a block from the Mississippi River and half a block from the Radisson Hotel and La Crosse convention center. The '50s retro Starlite Lounge upstairs at Billy's makes it an ideal getaway for conventioneers crashing at the Holiday Inn next door. All it needs is the cast of the television hit *Mad Men* to complete the era's ambience.

Country Garden Restaurant & Bar, 913 W. Exchange St., Brodhead, WI 53520; (608) 897-4483; Casual American; $. This is a traditional small-town diner, with good, solid food and decent pricing. Every diner seems to know everyone else. Don't come here expecting fast food; you'll find a different pace of life, and any entree is worth the slight wait. Be sure to get a side of biscuits. The waitresses know their business and always seem to have a smile and a friendly hello.

Eddie's Irish Pub, 800 S. Marquette Rd., Prairie du Chien, WI 53821; (608) 326-6625; eddiesirishpub.com; Casual American; $–$$. Potato skins, fried dill pickles, or buffalo wings make for a grand backup to an imperial pint of Guinness. That's 20 ounces of stout, but who is counting? At least not at Eddie's. The Galway Bay fish sandwich is another nod to the Auld Sod, as are Flanagan's fish-and-chips. You might not find jalapeño poppers stuffed with cream cheese at the end of the rainbow, but you can munch them here. End a visit with a Molly's Delight, concocted from coffee, Bailey's Irish Cream, Amaretto, Kahlúa, and whipped cream. Irish eyes will be dancin' after that.

Home-A-Gins, 120 N. Centre St., Mount Hope, WI 53816; (608) 988-4417; Casual American; $. Mount Hope is a tiny crossroads in Grant County, a sneeze south of US 18, just east of Patch Grove and 5 miles west of Mount Ida, for you GPS devotees. The Home-A-Gins has plenty of rough edges, replete with a long well-knicked bar, scattering of battered tables, and lots of farmers. But every country-and-western entertainer in the world would love singing over there in the corner because this audience would get it. This is casual at its best, where breakfast eggs are done right and beef jerky is as good as its high salt content suggests. Look for the gals in their cow-barn work boots and the sunburned guys in baseball caps, whose callused hands can palm a basketball. Nope, no Wi-Fi, but there is plenty of conversation about birthing calves, discussed over huge slices of toast and thick, black coffee that could clean your carburetor faster than a team of tractor pullers. Good beer, too. But please, no pitchfork jokes.

Katina's Kitchen, 205 W. Main St., Dickeyville, WI 53808; (608) 568-9965; Casual American; $–$$. The "I Hope You're Hungry Ham Steak" sets the scene at one full pound for this piggy part. But the corned beef hash deserves as much applause. The pink building, with a sign on the side that proclaims DINER, jumps out at you when cruising south along US 61/State Highway 35. If you love caramel pecan pancakes, or are merely experimenting with roadside restaurant breakfasts, Katina's is a real heaven. Folks come from around the world, probably, for the stone gardens and stay for the hash browns. If they ask where Katina's is, the entire town population of about 1,000 can point the way. A hefty breakfast here will fortify you for a tour of the Dickeyville Grotto on the grounds of Holy Ghost Parish. Father Matthias Wernerus, parish pastor from 1918 to 1931, kept himself busy with this stonework. His memorial was constructed between 1925 and 1930, dedicated to his love of God and country.

Lakeview Marina Bar & Restaurant, 32319 County Road K, Prairie du Chien, WI 53821; (608) 326-2711; Casual American; $–$$. Overlooking Greymore Lake, the restaurant serves lunch and dinner with the standard fare, but all well prepared. The bar is always bustling, packed with locals and tourists, happy anglers, speed boaters, and tired cyclists. If motoring, drive north 3.5 miles from Prairie on County Road K. Better yet, merely dock your cruise ship or bass boat and walk in to Lakeview. As a lure, for every drink you buy during happy hour, you get a chance to win happy hour prices all day long for a week. The drawing is held every Friday for the following week. Since the marina patrons hail from each side of the Mississippi River, both Wisconsin Badger and Iowa Hawkeye football games are shown on the television to keep the cross-border peace.

Maggie's on Main, 205 Main St., Onalaska, WI 54650; (608) 519-2200; maggiesonmain.com; Bistro; $$. The restaurant is quickly found on the corner of State Highway 35 (the Great River Road) and Main Street, offering home-cooked tastes for breakfast, lunch, and dinner. The eatery was named after Chef-Owner Mary Cody's beloved Maggie, a Labrador retriever pal of 14 years. Maggie's is near the Great River Bike Trail, so when the hungries hit, you can rush over via pedal power or order ahead of time and they'll prepare a picnic lunch for you. The restaurant is also directly across from the Great River Landing, making it a snap for fisherfolk to drop by. The breakfast sandwich is popular with both on-the-go cyclists and boaters, with scrambled eggs and a choice of bacon, ham, or sausage patty and cheddar cheese served on a buttermilk biscuit or a toasted English muffin. For folks with more time on their early morning hands, try one of the seven All-in-One Skillet Scrambles, which consists of three eggs whipped to a frenzy, along with hash browns and toast or an English muffin. The Bacon Bleu is among the best, made with crumbled blue cheese, smoked bacon, and fresh tomatoes. The glazed baby-back ribs are winners for an evening dinner experience; end a meal with house-made apple pie. If Maggie were still around, she'd approve of either. Bring the kids for Thursday's family night, with all-you-can-eat spaghetti snazzled up with vitamin-heavy homemade red sauce, plus plenty of garlic bread to ward off the night creatures.

Picadilly Lilly Diner, E2513 County Rd. JJ, Spring Green, WI 53588; (608) 583-3318; Casual American; $. The menu primarily consists of soup, chili, hot dogs, cheeseburgers, Philly cheesesteaks, and related quick-service fare. All are scratch-made. For breakfast, try the biscuits and gravy or the pancakes. Dishes are also available for takeout, or you can place your order in advance. Fly in, fly out. The diner is located at the area airport and is only open for breakfast and lunch.

Pier 4 Cafe & Smokehouse, 600 N. Main St., Alma, WI 54610; (608) 685-4964; pier4cafe.com; Casual American; $–$$. The Pier's pork and beef dry rubs are praised by critics at AAA and *Midwest Magazine* and by other reviewers; they are available online as well as on-site. The German potato pancakes here are *wunderbar* for breakfast, especially sided with links or bacon. If you feel up to the challenge, dig into the Danimal, which is a 3-pound stack of husky pancakes. Eat it all in 30 minutes or less, and it's free. They promise that if you gobble it all down in less than 14 minutes, they'll name the item after you. Nobody says anything about post-pancake rehab. Don't expect to try this on Tues because the restaurant is closed that day. Platters of ribs, brisket, and pulled pork are among the smoked-to-perfection goodies also found in the kitchen. Consider takeout since the Pier is open only from 6 a.m. to 2 p.m. Look for the sign of the flying pig hanging outside what the locals call the "best breakfast and barbecue by a dam [*sic*] site." Find out for yourself, sitting down to enjoy a slathered slab in the screened-in patio overlooking Lock and Dam No. 4 on the Mississippi River.

Red Rooster Cafe, 158 High St., Mineral Point, WI 53565; (608) 987-9936; Casual American; $. You can be sure of getting good eats at the Red Rooster. No "yolk"! The breakfasts here are the talk of Western Wisconsin, a region of foodophiles who knows their cafe food. This hole-in-the-wall is the archetypical diner, one where you can get a real Cornish pasty, a traditional meat pie lunch favored by the area's miners back in the good old days when Mineral Point was a hub of the state's lead business. Quaint, full of knickknacks, a simple menu, good gravy, mashed potatoes with real lumps, and friendly staff. All pluses for the hungry traveler.

Rudy's Drive-In, 1004 La Crosse St., La Crosse, WI 54601; (608) 782-2200; rudysdrivein.com; Burgers; $. Everything here seems big. For example, there is a Monster Burger, a triple burger with double cheese, lettuce, tomato, and Rudy's special sauce; the Super Burger, a double burger with lettuce, tomato, melted cheese, sauce, and slice of bacon if you wish; and finally the double cheeseburger, a real gutbuster. For those of you on a health kick, but who still want an old-fashioned drive-in experience, consider the turkey burger, a one-third pound of low-fat white meat with lettuce, tomato, and pickle on a whole wheat Kaiser bun; a buffalo burger, made of 100 percent buffalo meat with lettuce, tomato, pickle, and a buffalo sauce; or a walnut burger developed at the **Historic Trempealeau Hotel** (p. 283). The latter is a seasoned walnut and cheese patty, served with lettuce, tomato, pickle, and honey mustard on a wheat Kaiser roll. You can also get trans-fat-free french fries. Take home a gallon of root beer to tide you over until your next trip to Rudy's. The drive-in regularly sponsors classic car reunions. Participants get free root beer floats for showing off their hip vehicles, whether an auto or a vintage motorcycle. The original Rudy's opened as an A&W root beer stand in Chippewa Falls in 1933 when a frothy beverage was only five cents. There were several other sites over the generations. Rudy's is still family owned.

Spring Green General Store, 137 S. Albany St., Spring Green, WI 53588; (608) 588-7070; springgreengeneralstore.com; Casual American; $–$$. A simple word, "charming," sums up the General Store. The four-bean chili is worth a drive from just about anywhere. Try a bowl with Monterey Jack or as a platter served over rice. You can get deli sandwiches all day. This is a great breakfast place with numerous egg dishes to mull. One specialty is the garlic dill cheese-curd scramble. You can kick back with a cup of coffee on the flower-bedecked front porch, if that's your dream morning. Yet the cinnamon toast here, with homemade maple cream cheese frosting, is a magnificent add-on. Every day offers specials for lunch, from a stuffed tomato platter to Greek pasta salad and a lot in between. You order at the counter, where you'll receive a world flag to place on your table so that the server can find you. Pay when finished at the main store checkout. The store itself has books, along with gifts, clothing items, herbs in bulk, and plenty of country-style odds and ends. There is also regular music.

Spring Lake Inn, 64040 County Rd. N, Prairie du Chien, WI 53821; (608) 326-6907; Casual American; $–$$. This unpretentious diner has a Friday fish fry that consistently receives rave reviews. The Saturday night prime rib hits the spot, as well. Be sure to get a doggie bag for leftovers because portions are doubly plentiful. This is a comfortably casual, clean, come-as-you-are country bar and restaurant that hits the spot whether for lunch or dinner. The restaurant is barely a few miles north of Prairie du Chien, so you won't have far to go.

Tranel's Canal St. Restaurant, 527 Canal St., Bloomington, WI 53804; (608) 994-3141; Casual American; $. All-you-can-eat hot wings and occasional his/hers pool tournaments make this a special caravansary. But then, their steak and lobster dinner also makes for a nifty Valentine's Day night out for you and a significant other. There's often a deejay or a band performing, along with Halloween parties that would delight a vampire.

Westby House Inn and Restaurant, 200 W. State St., Westby, WI 54667; (608) 634-4112; westbyhouse.com; Traditional American; $–$$. Take in lunch or tea in the Westby House tearoom, which is open to the public with seasonal hours. Among the most popular menu items are the house chicken salad, the Reuben, and a Westby Melt, made with ham or turkey with swiss cheese. This 1890s Queen Anne–style home is quaint and cozy, the perfect locale for afternoon tea, with a traditional offering of several varieties of small sandwiches, scones with Devonshire cream, cakes, and pastries. Tea from an extensive list of brews is served in china pots. Reservations are required. Be aware that the restaurant and tearoom are closed Nov through Apr. However, the Inn holds an annual Valentine's Day four-course romantic dinner. Be sure to sign up early.

Landmarks

Freight House Restaurant, 107 Vine St., La Crosse, WI 54601; (608) 784-6211; freighthouserestaurant.com; Supper Club; $$. When in La Crosse, consider stopping in at the Freight House Restaurant, a National Historic Site. The building was originally constructed in 1880 as the Milwaukee Road freight house. The site was renovated in 1978 and has become one of the area's premier steak and seafood restaurants. Prime rib, chicken, steak teriyaki, seafood, and vegetarian items pack the menu. Seasonal vegetables are offered, and you should head to the salad bar, an integral addition for all meals. *Wine Spectator* magazine has given the Freight House an Award of Excellence. The restaurant features an extended domestic and imported wine list, with many vintages by the glass, plus flights, to help you keep up your "spirits." For winter nights, snuggle up next to the fireplace, and listen to the local musicians performing on Friday and Saturday night.

Hayloft Cafe, E4830 US 14, Spring Green, WI 53588; (608) 588-3540, theroundbarnlodge.com; Casual American; $–$$. As they say here, "we offer a little history and a lot of class." This old round structure, originally called the Round Barn Restaurant, became a full service eatery in 1952, with a lodge added in 1974. The complex has been enlarged and renovated several times since then. You can order breakfast all day, with daily lunch specials that range from swiss steak

to liver and onions. Kids love the Thursday pizza buffet. The cafe's homemade soups always get a nod of approval. This is a great drop-in when touring the region's tourist attractions such as the quirky House on the Rock museum, architect Frank Lloyd Wright's home and studio, the American Players' Theater, and area parks.

The Historic Trempealeau Hotel, 150 Main St., Trempealeau, WI 54661; (608) 534-6898; trempealeauhotel.com; Traditional American; $–$$. This funky old hotel, dating from 1888, serves some of the most delicious, made-from-scratch food on this stretch of the Great River Road. The kitchen uses local and seasonal ingredients whenever possible. Among the providers are the Deutsch Family Farm in Osseo; Keewaydin Organics, Viola; Featherstone Farms, Rushford; the Tomato Patch, Melrose; and at least three from the Trempealeau area, such as Elmaro Vineyard, Ecker's Apple Orchard, and Schwertel Farms. The cheery dining room looks out at the Mississippi River, making for a fine view while enjoying a locally caught perch or the hotel's signature walnut burger, a delicious meatless patty made from chopped walnuts, which you can also purchase at outlets around Wisconsin. Live music is regularly held on the deck or a bandstand on the lawn where the hotel's Reggae Fest and the annual Blues Bash hold forth in the summer. Nearby is Perrot State Park with its Native American mounds for exploring. After a day of such adventuring around the neighborhood, return to the hotel for an upstairs stay in one of several small European-style rooms, each with handmade quilts and antique furniture. Closer to the river is the Pines Cottage, equipped with a Jacuzzi. Before checking out, stash a supply of those burgers in your car's cooler for home eating. You can purchase them in frozen four-packs at the hotel.

Pete's Hamburger Stand, 118 W. Blackhawk Ave., Prairie du Chien, WI 53821; peteshamburgers.com; Burgers; $. Pete's is open only on Fri, Sat, and Sun, continuing a century of serving burgers in one venue or another around town. Pete's was initially started by Pete Gokey, who discovered that his burger prep for firemen's picnics was especially popular when the patties were simmered in water and onions before frying. Eventually, he worked his way through the area's saloons and then on to street carnivals. He eventually built a traveling trailer for touring the river towns over the summer before settling down to set up shop in Prairie. Remember, these were the days before Big Macs and Kentucky Fried anything. Pete's menu today is hamburgers— that's all. Oh, soda and chips, too. The little stand has been adjacent to Stark's boat sales in Prairie since 1955 and is currently operated by the original Pete's great-grandkids.

Piggy's Restaurant, 501 Front St. South, La Crosse, WI 54601; (608) 784-4877; piggys.com; Barbecue; $$. The hardwood smoker at Piggy's is always busy, stoked with hickory and applewood from the nearby bluffs. Among the perfect smokes are prime rib, ribs, pork chops, swordfish, and chicken. The kitchen and service staff can accommodate special dietary restrictions, from lactose through gluten, nuts, seafood, and anything in-between. The menu changes seasonally, but the homemade soups retain their tasty touch. The attached lounge has a full schedule of live music on weekends. Get on down and tune in to the Dust Bowl Blues Band or Doghouse Jon and the Misbehavers after a platter of  filet and bacon-wrapped shrimp. The music and meal are best accompanied by a David Bruce 2010 Sonoma Pinot Noir.

Furthermore Beer, 525 E. Madison St., Spring Green, WI 53588; (608) 588-3300; furthermorebeer.com. The brew headquarters are in the Furthermore Beer Barn, which has a most unflattering nickname (look it up). Subsequently, beers from here are just as idiosyncratic, quirky, and refreshing as the company's lifestyle. Fresh-pressed, hard apple cider is a seasonal treat. Furthermore has a tristate reputation for great summer and autumn parties and jam sessions where you can grill your own food and rock around the clock, almost. No stage, so you can sit up close and cozy. Be sure to bring a lawn chair or a blanket on which to sit while sucking down a bottle of Makeweight, a triple pale mashup made with Flanders yeast tempered by Yankee and Brit brands and Oregonian hops. What a way to spend a day.

Lake Louie Brewing, 7556 Pine Rd., Arena, WI 53503; (608) 753-2675; lakelouie.com. Among numerous Wisconsin's microbreweries, Lake Louie's offerings are at the top of the six-pack. The brewery is small, like Lake Louie itself, which is actually a quarter-acre pond. Fear not. The brews here pack a big punch. Owner Tom Porter had a midlife crisis in the late 1990s and left the soft life as an engineer to make a name for himself as a brewer. Right choice, Tom! Besides, with a name like Porter, what else could he have done? He can now brag that his Lake Louie is the largest brewery in Arena. Albeit a lofty claim, Lake Louie is truly the only brewery in Arena. Porter now has a far-ranging rank of beers, from ales to heavier brews. Among the best is the Warped Speed Scotch Ale that more or less harkens back to Scottie, the Scottish engineer on the television hit *Star Trek*. Lake Louie's funniest label is a Kiss the Lips IPA, from the lyrics in the country song, "It's hard to kiss the lips at night that chew your ass out all day long." Even so, this is still lip-smacking good. Check the website for the

Hit the High Road, Get Your Veggies at the Market

Cameron Park Farmers' Market, at the Hanifl Marketplace on King Street between 4th Street South and 5th Avenue South in downtown La Crosse, Fri, 4 to 8 p.m., late spring through Oct 25; (608) 433-6708; cameronparkmarket.org.

Dodgeville Farmers' Market, Municipal parking lot next to the United Methodist Church on Iowa Street, Sat, 8 to 11 a.m., mid-May through end of Oct; (608) 553-2625.

Ferryville Market in the Park, Sugar Creek Park, State Highway 35, south end of town, Sat, 9 a.m. to 3 p.m., mid-May through end of Oct; (608) 734-3400; visitferryville.com.

Gays Mills Farmers' Market, Gays Mills Lions Park, Main Street near the bridge, Wed, 2:30 to 6 p.m., May 15 through Oct 16; (608) 624-3409; gaysmillsfarmersmarket.com.

Mount Horeb Farmers' Market, 110 N. 2nd St., downtown under the water tower, June through Sept, Thurs, 3:30 to 6:30 p.m., June through Sept; (608) 437-2582.

Platteville Farmer's Market, Platteville City Park on Market Street, Sat, 7 a.m. to noon, May through Oct; (608) 732-8625; platteville.org.

occasional Saturday tours; the brewery otherwise is not open to the public but sells its products statewide.

Ma's Bakery, 450 Canal St., Bloomington, WI 53804; (608) 994-3171. You can walk in as early as 4 a.m., pour your own coffee, sit

Bottomless Caffeine, Anyone?

Coffee Break Festival, (888) 873-7912; stoughtonwi.com. Held in Mandt Park in mid-August, this fest celebrates your favorite java. Sample brews from a variety of coffee roasters and stay kicked all day, which keeps you going through the car show, arts and crafts fair, 5K Java Jog, and 1-mile FunRun, plus plenty of music. The town was settled by Norwegian immigrants and claims to be the birthplace of the coffee break. According to town legend, the area's farm wives took time out from their work to enjoy a midmorning and a midafternoon caffeine-enhanced brew. Naturally, thus a fest was born.

The Koffee Kup, 355 E. Main St., Stoughton, WI 53589; (608) 873-6717; $. Supposedly this little building has operated as a restaurant since 1912. Each table gets its own coffeepot, a perfect accompaniment for a classic breakfast of eggs, toast, and bacon, or you can still indulge in a three-veggie omelet. The Kup's clam chowder is considered "the best in the world," by diehard chowderheads. There is some counter seating and a mix of tables and booths.

at the big communal table in the middle of the room, and order a still-warm-from-the-oven pastry. This is aromatherapy via the goodly perfume of baking cookies. The guys from the feed mill, a truck driver or two, several farmers, and folks on their way to the Mississippi for a day of fishing most often make up the early crowd.

Organic Valley Family of Farms, 1 Organic Way, La Farge, WI 54639; (888) 444-6455; organicvalley.coop. When they say "organic" here, they mean "organic." The company is a major producer of some 200 items, including high-quality milk, cream, yogurt, butter, soy, produce, and other items. None have hormones, traces of pesticides, and other non-healthful additions to the food chain. This is a cooperative of sustainable family farms, linked to numerous other food-savvy organizations such as the Chefs' Collaborative and Farm Aid. These are farmers on a mission: to produce and promote good food. One way they do this is hosting a kitchen and pantry tent at the Kickapoo Country Fair, the Midwest's largest organic food festival, held in late July in LaFarge. See Abbie Corse's recipe for **Muffins** on p. 310.

Rooted Spoon Culinary/Kitchen Table, 219 S. Main St., Viroqua, WI 54665; (608) 637-2223; rootedspoon.com. This catering company offers seasonal menus, using ingredients provided by area farms, cheese producers, butchers, and bakers. Among them are **Driftless Organics** (p. 289), **Organic Valley Family of Farms** (p. 287), Snow Goose Farm, Big River Beef, Harmony Valley Farm, Organic Prairie, Ridgeland Harvest, **Cress Spring Bakery** (p. 289), Tochko Bread, Viroqua Food Co-op, **Underground Food Collective** (p. 207), **Black Earth Meats** (p. 241), Premier Meats, Uplands Cheese, Castle Rock Organic Farms, and Hidden Springs Creamery. All the food is handcrafted from scratch and served either on-site or for off-site weddings or other special events. Rooted Spoon is housed in the old Main Street Station in downtown Viroqua, where it hosts a brunch on the second Sunday of most months. Food is also often served at art openings and film screenings held in its hall. Kitchen Table is an event space and dining room where meals are customized for groups by the Roosted Spoon crew.

Rural Route 1 Popcorn, 101 US 18, Montfort, WI 53569; (800) 828-8115; ruralroute1.com. This popcorn purveyor was launched in 1983, when Elmer Biddick got into the business and put 25 acres of his farm into popcorn production. Now several hundred of the family's 3,000 farmed acres are dedicated to producing gourmet

Farm Stands Stand Out for Freshness

Bures Berry Patch, 3760 W. Brigham Rd., Barneveld, WI 53507; (608) 924-1404; buresberrypatch.com.

Campo di Bella, 10229 Sharp Rd., Mount Horeb, WI 53572; (608) 320-9287; campodibella.org.

Driftless Organics, 50561 County Rd. B, Soldiers Grove, WI 54655; (608) 624-3735; driftlessorganics.com.

Flemming Orchards, 46054 Hwy. 171, Gays Mills, WI 54631; (608) 735-4625; flemingorchards.com.

Small Family Farm, S2958 W. Salem Ridge Rd., LaFarge, WI 54639; (608) 625-4178; smallfamilycsa.com

popcorn. Standard varieties of white and yellow popcorn are grown, sold in packages varying in size from 2 to 25 pounds. The company makes caramel corn and other flavors, as well as several varieties of microwavable corn. If you really love popcorn, and who doesn't, you can select your own tin and fill up to 6 gallons of popped corn. The retail store also has jewelry, knickknacks, toys, and kitchen utensils. Authors often drop in for book signings. And popcorn.

Valley Fish & Cheese, 304 S. Prairie St., Prairie du Chien, WI 53821; (608) 326-4719; valleyfishmarketpdc.com. The subtle perfume of hickory-smoked fish and turtle meat permeates the showroom at Valley Fish Fresh and frozen buffalo, carp, chubs, sturgeon, catfish, perch, and other fish, and Wisconsin cheeses, crackers, and condiments burst from cold storage display cases and range along the shelving. Jars of tasty pickled walleye, bluegill, and herring beckon. Owner and chief angler Mike Valley, one of the few remaining commercial fishermen on the upper Mississippi, prepares catfish bologna, snapping turtle beer sticks and a long list of jerkies made from salmon, beef, bison, and alligator, among other meats. If you need pork hocks or turkey gizzards, drop in and load up. Valley earned his fins from a lifetime on Ol' Man River, whose rough, black waters are a block to the west. If you can catch him away from his nets and poles, he has numerous stories to relate about the back sloughs and wetlands of the mighty waterway. His rustic building, packed with duck decoys and related carvings, is located on the interstate bridge near Wisconsin's tourism information center on US 18. If you need another reference point, look for the self-described world's largest handcarved muskie on the lawn outside. The monster was carved from black willow by Valley and pal Ted Parker, with the fins and tail from white pine. The muskie is 126 inches long and weighs more than 400 pounds. The store is open from March 1 through Dec 31.

The Wine Guyz, 122 King St., La Crosse, WI 54601; (608) 782-WINE; wineguyz.com. Because it opened way back in 2005, the Guyz is considered La Crosse's first full-fledged wine bar, one where you can indulge in a glass or a full bottle. There is also a wine shop, gourmet cheeses and meats, and other food items. Wine tastings are available with advance reservations, most of which have food pairings. Each month, a local artist is featured, whose exhibition is kicked off with a "meet the artist" party. Food is limited mostly to heavy appetizers such as panini, pizza, and cheese trays when sitting at the bar. But the wine list is amazing, as well as the beer selection. The Guyz, which is quite casual and not snobbish, has become one of La Crosse's most popular meet 'n' conversation locales for wine lovers. There is a deli in the back for takeout. When you leave with your sandwich, don't forget to take your Jam Jar Sweet Shiraz, sent in from South Africa.

Recipes

Grilled Kabocha Squash with Prosciutto & Truffle Honey

For years, Braise restaurant Chef-Owner David Swanson has been encouraging farm-to-table resources and has been a strong advocate of locally sourced fresh produce for everyone's table. His dedication to the cause of good food extends to all the menu items at his restaurant. Swanson also runs a culinary school that attracts food lovers from around the Greater Milwaukee area. In addition, Swanson works closely to link farmers and other restaurateurs, ensuring that the best produce, cheeses, meats, and other foods are produced, delivered, and served.

Serves 4

Truffle Honey

3 tablespoons honey   1 tablespoon white truffle oil

Mix together in bowl, set aside.

Squash

1 medium kabocha squash   Salt to taste
¼ cup truffle honey (see
   recipe)

Cut squash in half, roast in 350°F oven for 20 minutes, depending on size, or until squash is almost cooked but still firm in the center. Remove from the oven and let cool. Remove the rind from the squash and cut it into wedges. Mix squash with half of the truffle honey; let marinate for 10 minutes.

Presentation

8 very thin prosciutto slices
1 tablespoon cracked black
pepper

4 ounces Parmesan cheese,
thinly sliced

Lay the prosciutto on a plate. Grill squash until tender when poked with a fork, season with salt. Place the squash on top of the prosciutto and drizzle with the remaining truffle honey. Dust with black pepper and top with finely sliced Parmesan.

Courtesy of Chef David Swanson of Braise (p. 58).

Sauerkraut & Bacon Bread Pudding

Chef Jan Kelly of Milwaukee's Meritage restaurant is a James Beard Foundation award nominee whose career was launched in a Southern California fine-dining family. Her parents were kitchen adventurers at home, and in 1972 they opened The Hobbit in Orange, California. Kelly's brother now owns it. Kelly started working at there, taking reservations and doing some kitchen prep chores. She came to Wisconsin in 1995 with her husband, Gary, a championship speed skater who had trained in the city. After working in several other Milwaukee restaurants, she opened the always-exciting Meritage in 2007, featuring interesting blends of ethnic dishes and contemporary themes.

Serves 4–6

Nonstick cooking spray
½ loaf thick-cut egg bread
½ loaf sourdough or French
    bread
1 cup diced bacon

1 medium onion, sliced
2 cups sauerkraut
5 eggs
4 cups heavy cream
Salt and pepper to taste

Spray a 10 x 12-inch pan with nonstick cooking spray. Cut the bread into 1½-inch cubes and put them into prepared pan. Cook bacon until crisp; remove it from the pan, leaving the bacon fat in the pan. Add the sliced onions and sauté until soft and lightly brown. Add sauerkraut, cooked bacon, and onions to the bread and mix lightly.

Preheat the oven to 375°F.

In a separate bowl, whisk the eggs and heavy cream together along with any bacon fat left from cooking the onions. Add salt and pepper to taste and pour the mixture over the bread, making sure to cover all the bread. Cover with foil and bake until the bread pudding is cooked through, approximately 45–60 minutes. Remove foil but keep it in the oven for several minutes until the bread pudding browns.

Courtesy of Chef Jan Kelly of Meritage (p. 112).

Pizza with Wisconsin Fontina & Artichokes

The Wisconsin Milk Marketing Board (WMMB) ensures and promotes the gold standard for dairy products produced in Wisconsin. The WMMB is a nonprofit marketing organization supported by the state's dairy-farm families. The board works hard to promote the sale and consumption of Wisconsin milk and dairy products. Among its many programs, the WMMB has developed a Traveler's Guide Map to America's Dairyland featuring the state's 126 cheese plants. The Wisconsin Dairy Council, the nutrition education arm of the WMMB, helps school food-service staff and teachers promote dairy products as part of a healthy diet. The WMMB has dozens of fabulous recipes at its website that it shares with food lovers who appreciate the quality of the state's milk and cheese industry.

Serves 4

- 1 pound frozen white bread dough, thawed according to directions but chilled
- 2 tablespoons olive oil, divided, plus extra for baking sheet
- 2 tablespoons wheat bran
- 1 large clove garlic, finely chopped
- ½ medium red onion, thinly sliced
- 1 (9-ounce) package frozen artichoke hearts, thawed, or 1 (14-ounce) can, drained and sliced lengthwise
- Salt and freshly ground pepper to taste
- 1 cup (4 ounces) shredded fontina cheese

Preheat the oven to 450°F. On a lightly oiled baking sheet, press the chilled dough into a 9 x 12-inch rectangle with raised edges. Brush with 1 tablespoon of olive oil. Evenly sprinkle the bran over the dough and press lightly. Sprinkle with the garlic. Arrange the onion in one layer over the dough; top with the artichoke hearts. Drizzle with the remaining 1 tablespoon of olive oil. Lightly season with salt and pepper to taste. Evenly sprinkle the cheese. Do not permit the dough to rise. (The pizza may be held briefly in the refrigerator before baking.) Bake for about 15 minutes, until the crust and cheese are lightly browned.

Courtesy of the Wisconsin Milk Marketing Board (wmmb.com).

Smoked Salmon with Spicy Noodles

Lucy Saunders is a writer, author and educator specializing in food and beer pairings, cooking with beer, and water conservation in the brewing industry. She is the author of five cookbooks, including Cooking with Beer, Grilling with Beer, The Best of American Beer & Food, *and* Dinner in the Beer Garden. *Saunders is also an instructor at the Chicago-based Siebel Institute on beer cuisine and organizer for the Great Lakes Craft Brewers Water Conservation Workshop (conserve-greatlakes.com).*

Fresh grilled salmon is also wonderful with these noodles, but as a pantry staple, Lucy uses a 3- to 4-ounce tin of smoked salmon to make this recipe. Don't be intimidated by the long list of ingredients, as it goes together quickly, in less than 30 minutes. Soba noodles are fast cooking, and the buckwheat variety adds great flavor, though white wheat soba are fine, too.

Serves 2

1 quart water
4 ounces soba noodles
Pinch of salt
2 tablespoons vegetable oil
1 tablespoon chile-sesame oil or 1 tablespoon toasted sesame oil and chile paste to taste
6 ounces shiitake mushrooms, cleaned and stemmed, sliced into bite-size pieces if large

¾ cup chopped red bell pepper (about 1 medium pepper)
¼ cup chopped green onions, or more to taste
1 (3½–4-ounce) can smoked salmon
¼ cup rice vinegar
2 tablespoons minced ginger
¼ cup toasted almond slices
¼ cup chopped fresh sorrel

Bring water to a boil in a 2-quart saucepan, and add soba noodles and salt. Bring to a simmer.

While the water heats, prepare vegetables: Place vegetable oil and chile-sesame oil in a large skillet, over medium-high heat, and add mushrooms, bell pepper, and green onions, stirring and cooking until just tender, about 3 minutes. Reduce heat to low. Add drained smoked salmon to vegetables in skillet, and toss with vinegar and ginger. Cook until salmon is warmed through. Check soba noodles for doneness, and drain well. Add hot drained noodles to the large skillet, tossing so vegetables and fish are mixed in. Garnish with toasted almonds and fresh chopped sorrel.

Pairing

A fun pairing is the Rogue Ales Morimoto Black Obi Soba Ale, which uses soba in the brew; otherwise, try a porter ale, such as Central Waters Mudpuppy Porter or Potosi Gandy Dancer porter, to pick up the smoky edge of the salmon without overwhelming the taste of the fish.

Courtesy of Lucy Saunders,
cookbook author and brew maven (beercook.com).

Polenta with Stewed Peppers, Ricotta & Feta Cheeses

Elizabeth Crawford has contributed numerous recipes to the Ruth Paull Lamb & Family Cookbook, one of the cookbooks created at FamilyCookbookProject .com. The project helps families and individuals create and preserve heirloom cookbook treasures, with more than 400,000 archived recipes. Pumpkin Pie Squares, Maple Nut Coffee Twist, Onion/Cucumber Salad, and Toasted Pumpkin Seeds recipes are among Crawford's best. When she decides to entertain, which is often, she can whip up a divine meal for friends even using leftovers. For a great meal, she emphasizes, "All you need are a few very, very good ingredients in your kitchen." Fresh produce, oils, vinegars, and spices are her stock in trade.

Serves 6

Polenta

5 cups water
1 cup polenta-grade cornmeal
¼ teaspoon baking soda

1 teaspoon fine sea salt
½ cup freshly grated Parmesan cheese

Bring the water to a rapid boil in a heavy pot. Slowly and constantly whisk the cornmeal into the boiling water (you want to avoid lumps). Add the baking soda, reduce the heat to medium low, and continue whisking an additional minute or two until the cornmeal starts to suspend in the water. Reduce heat to low and cover. Stirring occasionally, continue cooking until the polenta is very creamy, about 20–30 minutes. (Using a diffuser under the pot helps to prevent sticking.) Remove the pot from the heat and stir in the salt and Parmesan cheese.

Stewed Peppers

¾ cup olive oil

4 bell peppers in assorted colors, thinly sliced

1 large onion, thinly sliced

2 teaspoons sea salt, plus additional as needed to taste

2 teaspoons dried rosemary needles or 1 large sprig of fresh rosemary

4 cloves garlic, thinly sliced

Freshly ground black pepper to taste

Heat a heavy sauté pan or pot over medium heat. Add the olive oil, peppers, onion, salt, and rosemary. Cover and reduce heat to medium low. Cook, stirring occasionally, for 30 minutes. Add the sliced garlic and continue cooking an additional 15 minutes. Add ground pepper and additional salt to taste.

Assembly

½ pound fresh ricotta cheese

½ cup grated soft feta cheese or freshly grated Parmesan cheese

½ bunch Italian parsley, coarsely chopped

Pour out the soft, warm polenta onto a large serving platter with a rim. Distribute the ricotta cheese over the polenta. Lift out the peppers with a slotted spoon and distribute them over the cheese followed by the feta or Parmesan cheese. Spoon over the additional olive oil remaining from the peppers and finish with the parsley. A few grinds of black pepper are good too.

Courtesy of Elizabeth Crawford,
cookbook writer, teacher, caterer & advocate of simple, healthy fare.

Gluten-Free Vegan Key Lime Pie

Executive Chef Joshua North of the Abbey Resort has two decades of kitchen experience under his belt, from dishwasher to executive chef. Joshua studied at the Cooking & Hospitality Institute of Chicago. He has worked in numerous kitchens along his career path; prior to the Abbey Resort Joshua spent more than 4 years as the head chef of the Hunt Club Restaurant at Geneva National. Chef North's favorite position in the kitchen to date was under Executive Chef Richard Knox as a saucier, who—appropriately named—is in charge of making all sauces in a large kitchen structure. For him, the culinary field is a passion and he emphasizes that quality cannot be sacrificed in any circumstance.

Makes one 9-inch pie.

Crust

2 cups toasted hazelnuts
½ cup flaked coconut

3 cups pitted dates
½ teaspoon sea salt

Filling

2 cups fresh Key lime juice
5 avocados, peeled and pitted

1 cup agave nectar
¾ cup coconut oil, melted

For the crust, combine all the crust ingredients in a food processor. Process the mixture until it is well blended; it will be a little bit chunky and sticky. When done, press the crust mixture evenly into a 9-inch springform pan.

For the filling, add all filling ingredients to a clean food processor; process till smooth.

To assemble, pour the filling into the crust and immediately cover with wax paper or foil (to preserve color). Refrigerate for a minimum of 2 hours prior to serving.

Courtesy of Executive Chef Joshua North and the Abbey Resort (p. 181).

Pub Mussels

Jody Erickson, chef of The Pub Restaurant and Wine Bar on Madeline Island, near La Pointe, Wisconsin, spends his summers melding fresh local ingredients with his culinary expertise and extensive international travels. Trained at The Culinary Institute in Napa Valley, Erickson often creates with Cajun spices, thanks to his deep passion for the southern cooking of New Orleans. His foods complement the dining areas at the restaurant, with its lakeside option in the spacious dining room, a comfortable lounge, or beachfront patio. Bistro lunches and regional-produce-themed dinners featuring Chef Erickson's creative dishes are served daily throughout the high season. Take-out meals are available for in-room dining, island picnics, and charter excursions.

Serves 5

- 5 pounds fresh mussels
- 2 tablespoons diced shallots
- 2 cloves garlic, minced
- 1 tablespoon butter
- 2 cups dry white wine
- 2 cups whipping cream
- 1 cup fish stock
- Chopped chives
- 1 tablespoon cold butter
- French bread for serving

Clean mussels in fresh water, soaking them for about 20 minutes; remove the beards, or the fibers emerging from the mussel's shell. Grasp the mussel in one hand, tightly hold the beard, yank it sharply toward the hinge end of the mussel, and then discard the fibers.

In a large pan, briefly sauté shallots and garlic in butter. Add the mussels and wine. Cover for approximately 5 minutes until the mussels open. Remove the mussels from the sauce, and cover and keep them warm. Add cream and fish stock and reduce it by three-quarters. Return the mussels to the reduced sauce, season with chives and cold butter, and serve immediately with warm French bread.

Courtesy of Jody Erickson of The Pub Restaurant and Wine Bar, Madeline Island (p. 258).

Grilled New York Strip Steak with Sungold Tomatoes, Fava Beans, Fresh Mozzarella & Basil Vinaigrette

Executive Chef Tory Miller of L'Etoile and Graze Gastropub restaurants on Madison's Capitol Square specializes in dishes made from locally grown, organic ingredients. With his extensive knowledge of Wisconsin's cheese, he is a Wisconsin cheese ambassador for the Wisconsin Milk Marketing Board. Miller is a graduate of the French Culinary Institute and worked in numerous restaurants before purchasing L'Etoile in 2005, initially partnering with his sister, Traci Miller. He is active in Slow Food USA and other food-related organizations, and has won numerous awards, including a coveted James Beard.

Serves 4–6

- 4 New York strip steaks, preferably from Fountain Prairie Farm
- Salt and pepper to taste
- 1 pint Sungold tomatoes, halved, preferably from Snug Haven Farm
- 1 cup fava beans, blanched and then peeled, preferably from Jones Valley Farm
- 1 red onion, sliced thinly
- 2 balls fresh mozzarella, diced, preferably from Farmer John
- 1 tablespoon chopped fresh oregano
- 2 tablespoons red wine vinegar
- 4 tablespoons extra-virgin olive oil

Season the steaks with salt and pepper. Grill the steak until it has reached desired doneness, so keep checking to ensure your favorite rare, medium, or well-done status. Remove from the grill and let rest for at least 5 minutes.

In a bowl, combine the tomatoes, fava beans, onion, and mozzarella. In another bowl, whisk the oregano, red wine vinegar, olive oil, salt, and pepper together. Drizzle over the vegetable mixture and toss to coat.

Basil Vinaigrette

1 pound fresh basil, blanched and dried	Juice of 1 lemon
1 clove garlic	1 egg yolk
¼ cup white wine vinegar	1 tablespoon Dijon mustard
	1½ cups extra-virgin olive oil

In a blender, combine all of the ingredients except the olive oil. Puree until combined. Continue blending while you drizzle in the olive oil. The final product should be thick and emulsified. Lightly drizzle over the steaks.

Courtesy of Executive Chef Tory Miller of L'Etoile (p. 216) & Graze Gastropub (p. 208).

Carrot, Fennel & Orange Soup

Linda Mutschler is the Milwaukee-based author of the easy-to-read, easy-to-use Fast Track to Fine Dining: A Step-by-Step Guide to Planning a Dinner Party *and other food writings.*

Serves 8

2 tablespoons butter

1 fennel bulb, trimmed and chopped, greens set aside for garnish

2 pounds of carrots, peeled and cut into ¼-inch slices

1 clove of garlic, minced

5 cups vegetable stock

Grated zest of ½ orange

½ cup orange juice

½ teaspoon kosher salt, or to taste

¼ teaspoon white pepper, or to taste

1 cup crème fraîche, divided

Melt the butter in a large soup pot. Add the chopped fennel and cook over medium heat, stirring occasionally, until softened, about 5 minutes. Turn the heat to low and add the carrots and minced garlic. Cover and cook, stirring occasionally, for 10 minutes.

Add the stock, turn up the heat, and bring to a boil. Cover and simmer for 20 minutes or until the carrots are soft.

Purée the soup in batches in the bowl of a food processor or blender until smooth. Return the soup to the cleaned-out soup pot. Add the orange zest and orange juice. Season with salt and pepper to taste. Stir in ½ cup crème fraîche and then gently reheat until heated through.

To serve, ladle the soup into bowls. Garnish with a small dollop or swirl of crème fraîche and top with a pinch of reserved fennel greens.

You can prepare the soup up to two days ahead. Cool, cover and refrigerate. Remember also to refrigerate the fennel greens for the garnish. To finish, reheat the soup gently and serve. This soup freezes nicely as well, so stop the prep before adding the crème fraîche. Cool the soup and freeze in an airtight container for up to three months. When ready, thaw the soup and place in a large soup pot and reheat gently, whisking often to make smooth. Once smooth, add the crème fraîche and heat through. Garnish with a dollop of crème fraîche.

For garnishes, you have several options. You can use a dollop or a swirl of crème fraîche. To make a swirl, place the crème fraîche in a small plastic bag, cut a small hole in the corner, and dip the corner slightly into the soup and squeeze out a little crème fraîche as you make the shape of a swirl. With regard to greens, if you make the soup ahead and don't have any leftover fennel, you can always substitute snipped chives instead. Preparation time is only 15 minutes, with cooking time at 35 minutes, making for a quick, delicious meal.

Courtesy of Linda Mutschler, dinner party planner and noted cookbook author.

Rushing Waters Stuffed Trout in Foil

Rushing Waters Trout Farm has been a fixture on the state's aquaculture scene since the 1940s. Located on 80 wooded acres near Palmyra, the complex's 56 ponds are fed with artesian spring water. The underground springs maintain a cold water temperature ideal for producing healthy rainbow trout year-round. With grass borders and earthen bottoms, the ponds contain a diverse ecosystem that provide the trout with access to food sources that mimic those found in the wild. You can also catch your own trout, which will be cleaned by the Rushing Water staff for take-home. The facility has its own on-site smoke house and a restaurant. Executive Chef Nathan Chappell prepares a wide range of menu offerings, including a smoothly wonderful smoked trout chowder.

Makes ½ pound per person.

Olive oil

Fresh trout (about a ½ pound per person)

Salt and freshly cracked pepper to taste

Additional favorite seasonings and garnishes as desired (optional)

Vegetables and herbs as desired (see suggestions below)

Butter

Cut enough heavy-duty foil squares to tightly wrap each portion of fish you are using. Place the shiny side of the foil down on your work surface and drizzle a bit of olive oil in the center. Season the trout; the best cut of fish is a boneless butterfly. Sprinkle the skin side of the fish with salt and freshly cracked pepper. Place the fish skin side down on the foil. You can customize your creation by

seasoning the flesh side of the fish, beginning with the salt and pepper. At this point, you can also add spices and fresh or dried herbs.

For the next step, top your fish with your favorite vegetable combination and a tablespoon of butter. Among Chappell's suggested flavor combinations are mushrooms, sweet onion, and thyme; lemon and fresh dill; tomato, garlic, fresh basil, and oregano; asparagus, leek, and fresh tarragon; and spinach, cooked bacon, and garlic.

To bake, preheat the oven to 450°F. Enclose the trout and seasonings in your foil packets and place them on a baking sheet. Roast in the oven for 15 minutes then carefully open the packets, allowing the hot steam to escape. Slide the trout and all its juices onto plates for immediate serving.

Courtesy of Chef Nathan Chappell, Rushing Waters Trout Farm (rushingwaters.net).

Pecan-Crusted Chicken with Kentucky Bourbon Sauce

Patty and Curt Robinson have taken the historic, rustic Union House and turned it into one of the top restaurants in Wisconsin, resulting in many awards and rave reviews. Today's diners can experience the same warm hospitality, delicious meals, and friendly service that immigrant Patrick Lynch provided for his customers when he first opened a restaurant in the same building more than 125 years ago. Chef John Mollet now takes a traditional dish and turns it into a dinner fit for royalty. The Union House is a favorite stop for visitors at the nearby Ten Chimneys historic home, where Broadway legends Alfred Lunt and Lynn Fontanne once lived.

Serves 6

1 cup finely chopped pecans

1 cup dried bread crumbs (made from day-old Italian bread)

6 (10- to 12-ounce) whole chicken breasts, halved, skinned, boned, and trimmed

Salt and pepper to taste

½ cup buttermilk

¼ cup (½ stick) clarified butter or vegetable oil, plus additional as needed

1 cup Kentucky Bourbon Sauce (see recipe)

Roasted-Garlic Mashed Potatoes (see recipe)

Preheat the oven to 350°F. Combine pecans and bread crumbs in a shallow dish for dredging. Season chicken with salt and pepper to taste. Dip chicken pieces in buttermilk, then dredge in crumb mixture, patting to coat. Heat butter in a large skillet; place coated chicken breasts in the butter. Do not crowd. Cook over medium heat, in batches if needed, adding additional butter as needed. Cook chicken until lightly browned on both sides, turning once after about 5 minutes. Transfer to a baking pan and bake in preheated oven 5–10 minutes, or until chicken is cooked through. Chicken should be firm to the touch but not hard. While chicken bakes, make Kentucky bourbon sauce and roasted-garlic mashed potatoes.

Kentucky Bourbon Sauce (About one cup)

¼ cup maple syrup

¼ cup bourbon

1 cup seasoned chicken stock

2 teaspoons cornstarch

2 tablespoons cold water

4 tablespoons whipping cream

In a small saucepan, combine syrup and bourbon. Heat to simmer, then reduce by half. Add stock and return to a boil. Combine cornstarch and water in a dish and mix well. Add to boiling mixture. Simmer until thickened, about 1 minute, then add cream and heat through.

Roasted-Garlic Mashed Potatoes

1 whole garlic bulb

Olive oil

6 large Wisconsin potatoes, peeled, cut, boiled until fork tender, and drained

6 tablespoons (¾ stick) softened butter

Salt and pepper to taste

Preheat the oven to 325°F.

To roast garlic, trim the ends from a bulb of garlic. Drizzle bulb with olive oil. Set in a small metal pan, cover pan with foil, and bake in the preheated oven for 1 hour, or until garlic is soft. Let cool.

Mash potatoes with butter and 1–2 tablespoons roasted garlic and then salt and pepper by hand. Do not whip with electric mixer; the potatoes should have small pieces in them.

To serve, place the cooked chicken breasts on a warm plate and serve with Kentucky Bourbon Sauce and roasted-garlic mashed potatoes.

Courtesy of Chef John Mollet of the Union House Restaurant (p. 195).

Muffins

This recipe comes from Organic Valley farmer Abbie Corse's great-aunt Florence, a woman whose love for her family was exemplified by her cooking. She would bring out a woven basket filled with muffins and covered with a lovely tea cloth. Corse's dad would practically clap with delight when he was a kid. Years later, Corse started making the muffins on Christmas Eve after everyone went to sleep, leaving them under the tree as a bit of holiday magic.

Makes a dozen muffins.

1 cup whole wheat pastry flour
1 cup uncooked quick cooking
    oats, preferably organic
1 tablespoon baking powder
2 teaspoons ground cinnamon
1 teaspoon ground nutmeg
½ teaspoon salt
1 large egg, preferably from
    Organic Valley

¾ cup whole milk, preferably
    from Organic Valley
½ cup (1 stick) unsalted butter,
    preferably from Organic
    Valley, melted and cooled
⅓ cup pure maple syrup
1 cup chopped peeled apple,
    preferably organic
1 cup golden or dark seedless
    raisins

Preheat the oven to 400°F.

Combine flour, oats, baking powder, cinnamon, nutmeg, and salt in a medium bowl; mix well. In a small bowl, beat the egg lightly. Stir in milk, butter, and syrup. Add to oat mixture, mixing just until dry ingredients are moistened. Stir in apple and raisins. Spoon the batter into 12 paper-lined or greased medium muffin  *cups (cups will be nearly full). Bake 16 minutes or until wooden pick inserted in center comes out clean. Cool 5 minutes in pan and transfer to a wire cooling rack. Serve warm or at room temperature with additional butter if desired.*

Courtesy of Abbie Corse, Organic Valley Family of Farms (p. 287).

Canoe Bay Potato Leek Soup

Chef Tom Ghinazzi came to Canoe Bay from Chicago, where he worked in several of the city's premier restaurants. A graduate of the Culinary Institute of America, Ghinazzi uses the resort's on-site garden for creating his dishes. The sophisticated haven was developed by Dan and Lisa Dobrowolski and is considered one of Wisconsin's top romantic getaways. The facility is designed for couples escaping the stress of everyday life. This is easy, lolling in one of the cottages, rooms, or villas, knowing that Chef Ghinazzi's breakfasts and lunches are delivered to your room. Dinner is prix fixe and on a first-come, first-served basis in the dining rom. So plan your arrival accordingly if really hungry. Ghinazzi also sponsors a chef's table in his kitchen, where you can watch all the action.

Makes 8 (16-ounce) servings

1 tablespoon olive oil
3 leeks, white and light green
    parts only, sliced
½ cup white wine
2 Wisconsin potatoes, peeled
    and cut in large chunks

3 quarts water
1 cup heavy cream
Salt to taste

In a large pot, heat the oil over medium-low heat. Add leeks, sweating them down until soft and translucent. Add white wine to the pot and reduce the mixture, still over medium-low heat, until almost dry. Add potatoes and water, simmering until the potatoes are fork-tender. Add the cream and blend the soup, 2 cups at a time, in a blender at medium to high speed until smooth (use caution while blending the hot soup). Season blended soup to taste with salt. You can adjust the consistency by adding more water as desired.

Courtesy of Chef Tom Ghinazzi of Canoe Bay Resort (canoebay.com).

Macski's Scotch Eggs

One morning at breakfast, Morganne L. MacDonald, president Macski's Highland Foods, and her husband, Vince Milewski, were brainstorming ideas for new Scottish foods that people would love. Their son Cian, then 13, hit on an idea that his parents had been thinking about. "What about something with haggis and eggs together?" he asked, and Macski's Scotch eggs were born. Traditionally, Scotch eggs are made with pork sausage, but it just didn't seem right to MacDonald and Milewski that something carrying a Scottish name wouldn't be made from Scottish sausage. They set out to remedy that small injustice. Haggis, a savory pudding make with sheep parts, is made to crumble. That meant some creativity in the recipe was needed to ensure proper adhesion. It didn't take long before they accomplished that with an egg wash and some panko bread crumbs. Macski's Scotch eggs have more flavor than traditional Scotch eggs, given the spicy nature of haggis. You can order the haggis, plus other Highland foods and clothing, from macskis.com.

Serves 6

1 pound Macski's Highland
    Haggis (in bulk)
2 raw medium-size eggs

6 hard-boiled medium-size
    eggs, peeled
Panko bread crumbs
Vegetable oil for frying

Bake the haggis in its casing according to the directions on the package. Allow it to cool, then refrigerate the haggis until it becomes firm; overnight is fine but even 1 hour to cool is sufficient.

In a large mixing bowl, beat 1 raw egg. Remove the haggis casing and gently combine package contents with the beaten egg in a bowl. Divide the mixture into six equal portions. In a small bowl, beat the remaining raw egg. Shape one haggis portion into a thin patty and wrap it around a hard-boiled egg, taking care to seal all the seams. Dip the covered egg in the beaten egg and then gently roll it in the bread crumbs. Repeat for the remaining hard-boiled eggs. Deep-fry the eggs in heated vegetable oil until brown and crispy.

Courtesy of Morganne MacDonald of Macski's Highland Foods (macskis.com).

Potato & Beer Soup with Bistro Flatbreads

Chef Christian Czerwonka emphasizes Cajun and Creole and new American dishes at his Christian's Bistro in Plover, Wisconsin. However, his potato and beer soup is a great traditional favorite for the state's residents who love the combination of Wisconsin spuds and beer. Prep time is only 20 minutes with a 45-minute cooking window. What's not to enjoy?

Serves 4–6.

3 tablespoons unsalted butter

¼ pound chopped bacon, preferably Nueske's (optional)

1 pound medium onions, diced

Salt and pepper to taste

¼ cup chopped celery

14 ounces Wisconsin russet potatoes, peeled and diced

1 quart chicken stock

1 cup heavy cream

2 (12-ounce) bottles beer, preferably local

1 tablespoon chopped thyme

Bistro Flatbread

Olive oil for the bowl

3 cups warm water

3 tablespoons sugar

6 teaspoons active-dry yeast

9 cups all-purpose flour, plus additional for kneading

9 tablespoons olive oil

4½ teaspoons salt

Flatbread Topping Suggestions

½ cup sliced grilled chicken breast

Oven-roasted tomatoes

Basil Pesto (see recipe)

Feta (or cheese of choice)

Basil Pesto

2 cup fresh basil leaves

2 cloves garlic

½ cup pine nuts

⅔ cup extra-virgin olive oil

½ cup freshly grated Parmesan cheese

Kosher salt and pepper to taste

In a 6-quart sauce pot, melt the butter over medium heat. Add chopped bacon, if desired, and cook until well browned. Add onions, salt, and pepper, stirring occasionally and cooking until the onions are tender, approximately 5 minutes. Add celery and cook an additional 5 minutes. Add potatoes and chicken stock. Bring to a boil, reduce heat to low, and cover and gently simmer until potatoes are soft, about 45 minutes. Then turn off the heat and puree the mixture with an immersion blender until smooth. Stir in heavy cream and beer. Season to taste with salt and pepper. Finish with fresh thyme.

For the flatbread, brush a bowl with oil and set aside. In separate mixing bowl, add warm water and sugar. Sprinkle yeast over and stir to dissolve. Let stand until it bubbles, about 10 minutes. Add flour, oil, and salt. Mix 1 minute. Transfer to floured surface. Knead until smooth, about 5 minutes.

Transfer the dough to the oiled bowl. Turn to coat it and cover with a dish towel or foil. Let rise in warm area (such as the top of your stove) for 1 hour.

Preheat the oven to 375°F. Divide the dough into round 4-ounce, rolled out, flattened portions; you should have 18–20 pieces, each about a ¼ inch high. (Halve the recipe for less dough or store extra in the freezer.) Place the dough rounds on a floured or cornmealed pizza stone; an inverted cookie sheet also works. Bake for 12–15 minutes.

To oven-roast tomatoes, slice them in half, season to taste with salt, pepper, and Italian herbs. Roast in a preheated 200°F oven for 3 hours.

To make basil pesto, combine the basil, garlic, and pine nuts in a food processor and pulse until coarsely chopped. Add the oil and process until fully incor-porated and smooth. Add cheese and mix until incorporated. Season with salt and pepper to taste.

Courtesy of Chef Christian Czerwonka of Christian's Bistro (p. 229).

Appendices

Appendix A: Eateries by Cuisine

Codes for Corresponding Regional Chapters:

(DOWN) Milwaukee Downtown
(RIVER) Milwaukee Riverwest
(CCITY) Milwaukee Central City
(WARD) Milwaukee Historic Third Ward, Walker's Point, the Fifth Ward & Bay View
(ESIDE) Milwaukee East Side
(MENO) Menomonee Valley
(NSIDE) Milwaukee North Side, plus Brown Deer, Shorewood, Whitefish Bay, Glendale, Fox Point & Mequon
(SSIDE) Milwaukee South Side, plus Cudahy, Oak Creek, Franklin & St. Francis
(WSIDE) Milwaukee West Side, plus Wauwatosa & West Allis
(WAUK) Waukesha, Brookfield, Pewaukee & Germantown
(DOOR) Door County
(EAST) Eastern Wisconsin
(MAD) Madison
(CENT) Central Wisconsin
(NORTH) Northern Wisconsin
(WEST) Western Wisconsin

Asian

Basil Restaurant, (CENT), 238
Ha Long Bay, (MAD), 209
Umami Moto, (DOWN), 29

Barbecue

Alamo Smokehouse, (CENT), 232
Double B's BBQ & Burgers,
    (WSIDE), 111
Piggy's Restaurant, (WEST), 284

Bistro

Allium Restaurant and Bar,
    (ESIDE), 76
Beedle's Bar and Restaurant,
    (WEST), 275
Bluefront Cafe, (DOOR), 137
Blue Spoon Cafe, (CENT), 238
Brasserie V, (MAD), 205
Buckley's Restaurant and Bar,
    (DOWN), 21
Cafe Benelux & Market, (WARD), 51
c.1880, (WARD), 58
Christian's Bistro, (CENT), 229
Dining Room at 209 Main, The,
    (CENT), 229
Elsa's on the Park, (DOWN), 33
Father Fats Public House,
    (CENT), 229
Filling Station, (RIVER), 45
Fratello's Waterfront Restaurant,
    (EAST), 161
Graze Gastropub, (MAD), 208

Harbor View Cafe, (NORTH), 256
Harvey's Central Grille, (NSIDE), 97
Honeypie, (WARD), 65
La Merenda, (WARD), 61
Maggie's on Main, (WEST), 278
Medusa Grill and Bistro, (EAST), 185
Pig in a Fur Coat, A, (MAD), 212
Rumpus Room, (DOWN), 28
Sardine, (MAD), 213
Tickled Pink Coffee Shop and Bistro,
    (EAST), 187
Trocadero Gastrobar, (ESIDE), 86
Wine Knot Bar & Bistro, The,
    (EAST), 188

British

Three Lions Pub, (NSIDE), 99

Cajun

Buzzard Billy's Flying Carp Cafe,
    (WEST), 275

Caribbean

Harbor Restaurant & Bar,
    (NORTH), 256
Jamerica Caribbean Restaurant,
    (MAD), 216

Casual American

Anvil Pub & Grille, (EAST), 155
Attebury's Pub and Eatery,
    (SSIDE), 102

Le Rêve Patisserie and Cafe,
(WSIDE), 115
L'Etoile, (MAD), 216
Pastiche Bistro & Wine Bar,
(WARD), 66

German
Chef's Corner Bistro, (EAST), 182
Golden Mast, The, (WAUK), 124
Hof Restaurant, The, (EAST), 145
House of Gerhard, (EAST), 184
Karl Ratzsch's Milwaukee's Land-
mark German-American Restau-
rant, (DOWN), 34
Mader's, (DOWN), 34
Weissgerber's Gasthaus, (WAUK), 124

Greek
Oakland Gyros, (ESIDE), 80

Indian
Taj Indian Restaurant, (MAD), 214
Taj Mahal, (CENT), 236

Irish
Black & Tan Grille, (EAST), 156
Brocach, (ESIDE), 77
County Clare Irish Inn, (ESIDE), 83
52 Stafford, An Irish Inn, (EAST), 172
Mulligans Irish Pub & Grill,
(SSIDE), 103
Pub, The, (EAST), 194
St. Brendan's Inn, (EAST), 166

Italian
Albanese's Roadhouse & Dominic's
Sports Lounge, (WAUK), 120
Cafe La Scala, (WARD), 52
Calderone Club, (NSIDE, DOWN), 96
Carini's La Conca D'Oro, (ESIDE), 82
Carmella's Italian Bistro, (EAST), 158
Casa Capri, (EAST), 180
Caterina's Ristorante, (SSIDE), 106
Centro Cafe, (RIVER), 45
DeRango's Pizza Palace, (EAST), 183
Galileo's Italian Steakhouse & Bar,
(DOOR), 138
Il Mito Trattoria e Enoteca,
(WSIDE), 112
Mangia Trattoria, (EAST), 185
Mimma's Cafe, (ESIDE), 84
Nessun Dorma, (RIVER), 46
North Avenue Grill, (WSIDE), 113
Papa Luigi's, (SSIDE), 104
Pasquale's International Cafe,
(EAST), 165
Pasta Tree Restaurant & Wine Bar,
The, (ESIDE), 84
Pitch's Lounge and Restaurant,
(ESIDE), 85
Ristorante Bartolotta, (WSIDE), 116
Rustico Pizzeria, (WARD), 55
Sala da Pranzo, (ESIDE), 85
Tenuta's Italian Restaurant,
(SSIDE), 191
Trattoria di Carlo & Pizzeria,
(SSIDE), 105

Trattoria Stefano, (EAST), 163
Tutto Restaurant Bar, (DOWN), 28
Via Downer, (ESIDE), 80
Wild Earth Cucina, (MENO), 93
Zarletti, (DOWN), 32

Japanese
Edo Japanese Restaurant,
(MAD), 206
Fushimi, (ESIDE), 78
Kanpai, (WARD), 54
Soon's Sushi Cafe, (EAST), 186

Jewish
Jake's Delicatessen, (CCITY), 42

Latin American
Antigua Latin Restaurant,
(WSIDE), 109

Mexican
BelAir, (WSIDE), 110
Botanas, (SSIDE), 71
Cafe Corazón, (RIVER), 44
Cafe el Sol/United Community
Center, (SSIDE), 71
Cafe Mexicana, (NORTH), 254
Cielito Lindo, (SSIDE), 71
Conejito's Place, (SSDIDE), 71
El Rey Foodmart, (SSIDE), 71
Fajitas Grill Centro, (DOWN), 25
Guadalajara Restaurant, (SSDE), 71
Highland House, (NSIDE), 98

La Canoa, (SSIDE), 103
Le Fuente, (SSIDE), 71
Le Perla Mexican Restaurant,
(SSIDE), 71
Mojo Rosa's Cantina and Pub,
(DOOR), 141
Mr. Senors, (ESIDE), 79
Poco Loco Cantina, (NSIDE), 99
Riviera Maya, (WARD), 66
Seester's Mexican Cantina,
(WAUK), 122
Taqueria El Fogoncito, (WSIDE), 114
Taqueria Los Comales, (SSIDE), 71
Terra, (SSIDE), 71

New American
Alchemy Restaurant, (MAD), 203
Cafe Calatrava, (DOWN), 22
Cafe Hollander, (ESIDE), 77
Cafe Soeurette, (EAST), 171
Cookery, The, (DOOR), 138
Coopers Tavern, The, (MAD), 206
Harry's Bar & Grill, (ESIDE), 78
Harvest Restaurant, (MAD), 215
Hinterland, (WARD), 54
INdustri Cafe, (WARD), 59
Lola's on the Lake, (EAST), 164
LuLu, (WARD), 67
Meritage, (WSIDE), 112
Mission Grille, (DOOR), 140
The Noble, (WARD), 60
Nostrano, (MAD), 210
Odd Duck, (WARD), 65

Ed Thompson's Tee Pee Supper
   Club, (CENT), 239
Eric's Porter Haus, (WAUK), 123
Fanny Hill Dinner Theatre,
   (NORTH), 262
Fireside Dinner Theatre, (EAST), 194
Fireside Supper Club, (NORTH), 255
Flannery's Wilhelm Tell Supper
   Club, (CENT), 230
Freight House Restaurant,
   (WEST), 282
Granary Supper Club, The,
   (EAST), 161
HobNob, (EAST), 184
House of Embers, (CENT), 239
Jake's, (WAUK), 125
Machut's Supper Club, (EAST), 172
Mr. G's Logan Creek Grille,
   (DOOR), 141
Red Cedar Lodge, (NORTH), 257
Richard's Restaurant & Bar,
   (CENT), 236
Riverstone Restaurant,
   (NORTH), 259
Robbins Restaurant, (EAST), 166
Roxy Supper Club, (EAST), 166

Swedish
Al Johnson's Swedish Restaurant &
   Butik, (DOOR), 144

Swiss
Glarner Stube, (CENT), 230

New Glarus Hotel Restaurant,
   (CENT), 234
Turner Hall, (CENT), 237

Thai
Thai Bar-B-Que, (SSIDE), 105

Traditional American
Alexander's, (DOOR), 137
A's Restaurant & Music Cafe,
   (EAST), 155
Bacchus, (DOWN), 32
Back When Cafe, (CENT), 227
Blind Horse Restaurant and Winery,
   The, (EAST), 157
Frontier Dining Room, (EAST), 193
Historic Trempealeau Hotel, The,
   (WEST), 283
Immigrant Restaurant, (EAST), 157
Inn at Cedar Crossing, (DOOR), 146
Jail House Restaurant, The,
   (EAST), 172
James Sheeley House Restaurant
   and Saloon, (NORTH), 257
No No's, (EAST), 173
Port Hotel Restaurant and Inn, The,
   (EAST), 173
Quivey's Grove, (MAD), 212
Remington's River Inn, (EAST), 166
Rhinelander Cafe & Pub,
   (NORTH), 259
Roxbury Tavern, (CENT), 239
Shoreline Restaurant, (DOOR), 142

Appendix B: Dishes, Specialties & Purveyors

Codes for Corresponding Regional Chapters:

(DOWN) Milwaukee Downtown
(RIVER) Milwaukee Riverwest
(CCITY) Milwaukee Central City
(WARD) Milwaukee Historic Third Ward, Walker's Point, Bay View & the Fifth Ward
(ESIDE) Milwaukee East Side
(MENO) Menomonee Valley
(NSIDE) Milwaukee North Side, plus Brown Deer, Shorewood, Whitefish Bay, Glendale, Fox Point & Mequon
(SSIDE) Milwaukee South Side, plus Cudahy, Oak Creek, Franklin & St. Francis
(WSIDE) Milwaukee West Side, plus Wauwatosa& West Allis
(WAUK) Waukesha, Brookfield, Pewaukee & Germantown
(DOOR) Door County
(EAST) Eastern Wisconsin
(MAD) Madison
(CENT) Central Wisconsin
(NORTH) Northern Wisconsin
(WEST) Western Wisconsin

Bakery

Angelic Bakehouse, (WAUK), 127
Bendtsen's Bakery, (EAST), 183
Clasen's European Bakery, (MAD), 219
Cress Spring Bakery, (CENT), 242
The Elegant Farmer, (EAST), 175
Greenbush Bakery, (MAD), 221
Larsen's Bakery, (EAST), 183
Lehmann's Bakery, (EAST), 183
Madison Sourdough Co., (MAD), 221
Main Grain Bakery, The, (CENT), 243
Ma's Bakery, (WEST), 286
O&H Danish Bakery, (EAST), 183
People's Bakery, (MAD), 224
Peter Sciortino's Bakery, (ESIDE), 88
Robin's Nest Cakery, (EAST), 190
StoneBank Baking Company,
   (EAST), 200
Sweet House of Madness, (EAST), 191
Tamara's the Cake Guru, (EAST), 178
Treat Bake Shop, (WSIDE), 117
Wild Flour Bakery, (WARD), 72

Bakery Cafe

Amaranth Bakery (WSIDE), 116
Ashland Bakery, (NORTH), 266
Bohemian Ovens Restaurant &
   Bakery, (NORTH), 253
Danish Mill, The, (DOOR), 138
Gotham Bagels, (MAD), 221
Linnea Bakery, (EAST), 190
Rolling Pin Bake Shop, (CENT), 245
Scaturo's Baking Company & Cafe,
   (EAST), 142

Breakfast/Brunch

Blue's Egg, (WSIDE), 110
Bogus Creek Cafe & Bakery,
   (NORTH), 253
Buckley's Restaurant and Bar,
   (DOWN), 21
Chuck's Place, (EAST), 171
Friendship House, (NORTH), 255
Frontier Dining Room, (EAST), 193
Harry's Restaurant, (EAST), 215
Kitchen Table, The, (CENT), 231
Koffee Kup The, (WEST), 287
Log Cabin Family Restaurant,
   (CENT), 231
Marigold Kitchen, (MAD), 210
Monty's Blue Plate Diner, (MAD), 217
Norske Nook, (NORTH), 265
North Avenue Grill, (WSIDE), 113
Old Post Office Restaurant,
   (EAST), 147
Paul Bunyan's Cook Shanty,
   (CENT), 233
Simple Cafe, (ESIDE), 80
Simple Cafe (EAST), 186
Sweetie Pies, (EAST), 153
Whispering Orchards & Cafe,
   (EAST), 171
White Gull Inn, (DOOR), 143

Breweries & Brewpubs

Black Husky Brewing, (NORTH), 269
Capital Brewery, (MAD), 218
Furthermore Beer, (WEST), 285

Burgers

Butcher

Cheesemonger

Roth Käse USA, (CENT), 246
Wisconsin Cheese Mart, (DOWN), 37

Chocolatier/Candy

Beerntsen's Confectionary,
(EAST), 174
Burke Candy, (ESIDE), 87
Craverie Chocolatier Cafe,
(EAST), 156
DB Infusion Chocolates, (MAD), 222
Door County Candy, (EAST), 150
Gail Ambrosius Chocolatier,
(MAD), 222
Jelly Belly Visitor Center, (EAST), 188
Legacy Chocolates, (NORTH), 268
Maurie's Fine Chocolates of
Madison, (MAD), 223

Coffee Shop

Black Cat Coffeehouse, (NORTH), 252
Colectivo Coffee, (WARD), 69
Door County Coffee & Tea
Company, (EAST), 150
Fiddleheads Espresso Bar & Cafe,
(EAST), 159
Java House Cafe & Micro-Roaster,
(EAST), 159
Mud Creek Coffee Cafe, (EAST), 165
Sprizzo Gallery Caffe, (WAUK), 122
Stone Creek Coffee Roasters,
(MENO), 95
Tickled Pink Coffee Shop and Bistro,
(EAST), 187

Cooking School

Lakeshore Culinary Institute,
(EAST), 176
Savory Spoon Cooking School,
(EAST), 152
Trattoria Stefano, (EAST), 163

Farmstand

Growing Power, (RIVER), 47
Sweet Corn Lady & Daughters,
(EAST), 191

Fish Boils

Greunke's Restaurant, (NORTH), 264
KK Fiske & the Granary, (DOOR), 140
Log Den, The, (DOOR), 147
Old Post Office Restaurant,
(EAST), 147
Pelletier's Restaurant & Fish Boil,
(DOOR), 148
Rowleys Bay Resort, (DOOR), 148
Scaturo's Baking Company & Cafe,
(EAST), 142
White Gull Inn, (DOOR), 143

Fishmonger

Charlie's Smokehouse, (EAST), 150
Ewig Brothers Fish Company,
(EAST), 175
Ma Baensch, (RIVER), 48
Rushing Waters Fisheries,
(EAST), 198
Susie Q Fish Market, (EAST), 178

Valley Fish & Cheese, (WEST), 289

Grocery

Brennan's Market, (MAD), 218

G. Groppi Food Market, (WARD), 70

Glorioso's Italian Market, (ESIDE), 87

Grandma Tommy's Country Store,
(EAST), 152

Hmong Asian Food Store,
(SSIDE), 107

Kenosha HarborMarket, (EAST), 189

Marchant's Foods, (NORTH), 268

Metcalfe's Market, (MAD), 223

Milwaukee Public Market,
(WARD), 55

Organic Valley Family of Farms,
(WEST), 287

Outpost Natural Foods, (RIVER), 48

River Valley Ranch & Kitchens,
(EAST), 197

Riverwest Co-op, (RIVER), 49

Slow Pokes Local Food, (EAST), 177

Viet HOA Supermarket, (WSIDE), 117

Willy Street Co-op, (MAD), 226

Ice Cream/Yogurt

Babcock Hall Dairy Store,
(MAD), 204

Ella's Deli and Ice Cream Parlor,
(MAD), 215

Flat Pennies Ice Cream,
(NORTH), 255

Herschleb's, (NORTH), 264

J. Lauber's Ice Cream Parlor,
(EAST), 196

Joe Jo's Pizza & Gelato, (EAST), 139

Kelley Country Creamery,
(EAST), 175

LaGrander's Drive In, (NORTH), 264

Milty-Wilty, (CENT), 234

Mullen's Dairy and Eatery,
(EAST), 195

North Point Custard, (ESIDE), 79

Sandy's Popper Ice Cream,
(EAST), 190

Ted's Ice Cream and Restaurant,
(WSIDE), 114

Wedl's Hamburger Stand and Ice
Cream Parlor, (CENT), 240

Wilson's Restaurant and Ice Cream
Parlor, (DOOR), 149

Pizza

Ang and Eddie's, (EAST), 155

Angler's Haven Resort, (NORTH), 252

Buffalo Phil's Pizza & Grille,
(CENT), 232

DeRango's Pizza Palace, (EAST), 183

Glass Nickel Pizza, (WAUK), 120

Grant's Olde Stage Station
Restaurant, (EAST), 145

Il Ritrovo (EAST), 162

Joe Jo's Pizza & Gelato, (EAST), 139

Moosejaw Pizza & Dells Brewing
Co., (CENT), 232

Pizza Man (ESIDE), 80

Index

farm stands (Door County), 151

farm stands (Eastern Wisconsin),
178, 198

farm stands (Milwaukee), 132

farm stands (Northern
Wisconsin), 271

farm stands (Western
Wisconsin), 289

Farmers' Market of Wausau, 249

farmers' markets (Central
Wisconsin), 247

farmers' markets (Eastern
Wisconsin), 176, 189, 199

farmers' markets (Green Bay), 161

farmers' markets (Milwaukee), 130

farmers' markets (Northern
Wisconsin), 270

farmers' markets (Western
Wisconsin), 286

Father Fats Public House, 229

Ferryville Market in the Park, 286

Festival of Flavors (Eagle River), 13

Fiddlehead Espresso Bar, 159

Fiddlehead's Coffee Bar, 159

Fiddleheads Coffee Roasters, 159

Fiddleheads Espresso Bar &
Cafe, 159

Field to Fork, 162

52 Stafford, 172

Filling Station, 45

Firehouse Restaurant, The, 160

Fireside Dinner Theatre, 194

Fireside Supper Club, 255

Fish Creek, 151

Fish Day (Port Washington), 170

Five Corners Farmers'
Market, 176

Five O'Clock Steakhouse, The, 41

Flannery's Wilhelm Tell Supper
Club, 230

Flat Pennies Ice Cream, 255

Flemming Orchards, 289

Fondy Farmers' Market, 131

food trucks (Milwaukee), 26

Forequarter, 207

Foundation, The, 50

Fox Point Farmers' Market, 133

Fraboni's Italian Specialties, 220

Franks Diner, 184

Fratellos Waterfront
Restaurant, 161

Fred & Fuzzy's Waterfront Bar and
Grill, 144

Freight House Restaurant, 282

Friendship House, 255

Fromagination Cheese Store, 220

Frontier Dining Room, 193

Furthermore Beer, 285

Fushimi, 78

G

Gail Ambrosius Chocolatier, 222

Galileo's Italian Steakhouse &
Bar, 138

Gays Mills Farmers' Market, 286

G. Groppi Food Market, 70